Buenos Aires

World Cities Series

Edited by
Professor R. J. Johnston and Professor P. Knox

Published titles in the series:

Forthcoming titles in the series:

Other titles are in preparation

Buenos Aires

Global Dreams, Local Crises

David J Keeling

Western Kentucky University, Kentucky, USA

JOHN WILEY & SONS

Chichester • New York • Brisbane • Toronto • Singapore

Other Wiley Editorial Offices

John Wiley & Sons, Inc., 605 Third Avenue,
New York, NY 10158-0012, USA

Jacaranda Wiley Ltd, 33 Park Road, Milton,
Queensland 4064, Australia

John Wiley & Sons (Canada) Ltd, 22 Worcester Road,
Rexdale, Ontario M9W 1L1, Canada

John Wiley & Sons (Asia) Pte Ltd, 2 Clementi Loop #02-01,
Jin Xing Distripark, Singapore 0512

Library of Congress Cataloging-in-Publication Data

Keeling, David J.
    Buenos Aires : global dreams, local crisis / David J. Keeling.
       p.   cm.—(World cities series)
    Includes bibliographical references and index.
    ISBN 0-471-94935-3 (ppc)
    1. Buenos Aires (Argentina)—Geography.   2. Buenos Aires (Argentina)—History.
  I. Title. II. Series.
F3001.K44 1996
    304.2'3'098211—dc20   96-10662
                                                   CIP

British Library Cataloguing in Publication Data

A catalogue record for this book is available from the British Library

ISBN 0-471-94935-3

Typeset in 10/12pt Palatino from author's disks by Mayhew Typesetting, Rhayader, Powys
Printed and bound in Great Britain by Biddles Ltd, Guildford and King's Lynn

This book is printed on acid-free paper responsibly manufactured from sustainable forestation, for which at least two trees are planted for each one used for paper production.

Contents

List of figures

List of tables

Preface

Buenos Aires has generated hundreds of books and articles on myriad aspects of life in the city over the past few decades. Why, then, should a geographer write another book about the city? First, in-depth analyses of Buenos Aires traditionally have been the domain of historians, political scientists, urban planners, economists, and sociologists. Detailed geographic examinations of the city are rare. Second, the majority of geographical analyses appear in languages other than English. Third, the few geographic studies of Buenos Aires available in English have focused primarily on the city's historical evolution (see, for example, Sargent 1974, Scobie 1974). Little attention has been paid to the spatial changes wrought on Buenos Aires that stem from the city's articulation over the past two decades with the contemporary world economy. Fourth, recent theoretical developments in urban research raise important questions about the role certain "world cities" such as Buenos Aires play as socio-spatial expressions of the world economy (Friedmann 1986). Finally, major economic and social restructuring in Argentina since 1991 have changed local and international perceptions of both city and nation profoundly, prompting many questions about the role of Buenos Aires in the emerging world city system and in the global economy. This book aspires to address some of these important issues by examining the characteristics that help to define Buenos Aires as a world city and by focusing attention on the implications of globalization for change in the city over space and through time.

World cities are distinct places. They exhibit a special dynamism and ambience, and they exert a control over certain global and regional activities that sets them apart from other urban centers. Although Buenos Aires lacks the global and regional control functions that distinguish London, New York, and Tokyo as dominant world cities, it does exert tremendous political, economic, and social control over an entire nation. Buenos Aires also has an impact on the actions and activities of many neighboring states. Moreover, Buenos Aires exudes a vitality and sophistication that have made the city a mecca for migrants, entrepreneurs, miscreants, entertainers, tourists, politicians, and others during much of its history. The hopes, dreams, and ambitions of generations of people and institutions have helped to shape the contemporary city.

Reciprocally, Buenos Aires itself has exerted tremendous influence over its residents and institutions, helping to define a unique and fascinating sense of place. To capture this intricate and intimate relationship, the study juxtaposes the effects of internationalizing the city against the day-to-day realities of managing an enormous and complex urban environment. Examining more closely the bidirectional links between the local and the global may help to shed light on the processes that shape and influence a city's position and involvement in the world city system and in the global economy.

The study does not pretend to be the definitive work on contemporary Buenos Aires. It offers but a snapshot of the city in space and time. As you read these words, businesses are changing, buildings are going up and coming down, people are migrating in and out of the city, and policies are being formulated that will change Buenos Aires in some way, shape, or manner. Buenos Aires, along with every other world city, is dynamic and in constant flux. Moreover, my own cultural, business, and academic backgrounds bias my interpretation of contemporary Buenos Aires. Although I have enjoyed a relationship with this wonderful and intriguing city that spans three decades, I do not view the city through the same lens as would, for example, a native *porteño* (resident of Buenos Aires). My particular interests and biases have led me to focus on certain aspects of the city's development, perhaps to the exclusion of other significant changes. This does not mean that the excluded processes are not important. They are. However, I have chosen to focus the research lens on certain themes to provide a more holistic picture of Buenos Aires and to tease out certain world city and world economy processes that are helping to reshape the contemporary city. I hope that the geographic interpretation of contemporary Buenos Aires presented in this book stimulates interest, argument, and discussion about the city and provokes more questions than answers. Buenos Aires is a fascinating, complex metropolis that merits further analysis as its citizens attempt to achieve their global dreams while struggling with myriad local crises.

A caution concerning statistics and other data is necessary here.

Although most Latin American countries have improved their methods of data collection and dissemination in recent years, statistics often can be unreliable and outdated. As Jorge Schvarzer (1992) noted recently, a paucity of basic data and an unquestioned reliance on official estimates have hindered the development of a critical mass of information that can provide a long-term picture. Many hypotheses about development processes in Argentina, for example, have been built on data that are not always confirmable or that diverge from estimations gleaned from other sources. In a parody of Gresham's law, as Schvarzer (1992, p. 170) wryly notes, "poor information displaces good data in the circulation of ideas." Thus, quantifications and data in the study serve primarily to illustrate trends and relationships and are not meant to be definitive evidence of a particular process. Readers can remain reasonably up to date on Argentine economic and political events by perusing the *Review of the River Plate*, the *Latin American Weekly Report*, the monthly reports of Argentina's Ministry of the Economy and Public Works and Services, and the annual *Statistical Abstract of Latin America* (see, for example, Wilkie and Contreras 1993).

Field research for the book was conducted during the northern summers of 1991, 1993, and 1994. Many people played an instrumental role in bringing this work to fruition. In Argentina, Dr. Juan Alberto Roccatagliata, general executive coordinator of the Argentine government's territorial reorganization project, provided logistical support, friendship, and innumerable introductions during my visits to Buenos Aires. Lucía Bortagaray, Verónica Arruñada, Albina Lara, Mónica Guastoni, Mabel Tamborenea Inza, Norma Marino, and Alberto Hugo Peláez at the offices of the Subsecretaría de la Acción del Gobierno in Buenos Aires provided valuable advice, information, and referrals. Hernán Untermann and Federico Andrejin, geography students at La Universidad del Salvador in Buenos Aires, assisted me during the 1993 visit with translations, and provided valuable insights into their generation's evolving sense of place. Marta Sanmarchi, Arturo Héctor Ramón, Luis Ainstein, Horacio A. Torres, César A. Vapñarsky, Carlos E. Reboratti, Elena M. Chiozza, Patricio H. Randle, Manuel Ludueña, Fernando López del Amo, María Adela Igarzabal de Nistal, and Alfredo Aguirre generously provided data, copies of publications, and personal insights into the machinations of city government and *porteño* life.

The staff and librarians at various provincial and local government offices (especially CONAMBA and CONICET), and at the Center for the Study of the State and Society (CEDES), Center for Population Studies (CENEP), Center for Urban and Regional Studies (CEUR), Institute of Argentine Railroads (FIADF), Association for the Promotion of the Study of Territory and Environment (OIKOS), and the National Institute of

Statistics and Census (INDEC), all in Buenos Aires, were generous with their time and expertise.

In the United States, Frank Richter and Ronald Sheck provided updated information on the privatization of Argentina's railroads and suburban transit systems. Alexander B. Murphy at the University of Oregon guided me through dissertation research on northwest Argentina and suggested that I consider writing about Buenos Aires for the World Cities series. My colleagues in the Department of Geography and Geology at Western Kentucky University provided logistical support, advice, and encouragement. I particularly thank Mark Lowry II, John O'Hara, Mary Snow, and Richard Snow for their constructive comments on several of the chapters. Tom Polanski, a geography graduate student at Western Kentucky University, produced most of the maps and provided valuable input on the content and interpretation of the graphics. The Interlibrary Loan staff at Western, along with Tom Polanski, diligently tracked down some of the more esoteric material. My friends at the University of Oregon – Greg Ringer, Sarah Shafer, and Nancy Leeper – kept me in beer and good humor as I began initial research for the project in 1991. Karen Lewotsky shared with me her unique geographic perspective, debated my treatment of several issues, and thoughtfully critiqued the initial proposal. *Gracias amiga y un fuerte abrazo.* I especially thank Ron Johnston and Paul Knox, editors of the World Cities series, and Iain Stevenson, at Wiley, for supporting this project. Their advice and editing skills proved invaluable as the manuscript threatened to take on a life of its own.

Finally, and most important of all, Dacia J. Urquhart deserves special recognition for guiding me through the past 2 years providing love, encouragement, editing skills, and copious quantities of tea and biscuits during my many interlocutions with the computer. All errors, interpretations, and nuances in translations from Spanish or other sources remain the responsibility of the author. Photographs are by the author unless noted otherwise.

This book is dedicated to Juan Alberto Roccatagliata
geographer, *porteño*, and railroad enthusiast

Juan Alberto's commitment to helping his country and fellow citizens achieve a better quality of life, and to promoting the discipline of geography as an essential component of the planning and development process, have set a standard for excellence and have provided inspiration to me and countless others.

1

Introduction

Many epithets have been used to describe Buenos Aires: the Pearl of the River Plate, the Paris of South America, the City of Good Aires, the Chicago of the Southern Cone, the Cultural Mecca of Latin America, the Queen of the Plata, and the Big Village. Among the great cities of the world, however, few had a beginning as inauspicious as Buenos Aires. The name given to the city's first incarnation in 1536 – the Port of Our Holy Lady Mary of the Fair Wind – reflected the hope and aspirations of its Spanish founders, not reality. Buenos Aires survived barely 5 years, little more than a collection of mud huts set up near the mouth of a meandering stream, the Riachuelo, on the right bank of the Río de la Plata. Food shortages, hostile indigenous peoples, and internal dissent forced the original settlers to abandon Buenos Aires in favor of the more secure and prosperous inland site of Asunción. A second incarnation of Buenos Aires in 1580, on ground to the north of the ill-fated first settlement, proved equally tenuous. Yet the settlement survived, not as a key center of the Spanish colonial trade and urban network, but as a minor outpost of Spain's New World empire.

For 300 years, Buenos Aires grew and developed at a relatively slow pace. Argentina's 1869 census, the nation's first, recorded approximately 223 000 people living in the area known today as the Greater Buenos Aires metropolitan region. By 1910, however, 100 years after Argentina's initial move toward independence from Spain, Buenos Aires had become the largest city in Latin America and second only to New York in the hemisphere. In addition, more than any other Latin American city, Buenos Aires straddled the line between Ibero-American tradition and western European culture and ideology. The city forged more links with Europe during the late nineteenth and early twentieth centuries than any of its regional contemporaries. *Porteños* and others often lovingly described Buenos Aires as the "Paris of South America," a reference to similarities in urban form, architecture, art, and culture. In reality, the morphology, economy, and urban dynamism of Buenos Aires had more in common with Chicago than Paris. Notwithstanding such comparisons, the transformation of Buenos Aires from a dusty, colonial town, *La Gran Aldea*, to a sophisticated world city, *La Gran Ciudad*, remains unmatched in scope or implication by any other Latin American urban center.

Today, Buenos Aires plays a pivotal role as Argentina's gateway to the world, as the Southern Cone's primary metropolitan center, and as an important regional node in the network of major world cities (Figure 1.1). The city is situated at 34° 20' south and 58° 30' west, approximately 270 kilometers from the Atlantic Ocean in the Río de la Plata estuary (Figure 1.2). Buenos Aires is the third largest Latin American city after São Paulo and Mexico City and it is one of the world city system's 10 major urban agglomerations (Table 1.1). With a metropolitan population near 13 million people in 1991 (Table 1.2), Buenos Aires dominates Argentina's economic, political, cultural, and social processes, and exerts a tremendous influence over national and regional development. Although Buenos Aires' share of Argentina's total population has declined slightly since peaking in 1970, approximately 40 percent of the nation's 32 million people live within the metropolitan area (Table 1.3). When you consider that Argentina has 2.8 million square kilometers of continental territory, Buenos Aires represents a staggering concentration of humanity in one city. Not surprisingly, Buenos Aires' hegemony over Argentina has played a powerful role in shaping population growth, economic development, mobility, political action, and social attitudes in the city over space and through time.

Following 50 years of growth and prosperity between 1880 and 1930, Argentina slipped into a six-decade period of political and economic instability. Buenos Aires began to lose its place in the world, even as it continued to grow rapidly as the country's primary urban center. Today, Buenos Aires is emerging from the shadows of Argentina's long-term instability to reassert itself in the regional and global urban network. Under the leadership of Carlos Menem and the *Justicialista* political party, and with an eye toward the contemporary world economy, since 1990 the federal government has attempted to globalize Argentina's economy and society. Globalization strategies include free-market economic policies, regional economic alliances, rapprochement with neighboring states, and state disengagement from many aspects of industry and services via privatization and deregulation ideologies.

The short-term benefits from globalizing Argentina's economy and

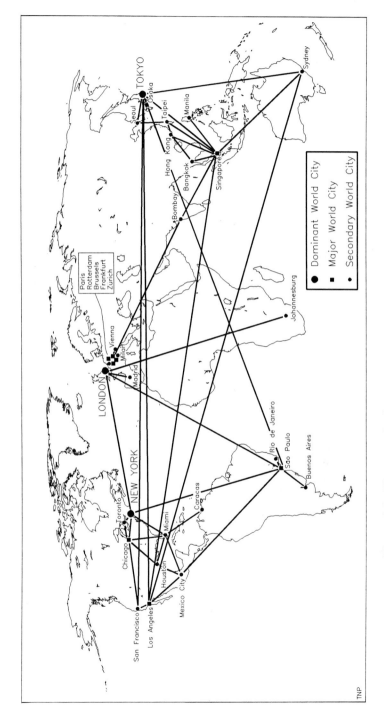

Figure 1.1 The network of world cities, 1994. *Source: After Friedmann (1986)*

Dominant World City

Major World City

Secondary World City

TOKYO
Osaka
Seoul
Taipei
Manila
Hong Kong
Bangkok
Bombay
Singapore
Sydney

Paris
Rotterdam
Brussels
Frankfurt
Zurich

Johannesburg

Vienna
Milan
LONDON
Madrid

Rio de Janeiro
São Paulo
Buenos Aires

Caracas

Toronto
NEW YORK
Miami
Chicago
Houston
Mexico City
San Francisco
Los Angeles

TNP

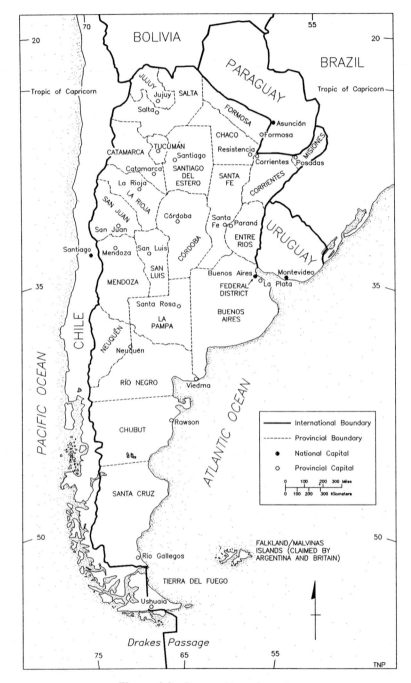

Figure 1.2   Buenos Aires, Argentina

Table 1.1 The world's 10 largest metropolitan areas, 1992

Rank	Metropolitan area	Country	Size (millions)	Average annual % change
1	Tokyo/Yokohama	Japan	31.0	1.04
2	Seoul	South Korea	18.0	3.50
3	New York	USA	17.4	0.16
4	Osaka/Kyoto/Kobe	Japan	17.1	0.44
5	Mexico City	Mexico	16.1	2.54
6	São Paulo	Brazil	15.5	1.71
7	Bombay	India	14.4	2.90
8	Los Angeles	USA	13.4	1.46
9	Calcutta	India	13.3	1.68
10	Buenos Aires	Argentina	13.0	1.15

Source: Rand McNally (1993).

Table 1.2 The population of Buenos Aires, 1991

Region	Population	Area (km^2)	Density (population/km^2)
Federal capital[a]	2 960 976	200	14 805
Inner Ring[b]	7 950 427	3680	2160
Middle Ring[c]	1 107 292	4561	243
Outer Ring[d]	804 381	31 174	26
Total	12 823 076	39 615	324

Source: República Argentina (1991).

[a] Comprises 21 school districts divided further into 47 *barrios* or neighborhoods.
[b] Comprises the original 19 municipalities of Greater Buenos Aires.
[c] Comprises the three municipalities of Greater La Plata and the six municipalities incorporated into the Greater Buenos Aires statistical region in 1991.
[d] Comprises the 23 municipalities of the urban periphery.

society are accruing primarily to Buenos Aires, not to other parts of the country. Additionally, the existence of severe local crises tempers the capital's aspirations to world city status. Social polarization, environmental degradation, deindustrialization, eroding middle-class lifestyles, rising unemployment, declining health and social welfare, collapsing infrastructure, and grinding poverty are changing Buenos Aires in profound and fundamental ways. Many observers argue that a direct causal link exists between declines in the quality of life in Buenos Aires and the globalization of the local economy. Others argue that globalization is the only acceptable medicine for Argentina as it attempts to reverse the effects of decades of economic, political, and social malaise. This study provides a comprehensive geographic survey of Buenos Aires against

Table 1.3 The relative distribution of population in Argentina by census year and by region, 1869–1991

Region[a]	1869	1895	1914	1947	1960	1970	1980	1991
GBAMA[b]	9.9	16.6	25.0	29.2	33.7	41.2	40.6	39.3
Pampas[c]	41.8	48.6	49.0	42.1	38.0	31.1	30.1	29.4
West	10.4	7.0	6.5	6.4	6.7	6.6	6.7	6.8
Northeast	9.1	9.2	5.5	8.8	8.1	7.8	8.1	8.7
Northwest	28.8	17.9	12.6	11.2	11.0	10.2	10.8	11.3
Patagonia	0.0	0.7	1.4	2.3	2.5	3.1	3.7	4.5
Argentina	100.0	100.0	100.0	100.0	100.0	100.0	100.0	100.0

Source: República Argentina (1991).

[a] GBAMA is the Greater Buenos Aires Metropolitan Area.
The Pampas region includes the provinces of Buenos Aires, Santa Fe, Entre Ríos, Córdoba, and La Pampa.
The West includes Mendoza, San Luis, and San Juan provinces.
The Northeast provinces are Corrientes, Chaco, Formosa, and Misiones.
Catamarca, La Rioja, Tucumán, Salta, Jujuy, and Santiago del Estero provinces comprise the Northwest.
Patagonia includes Neuquén, Río Negro, Chubut, Santa Cruz, and Tierra del Fuego provinces.
[b] From 1970 onwards, GBAMA includes the population of the Middle and Outer Rings previously counted in the Pampas region.
[c] Includes the population of the Middle and Outer rings of GBAMA until 1970.

the backdrop of these changes, and attempts to shed light on the processes that are shaping the city's involvement in the evolving global economic and urban systems.

Many of the terms used to describe Buenos Aires and its residents often are used interchangeably. To maintain clarity of meaning, throughout the book the 47 *barrios* (neighborhoods) that comprise the downtown core of Buenos Aires are referred to as the "Federal District." Greater Buenos Aires refers specifically to the municipalities that ring the downtown core. Reference to either Buenos Aires or the Greater Buenos Aires Metropolitan Area (GBAMA) includes both the Federal District and the suburban municipalities. Although the term *porteño* traditionally has been used to describe only those residents of the Federal District, it is used more broadly here and refers to any resident of the city.

A framework for analysis

In recent years the relative dominance of the nation-state in global processes has given way to new space–time patterns where both the multinational–global and the regional–local scales have risen to prominence. Although corporate, financial, and political activity at the global scale play crucial roles in structuring daily urban life, geographers and others are finding that regional and local responses and restructuring processes also are important. Devolution, decentralization, and localization forces are counterbalancing globalization processes. As a result, the local–global continuum of economic and urban relationships is realigning itself over space and through time. Viewing local and global activities as contradictory forces, however, is much too simplistic an approach. In reality, these activities are generating complex dynamic tensions in urban environments, tensions that are creating distinct spatial patterns of growth and change. Nowhere are these tensions more evident than in world cities, which function as dominant loci of regional and global economic relationships and processes. World cities, therefore, provide an excellent milieu for examining the dynamic forces at work along the local–global continuum.

The task of geographers, urban planners, and others in recognizing, analyzing, and addressing the dynamic tensions in world cities is both difficult and challenging. Over the past decade, however, theoretical and empirical studies of world city development, growth, and change have placed the tensions between local and global processes at the forefront of urban research (King 1990, Lo 1992, Sassen 1991, Shachar 1994). Such studies have drawn heavily from the world city paradigm, which posits that certain cities play a distinct role in articulating regional and national economies in the global system (Friedmann and Wolff 1982, Friedmann 1986). World cities develop hierarchical relationships that rise and fall over time according to their control and mediary functions in the system. As commanding nodes in the world economy, world cities are defined by dense patterns of interaction of people, goods, and information. World cities increasingly have become interconnected through the internationalization of labor and capital, which stems from their role as basing points for global and regional socioeconomic activity. Thus, a distinct bidirectional relationship exists between world city development and globalization forces.

As key centers for the control and mediation of global finance, world cities develop a very rich social and physical infrastructure. World city status also endows considerable benefits related to the development of high-growth sectors of the economy. It is not surprising that many entrepreneurial cities and city regions have engaged recently in the frenzied construction of science and research centers, megamalls, recreational theme parks, and conference facilities in an attempt to capture some of these important benefits. Cities also are busy organizing urban spectacles as they strive to bolster their position in the race for global yen, ECU, deutsche mark, or dollar investments. Hosting major conferences, world fairs, international or national sporting activities (for example, the soccer World Cup, the Olympics, or the Pan-American games), and similar events can attract major investment capital and can have a lasting impact on a city's landscape. However, tensions between local needs and global ambitions frequently arise from these activities. Thus, although the broad conditioning relationships imposed by global metropolitanism and capitalism are important, it is their articulation with local political, economic, and social structures that is crucial to understanding the geographic implications of world city and world economy involvement for cities like Buenos Aires.

Caution is required when drawing from generalizations put forward in the world city paradigm. The recipe for world city status includes myriad ingredients. National government functions, major ports, trading centers, luxury hotels and restaurants, international headquarters and offices, major airports, cultural icons, pools of specialized labor, significant portions of the nation's wealthiest and poorest people, control functions over the flow of labor and capital, and a powerful local mythology or "sense of place" are just a few of the criteria that help to define a world city (Hall 1966, Lo 1992). Many cities have some or all of these ingredients, yet exert limited influence in the world city system. Contemporary Buenos Aires certainly exercises little of the international or even regional control functions that world city status proposes. However, a staunch belief in the potential benefits accruing from involvement in the global economy underpins Buenos Aires' drive toward world city status. The government of Argentina considers world city status to be a guarantee of increased levels of prosperity and power. Failure to attain a major role in the world city system would condemn both city and nation to a secondary position in the emerging hemispheric and global economy. Therefore, as Argentina's primary city, the Southern Cone's most important urban center, and the focus of growing international financial and economic activity, Buenos Aires offers fertile ground for an analysis of the dynamic tensions resulting from increased involvement in the global urban and economic systems.

A thematic–spatial approach treats the myriad components of Buenos Aires as an interactive, integrative whole (Figure 1.3). This approach suggests that a highly generalized set of central relationships is at work in and among world cities. Place, global capital, and the international division of labor function as central pillars in the world city system. Interaction between these three components is inextricably intertwined with, and shaped by, political, social, cultural, and environmental processes. The constantly expanding and contracting interface between the various components, represented by the dashed lines, determines the strength of the relationship and its possible impact on a city. Weak interfaces between labor, capital, and place can inhibit the development

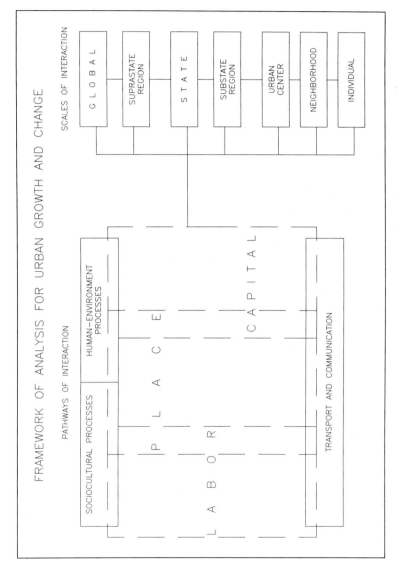

Figure 1.3 A framework of analysis for urban growth and change

of relationships within the hierarchy of world cities. For example, if global capital has a weak interface with an urban center, theoretically little globally induced urban restructuring is likely to occur. In South America, both Lima and La Paz are huge cities, with about 5 million and 2 million inhabitants, respectively, yet they exhibit little physical evidence of a strong interface with the circuit of global capital. Rarely are these cities mentioned in discussions of world city and world economy processes. Finally, transport and communication operate as the foundation upon which the central pillars of the world city system rest. Transport facilitates the movement of people, goods, and information through the system and is a necessary, although not sufficient, component of world city genesis, growth, and change.

To understand Buenos Aires' evolving world city role, and to appreciate the implications of the city's articulation with the contemporary world economy, the study addresses a series of interlocking and recursive themes that draw on the general relationships outlined in Figure 1.3. First, the city functions as a palimpsest. Buenos Aires' geohistorical background and experiences have helped to shape a rich cultural and physical urban mosaic. An analysis of the city's distinct growth stages sheds light on the historical inertia embedded in the way labor, capital, and place interact today. The past sets the stage for the present (see Chapter 2).

Changes in the city's urban environment are occurring as global capital reshapes the local marketplace and alters the production mix of goods, services, and information. At the same time, historical inertia in the local political, social, and economic arenas is conditioning institutional and individual responses to globalization and is influencing the way changes are occurring in the city. The urban environment, then, can be thought of as the theater within which the daily drama of human life is played out (see Chapter 3); however, it is definitely not a static vehicle. Past and present images linger, the external and internal scenery change constantly, and the theater's context is in a dynamic state of flux.

The actors in this daily drama are the institutions and people of Buenos Aires. Politicians, planners, policy makers, and housing providers, among others, play a pivotal role in shaping the urban landscape (see Chapter 4). As Allan Pred (1985) puts it, the physical evolution or becoming of a place is inextricably intertwined with individual biographies. Individuals, families, communities, neighborhoods, and institutions act and interact at myriad levels. They write, choreograph, and direct the script of the play of life, and they constantly are shaping and reshaping the theater within which the play takes place. Moreover, the players on the stage also function as the audience for other parts of the daily play of life.

A central theme of the study is the changing composition of the city's labor force. The structure and dynamics of the city's production and employment sectors directly reflect Buenos Aires' global, regional, and local economic functions and relationships. Individual and institutional processes shape the division of labor at both local and international levels. Additionally, the international division of labor helps to shape global capital circulation. Capital is another fundamental component of the forces that shape and reshape people, places, and landscapes. The urban environment reflects the ebbs and flows of capital circulation that are occurring as Buenos Aires develops into a concentration and accumulation site for international, regional, and local capital (both tangible and intangible). Indeed, global capitalism can be linked, in part, to the sociospatial polarization that is occurring in contemporary Buenos Aires (see Chapter 5).

Transport and communication services and infrastructure in Buenos Aires facilitate and condition interaction between people, institutions, labor, capital, and the urban environment. The level of connectivity experienced by Buenos Aires along the local–global continuum plays a crucial role in shaping relationships between the city and other urban centers. Transport and communication also help to shape the response of individuals and institutions to the forces of change. The long-term success of globalization forces in Buenos Aires and the city's incorporation more fully into the world city and world economy systems depend, in large part, on its response to increased demands for transport and communication services and infrastructure. Buenos Aires' ability to achieve its global dreams while managing successfully its myriad local crises requires enhanced levels of accessibility and mobility along the entire local–global continuum (see Chapter 6).

The elements outlined above have important consequences for human–environment relationships in Buenos Aires. Indeed, Buenos Aires' involvement in the global economy and its continued evolution as a world city are generating social and environmental costs at rates that are exceeding the fiscal capacity of both city and state. The spatial dynamics of environmental alteration in Buenos Aires play an important role in shaping the city's response to globalizing forces (see Chapter 7).

Finally, the experiences of place and landscape help to shape individual and community mythologies and "sense of place" (Relph 1976). Cultural mythologies stem from the customs, institutions, individuals, cultural phenomena, icons, and religious rites, whether real or perceived, that help to define and explain people's relationship with place. In Buenos Aires, cultural mythologies surrounding the tango, the gaucho, and Evita Perón, for example, play a powerful role in the relationship between city and resident. Commodifying these local mythologies and icons helps to shape societal structures as well as to influence the way individuals and institutions respond to external processes (see Chapter 8). Thus, the meanings attached to a place, and what happens in and to a place, are inseparable components (Pred 1985). As expressions of geographical activities and phenomena, they reveal the quality of human awareness about places and landscapes (Tuan 1974; 1976). Sense of place, in turn, is both shaped by and helps to shape the very structures that mold, motivate, and drive societies (Giddens 1984). The present becomes the past, another layer on the palimpsest, and it exerts a powerful influence over future changes in the urban environment.

Two possible broad and generalized development scenarios are suggested for Buenos Aires in the immediate future. Centralized development could result from Buenos Aires' continued evolution as a world city in the emerging global economy. The city could become more vertically integrated at the regional and international levels, with increased practical and perceptual separation from the rest of Argentina. At the same time, local activities increasingly could become disarticulated from the city's regional and global activities, which might lead to new, severe social and economic crises in both city and nation. Decentralized development, on the other hand, could spread the growth stimuli of global economic involvement to all regions and sectors of Argentina. Integration at both vertical and horizontal scales could help to reverse the bifurcation of Argentina and could mitigate the overwhelming economic, political, and social dominance that Buenos Aires exerts over the entire country. Which of these two scenarios is likely for Buenos Aires? In the following chapters, the forces that are shaping the city's global dreams and local crises are examined in detail and the spatial dynamics of growth and change in Buenos Aires are brought to center stage.

2

Historic Buenos Aires: urban growth and change, 1580–1990

Since its genesis in 1580, Buenos Aires has experienced an extraordinarily rich and detailed history of growth and change. A brief chapter on the city's history cannot do justice to 400 years of urban evolution, but it can provide a general framework for analyzing the contemporary city. Studies by Charles Sargent (1974), James Scobie (1974), Kathleen Wheaton (1990), Margarita Gutman and Jorge Hardoy (1993), and Manuel Ludueña (1993) offer excellent detailed histories and overviews of Buenos Aires. Their work provides the foundation upon which this chapter's analysis rests. The major components of the city's history are examined for each of six important periods of urban development. The chapter highlights how the spatial dynamics of Buenos Aires were shaped during these distinct epochs. It also illustrates how a number of general culture traits and attitudes became embedded in the city's political, social, and economic structures, influencing how the actors in Buenos Aires' play of life respond to global, national, and local issues. Embedded traits and attitudes condition the way the play of life is scripted and promote important physical and contextual changes in the theater (urban environment) within which the play takes place. Although these traits and attitudes have been modified over time, they still are evident in many aspects of life, livelihood, and governance in Buenos Aires.

Isolated settlement, 1580–1680

Buenos Aires owes its existence to geography and politics. Rivalry between Spain and other European powers during the sixteenth century encouraged the Spanish Crown to seek out strategic positions on the southern landmass of the New World. The Crown saw the Río de la Plata region as a possible Atlantic gateway between Spain and the perceived mineral riches of the Andean highlands. A fortified settlement along the Plata estuary could serve as a barrier to Portuguese advances in the Southern Cone and as a possible administrative center for Spanish activities in the region. In 1536, Pedro de Mendoza led 1500 men, the largest expedition at that time from Spain to the New World, up the wide, muddy Plata estuary looking for a suitable spot to establish a city. Mendoza's attempt at city building failed, as the site was abandoned after 5 difficult years. However, Buenos Aires rose again in 1580 when Juan de Garay and 60 followers arrived from the interior town of Asunción to reestablish the settlement. Garay believed that a coastal settlement could mount an effective challenge to the growing economic and commercial power of the interior and draw trade to the Atlantic route.

Both the 1536 and 1580 sites were located on the only stretch of high ground along the Río de la Plata's right bank adjacent to both a deep anchorage for oceangoing vessels and a source of fresh water. At approximately 27 meters above sea level, the settlement's initial location provided protection from high water and a slightly elevated view of the estuary for defensive purposes. South of Buenos Aires, a broad, low alluvial plain stretched out from the coast, unsuitable for settlement because of flooding and a lack of natural defenses. Higher ground to the north lacked an adequate deep-water anchorage and lay too close to the expanding, silt-laden Paraná delta. The area's two major streams, the Reconquista and Matanza, provided fresh water and served as anchorages and shelter for small craft traveling the Paraná. The lower reaches of the Matanza, known as the Riachuelo or little river, were next to both high ground and a deep anchorage area called *el pozo* (the hole). This became the anchorage spot of choice for larger oceangoing vessels.

Juan de Garay's original plat, a rectangular grid of approximately 15 blocks along a north–south axis and nine blocks to the west, drew primarily from royal instructions on town foundings. The Laws of the Indies, promulgated in 1573, outlined 28 rules and regulations that guided the establishment of plazas, the disposition of public buildings, and the cardinal directions of the main streets. Around the central plaza (known today as the Plaza de Mayo), the settlers laid the foundations for a fort, church, jail, and *cabildo* (municipal council chamber). Forty blocks centered on the plaza were subdivided into *solares* or quarters and assigned to 64 of the principal settlers. Streams to the north and south of the settlement served as practical areal limits to Garay's original plat. Larger lots outside the core were set aside for subsistence agriculture and as a source of forage for horses. Early immigrants to the new settlement from both Spain and the interior included commoners, farmers, merchants, clerics, soldiers, and clerks. At the end of the sixteenth century, approximately 1100 people maintained permanent residence in Buenos Aires.

By the time Buenos Aires began to function as a viable port and settlement, the administrative, economic, and transport networks of Spain's American empire had become well established. Administratively, Buenos Aires fell under the jurisdiction of the Royal Governor of Asunción, although the local *cabildo* handled municipal matters in the city. Commercial power, however, centered on Lima, Mexico City, and the Caribbean ports. The Spanish Crown dictated the official supply route to the silver mines of Upper Peru, a long, circuitous route via the Caribbean, Pacific Coast, and Lima (Figure 2.1). Nearly 2500 kilometers of rugged mountain terrain separated Lima from the Potosí silver mines. In contrast, much of the 2000 kilometers between Potosí and Buenos Aires covered relatively level ground. Buenos Aires offered serious competition to cities along the official supply route. Merchandise could be shipped from the Atlantic coast to Potosí in 2 months, whereas a journey between Lima and Potosí took nearly 4 months.

Despite the existence of an official supply route, illegal silver from the mines of Potosí trickled down the "backdoor" route to the Atlantic, encouraging contraband trade in Buenos Aires. Spain responded in 1618 by establishing a customs barrier 700 kilometers northwest of Buenos Aires, at Córdoba, to prevent European imports from reaching Potosí via the Atlantic coast. Four years later, the Crown further restricted Buenos Aires' growth by revoking the city's license to trade with Brazil. Nonetheless, Spain recognized the strategic importance of control over the Río de la Plata estuary. When Spain established the customs barrier in Córdoba, it also designated Buenos Aires as the seat of a governorship controlling a vast littoral region that included present-day Uruguay.

Northern merchants tried every political and economic maneuver available to restrict the growth of Buenos Aires and to prevent the Atlantic coast from usurping their commercial monopoly. In Tucumán and Potosí, Spanish merchants also formed alliances with Portuguese merchants to control the flow of illegal silver and agricultural products in the region. As a result, most *porteños* had little success in participating in the illicit movement of silver between Potosí and the coast. Manuel Trelles (1863, p. 23) observed that "the poor settlers [of Buenos Aires] were reduced to the miserable condition of picking up the crumbs of the commercial feast."

Distance from interior settlements and poor communication allowed Buenos Aires to develop considerable autonomy and economic self-

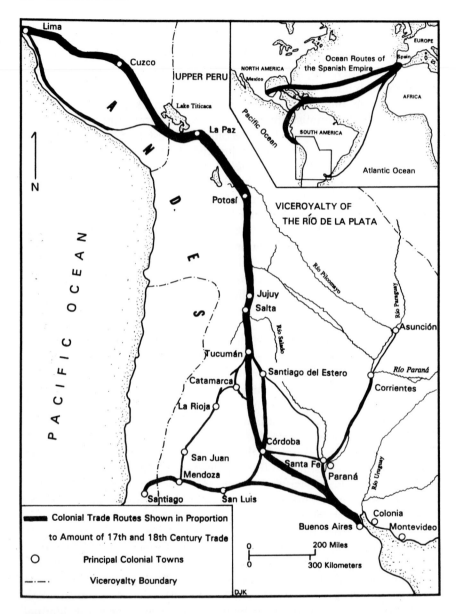

Figure 2.1   Southern Cone trade routes during the Spanish colonial period. *Source:* After Scobie (1971)

sufficiency, despite external efforts to restrict growth in the Plata region. Smuggled silver found its way in ever-increasing amounts to the city and encouraged much illegal trade with the Portuguese, Dutch, French, and English. In return for silver, Buenos Aires received and shipped north imported fineries and manufactures, as well as locally produced leather, mules, and agricultural products. Hides and animal fats also were processed and exported from Buenos Aires. This mixture of contraband and agricultural trade encouraged steady growth in the city during the seventeenth century. By 1660, Buenos Aires counted approximately 3500 inhabitants. Twenty years later, the population surpassed 5000 (Moreno 1939). Notwithstanding steady population growth, areally Buenos Aires remained focused on the central plaza and the surrounding 40 blocks. Most *porteños* lived in simple adobe huts, although the occasional brick house had begun to appear on the landscape, lending an air of permanency to the city. Buenos Aires had established firm roots in the Río de la Plata region despite being small, isolated, and relatively insignificant.

Commercial center, 1680–1776

Buenos Aires survived its first 100 years, but was viewed as little more than a collection of shacks in swampland. Located at the end of a long chain of towns stretching from Peru to the Atlantic Coast, the city remained far less important than the interior towns of Córdoba, Salta, and Tucumán (see Figure 2.1). Nonetheless, during the second half of the seventeenth century, Spain began to recognize Buenos Aires' increasing control over the region's interior markets and ordered the customs barrier in Córdoba moved north to Salta and eventually to Jujuy (1676). A major turning point in the city's development occurred in 1680, when the Portuguese founded Colônia dô Sacramento across the Plata estuary from Buenos Aires. The Portuguese trading center spurred the flow of Africans and contraband into the Plata estuary. Even distant Chile found itself drawn slowly but inexorably into the littoral's expanding realm of commercial influence. Buenos Aires began to emerge as a successful regional entrepôt, relying largely on smuggling. The city controlled the supply of imports, functioned as the region's largest and most dynamic urban market, and was the main export point. Buenos Aires also controlled the flow of finance capital throughout the region and received most of the area's tax revenues. Financial and areal growth in the city's commercial activities encouraged a 50 percent increase in population between 1680 and 1700.

Buenos Aires' growth during the seventeenth and eighteenth centuries must be viewed against the backdrop of the emerging European world economy that expanded after 1450 to encompass much of the globe (Wallerstein 1980). Buenos Aires functioned as part of the emerging world economy almost from its genesis, but really became involved after 1680 with a quickening of the pace of trade in the Río de la Plata estuary. Without its insertion into the North Atlantic economy, Buenos Aires may well have withered and died or, at best, remained an isolated, insignificant settlement. However, the city thrived with its growing role as regional entrepôt and primary connector between the exportable resources of the interior and the expanding European world economy.

As Buenos Aires grew, it developed a part symbiotic, part parasitic, mutual yet antagonistic relationship with the interior that still is evident today. Each area jockeyed to maintain economic and political control over the hinterland. Commercial interests in the interior aspired to dominate trade between Peru and the Atlantic coast. Merchants frequently petitioned the Spanish Crown to incorporate Buenos Aires into the jurisdiction of Tucumán. *Tucumeños* long had lobbied strongly for a southern approach to Peru rather than the long, cumbersome, and expensive route via the Isthmus of Panamá. While the *porteños* and *tucumeños* struggled to control trade in the region, the agricultural producers of the interior began to protest against the monopoly held by Seville–Lima merchants and the exorbitant prices charged for goods in Potosí. However, the powerful Seville–Lima merchant groups were not ready to let their trade monopoly go without a strong fight (Rodríguez 1956). Under pressure from the northern merchants, Spain rejected the request for a new southern route and reaffirmed the official supply route via Lima and the Caribbean. The Crown argued that it could not provide sufficient protection during the long land and sea voyage via Buenos Aires and the South Atlantic.

Despite Buenos Aires' official relegation to the backwaters of Spain's New World empire, the Crown relied on the strategic location of the port city. Buenos Aires thus presented Spain with a paradox. The coastal city functioned as a vital line of economic defense against smugglers who siphoned off the wealth of Potosí. Contraband flowed into the port in ever-increasing volumes as the southern "backdoor" route to the Atlantic developed into a cheaper and more efficient transport corridor. Yet the Crown's closed-port policy did not attract settlers to Buenos Aires, as little economic incentive existed for immigrants. Therefore, Buenos Aires grew during the eighteenth century with an almost Janus-like or split personality. *Porteños* were acutely aware of their importance to the economic defense of Spain, but also they needed to make a living. The term "obedezco pero no cumplo" became ever more fashionable in the city: "I hear what Spain says and understand its needs, but I need to do whatever is necessary to survive given the local conditions." *Porteños* developed an array of skills designed to avoid rules, regulations, and taxes that continue to be exhibited to this day.

Throughout the eighteenth century, Spain gradually increased the commercial and administrative responsibilities of Buenos Aires, laying the foundations for the late nineteenth century pattern of urban growth that James Scobie (1972) characterized as commercial–bureaucratic. Toward the mid-eighteenth century, the Spanish Crown started to permit a small legal flow of bullion through Buenos Aires so that it could recover the "royal fifth," the 20 percent tax that it lost through smuggling. Buenos Aires also grew in strategic importance as Portugal, Britain, France, and the Netherlands continued to make inroads both economically and territorially into Spain's American empire. The city flourished with its increased political power and economic importance, and by 1750 the population had reached 14 000.

In the ideal habitat of the Pampas, horses and cattle multiplied rapidly to become the backbone of Buenos Aires' commercial activities. A significant export of hides and animal fats laid the economic foundation for the development of an agricultural and merchant class who quickly became the city's power brokers, urban élite, and decision makers. Wealth from the smuggled silver and from the Pampas' bounty started to circulate in Buenos Aires, playing a major role in the city's trans-formation. Status symbols and ostentatious displays of wealth became *de rigueur* for the Buenos Aires élite, who now strolled the streets clad in the finest French silks, consumed large quantities of expensive imported European goods, and built elegant two-story brick houses near the central plaza. The largest houses in the center belonged to wealthy merchants and to the *estancieros* (landowners) who controlled vast swathes of Pampas land yet headquartered themselves in the city. In the urban hierarchy of Buenos Aires, the closer one lived to the *cabildo* (seat of power), the more prestige one had in society. On the fringes of Buenos Aires and its society lived *la gente perdida* (the lost people) – fleeing criminals, escaped slaves, deserting militiamen, and partially assimilated Querandí and Puelche indigenous peoples. Many of these people found sporadic employment on the small farms and orchards that ringed the urban periphery.

The development of an urban élite helped to strengthen certain incipient cultural traits and attitudes in the city. Members of the upper classes increasingly scorned manual labor, while lawyers, priests, and educators were held in high esteem. A sense of admiration developed for the roguish or clever man, for examples of *viveza criolla* (native cunning), and for the continuous and open display of virility and manliness (*machismo*) (Scobie .1974). These learned beliefs and values shared by *porteños* became embedded in the social structure of Buenos Aires over the coming decades, helping to maintain élitist control over politics, finance, education, investment, and physical change in the city.

Buenos Aires also grew as an important slave port during the eighteenth century. A major slave compound developed north of the urban core on the site that eventually became the major railroad terminal (Retiro). *Porteños* blamed the compound as the source of periodic epidemics that swept through the city. In reality, sanitary conditions were appalling throughout the urban area, not just in the working-class districts. Slave trading, smuggling, and exports spurred the development of a proto-industrial economy in the working-class neighborhoods. Silversmiths, cobblers, tailors, masons, builders, and carpenters used imported and domestic materials for their trades and satisfied much of the city's basic industrial needs. Unfortunately, little of the capital flowing from the land or from silver found its way back into the industrial economy or into urban infrastructural improvement. Investments were made either in additional land or merchandise, where quick and profitable returns on capital were assured, or in the consumption of luxury, imported goods. This trait continues today, with a general lack of native entrepreneurial capital circulating in the city. Investments in speculative real estate development, ostentatious consumption, or off-shore banks are the norm, rather than investments in business, infra-structure, and economic development. Thus, despite proto-industrial growth, Buenos Aires remained very much a big village (*La Gran Aldea*) until well into the mid-nineteenth century.

Administrative center, 1776–1810

In 1776 Spain dispatched a major military expedition to expel Portu-guese and English merchants from the Río de la Plata's left bank. At the same time, Buenos Aires became the capital of the newly created Viceroyalty of the Río de la Plata, controlling an area that embraced present-day Bolivia, Argentina, Paraguay, Uruguay, and northern Chile. With this profound change of economic and administrative policies, theoretically Buenos Aires now dominated all trade and political activity for thousands of miles. Rather than people, goods, and information traversing the rugged mountain route between Potosí and Lima, traffic focused increasingly on the trunk line between Buenos Aires and Upper Peru. Within the space of a few years, the road north from Buenos Aires across the dusty pampas became the most important transport route in the Southern Cone. Nearly two centuries after its second incarnation,

Buenos Aires had achieved one of Juan de Garay's principal objectives – economic, political, and administrative control over the entire region.

Concomitant with its new importance, the development of Buenos Aires now moved into a higher gear. Lawyers, priests, military officers, bureaucrats, artisans, slaves, soldiers, merchants, and prostitutes swelled the city's population to 40 000 by the end of the eighteenth century. Agricultural and merchant capital continued to circulate more freely in Buenos Aires, changing the city's urban morphology. New, more ostentatious buildings were constructed in the urban core. Real estate values tripled during the last years of the eighteenth century as Buenos Aires enjoyed a sustained property boom (Rock 1987). Several theaters opened in the downtown area, as well as a hospital and an orphanage. In 1778, the new viceroy instigated public works improvements in the central area, including the construction of sidewalks and the paving of streets. Ten years later, public street lights began to illuminate the civic center, giving the city a glow of progress and respectability. By 1794, 20 *barrios* (neighborhoods) had been delimited in the city, and the government moved to make the streets safer for pedestrians by controlling the circulation of big oxcarts through the narrow streets. Students were admitted to Buenos Aires' first secondary school (1783), art school (1799), school of medicine (1799), and naval academy (1799), and the newspaper *Telégrafo Mercantil* (1801) began to circulate regularly.

Despite improvements in the city's public face, Buenos Aires still suffered generally from poor infrastructure. Public toilets, water pipes, and street cleaning were almost nonexistent and the city continued to have terrible sanitation problems. Drinking water came from the same river water used for bathing and sewage. Disease was endemic. Moreover, the absence of an adequate and functional system of docks in Buenos Aires proved to be a major barrier to economic growth. Shallow waters in the Plata estuary kept large vessels anchored offshore. Goods had to be ferried back and forth to oceangoing vessels in small boats, an extremely costly and inefficient process.

As the nineteenth century dawned, Buenos Aires could distinguish four general zones: (i) a civic center around the central plaza; (ii) a wealthier neighborhood to the south; (iii) a ring of eight churches surrounding the civic center, reflecting the importance of religion in *porteño* society, each serving as the focal point of individual *barrios*; and (iv) a sparsely populated periphery, where proto-industrial activities (brickworks, tileworks, lime kilns) mixed with small stores, open areas for cart storage, and small orchards and farms. Two axes of urban growth began to take shape in Buenos Aires, one along the coast and the other to the west along the present-day arterial of Avenida Rivadavia.

A heightened level of antagonism evolved between city and interior as

Buenos Aires grew and changed, presaging the development pattern that would bifurcate Argentina during the coming century. Buenos Aires' growing economic and political power eroded the ability of the interior to develop a sustainable intraregional and local economy. After two centuries of close ties between Argentina's interior towns and their northern neighbors, the commercial–bureaucratic tentacles of Buenos Aires began to reach out and draw the interior inexorably toward the coast. An attitude of superiority now pervaded Buenos Aires' relationship with other urban centers. Moreover, after the creation of the viceroyalty, friction increased between *criollos* (American-born Spaniards), who owned land, and *peninsulares* (European-born Spaniards), who were the city's officials, bureaucrats, and merchants. This clash laid the foundation for the 1810 seizure of power in Buenos Aires by the *criollos*. War with Britain in 1796 had cut Spain's Atlantic trade routes, with disastrous consequences for Buenos Aires' merchants. Warehouses began to overflow with rotting goods, trade collapsed, and the circulation of capital slowed nearly to a halt. Spurred on by Napoleonic control of Spain that severed the line of imperial authority, *criollo* citizens replaced the Spanish-born viceroy and *cabildo* with their own junta and took effective control of the city on May 25, 1810.

Emerging national capital, 1810–1880

Geopolitical struggles marked the early years of Argentine independence. Upper Peru, Paraguay, and Uruguay renounced Buenos Aires' control almost immediately after the local junta took over, leaving the city to administer territory roughly equivalent to contemporary Argentina. Internal dissent also wracked the new country. Political clashes between Unitarists, who favored a strong central government in Buenos Aires, and Federalists, who wanted to preserve regional autonomy and protect local economies, dragged on for over 60 years. As internal bickering continued over political and economic control of the new republic, Buenos Aires consolidated its position as Argentina's premier urban center. Buenos Aires now functioned as Argentina's gateway to the world and as the world's doorway to Argentina.

Merchants and *estancieros* in Buenos Aires envisioned vast profits from opening up the entire country to free trade. *Porteños* knew that English woollen ponchos from Manchester and knives from Sheffield could be purchased at a fraction of the prices charged by interior towns for the same products. The time and cost of transporting goods from the provinces to Buenos Aires placed the interior economies at a severe competitive disadvantage regarding English products. Not surprisingly, provincial leaders were less than enthusiastic about free trade, as it would effectively destroy the provincial economies and subjugate the interior to Buenos Aires. Unfortunately for the interior, Juan Manuel de Rosas, a *porteño* and Argentina's wealthiest *estanciero*, emerged as the country's strong man from 1829 to 1852, firmly placing the parochial interests of Buenos Aires above the provinces (Lynch 1981). Buenos Aires grew steadily as the interior languished in poverty and relative isolation.

Early nineteenth century Buenos Aires comprised 29 distinct *barrios* equivalent to 464 *manzanas* (blocks), although only 360 blocks had openings to the street. Avenidas Victoria (now H. Yrigoyen) and Federación (Rivadavia) served as the principal axes of communication westward from the central plaza, while Avenida Buen Orden (B. de Irigoyen) formed the boundary between the city's urban and suburban zones. Beyond Avenida Entre Ríos, homes began to intermix with estates and country houses. South of the central plaza, an important nucleus of industrial and commercial activity grew along both banks of the Riachuelo and in the *barrio* of Barracas. This area experienced rapid growth after 1815 with the introduction of new techniques in the *saladeros* (meat-packing plants) and with the construction of warehouses for chinchilla and nutria tanners and hide exporters.

Throughout most of the nineteenth century, the commercial nucleus of Buenos Aires remained centered on the main plaza, with the most intensive activity occurring on the south side. To the west, along Avenida de Mayo, clustered the shops of English and Irish merchants. Most of the city's 80 000 inhabitants lived around the Plaza de Mayo and in adjacent blocks. Unfortunately, improvements in the city's sanitary conditions did not accompany steady population growth in the downtown core. For example, Buenos Aires in the 1860s suffered a mortality rate of 42 per 1000, double that of London. A major yellow fever epidemic in 1871 struck heavily in the southern *barrios* of Constitución, San Telmo, and La Boca, accelerating the northward shift of wealthy *porteños* begun several years earlier. The *porteño* élite now preferred the northern *barrios* of Palermo, Belgrano, and Barrio Norte for several reasons: (i) proximity to the central plaza with its governmental functions; (ii) access to the growing banking district north of the plaza; (iii) access to the many shops and businesses catering to the upper classes located along, and adjacent to, Avenida Florida, which ran north from Avenida de Mayo; and (iv) the existence of several well-maintained plazas in the northern area that served as open space for promenades and entertainment (Sargent 1974). Many of the houses abandoned by the élite in the southern *barrios* were taken over by immigrants and the urban poor and turned into *conventillos* or tenement houses. This process led to the remarkable juxtaposition in the densely populated urban core of crowded *conventillos* next to spacious mansions, banks, and other imposing public buildings.

The pace of Buenos Aires' incorporation into the expanding world economy accelerated between 1852 and 1880, spurred by several important events. Following the overthrow of Rosas in 1852, a liberal-oriented, progress-minded succession of leaders helped to formulate and implement Argentina's 1853 Constitution. The Constitution's major theme was "to govern is to populate . . . educate, improve, civilize, enrich, and grow spontaneously and rapidly." Second, political stability in Argentina encouraged an inflow of British investment capital. This proved important for both Buenos Aires and the nation because Argentinos were reluctant to invest their own capital in infrastructural improvements and new technologies. Safe and rapid returns from investments in land and agricultural production were preferred over investments in "speculative" technologies such as railroads, trolleys, and port works.

Third, after 1862, Buenos Aires functioned both as the seat of national government and as the capital of Buenos Aires province, essentially controlling the vast majority of the fledgling nation's wealth and economic potential. Fourth, European immigrants began to arrive in ever-increasing numbers, a process that would alter profoundly the ethnic and social characteristics of Buenos Aires over the coming decades. Finally, urban transport development changed the entire space–time dynamic of Buenos Aires and provided the impetus for the city's rapid areal and economic growth after 1870. Construction on the first railroad in Buenos Aires, the Ferrocarril del Oeste, began in 1854. Eight years later, the line extended approximately 40 kilometers west via Flores and Merlo to the speculative railroad plat of Moreno. Lines also ran north from Retiro toward the Paraná delta at Tigre and south from Plaza Constitución toward La Plata and Chascomús (Figure 2.2).

Charles Sargent (1974) has examined in detail the powerful link between urban development and transport in Buenos Aires. His authoritative analysis illustrated how transport innovations, population growth, and real estate development coalesced between 1870 and 1930 to transform the traditional concentric frame of Buenos Aires into a multi-nucleated, sectorially differentiated city more akin to Chicago than to other Latin cities. Tramways running first in the civic center (1869) and then between La Boca and Barracas (1870) prompted poorer residents to move to the southern working-class *barrios*. Railroads and tramways running west and north from the center also encouraged the gradual movement of the growing middle-class sector toward Belgrano and Flores (Figure 2.3). By 1900, Flores had become the city's most important middle-class residential area for government, commerce, and banking

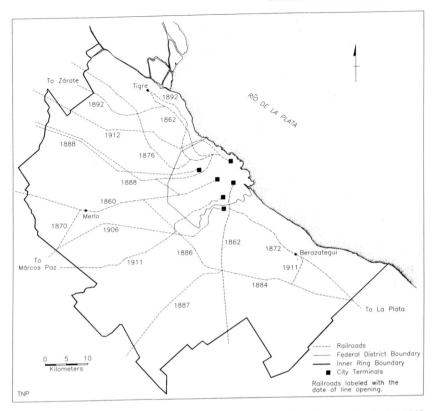

Figure 2.2 The growth of Buenos Aires' suburban railroad network, 1854–1912.
Source: After Sargent (1974)

employees. Land speculation along transport routes stimulated areal expansion in Buenos Aires as well as rapid population growth outside the core. Although the city's population had grown steadily since independence, recording an increase of 667 percent between 1810 and 1880, demographic change moved into high gear after the 1860s (Table 2.1). Not only were foreign migrants flowing into Buenos Aires, but the trickle of people moving from the increasingly impoverished interior threatened to become a flood.

Federal capital and expanding metropolis, 1880–1945

The fifth stage of Buenos Aires' urban development occurred against the backdrop of national territorial and political integration, the incorporation of Argentina fully into the world economy, and the adoption of

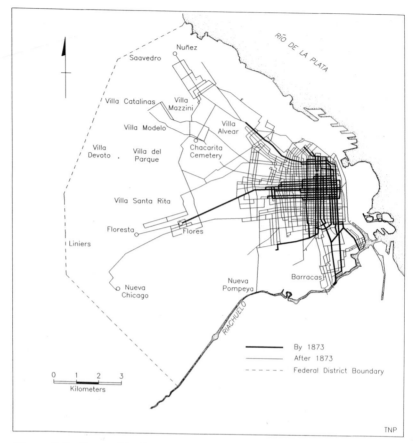

Figure 2.3   Buenos Aires' tramway network, 1900. *Source:* After Sargent (1974)

European models of progress and modernization. From this period emerged two powerful themes that have shaped development policies and ideologies to this day: (i) a belief that Buenos Aires represented the civilized, modernized European world and that the interior was barbaric and backward, and (ii) a belief that what was good for Buenos Aires was good for Argentina. In other words, all of Argentina should aspire to be like the sophisticated, cosmopolitan, Europeanized capital.

Urban development ideology in Argentina traces its roots to the early nineteenth century, when European models of progress and modernization nourished to maturity the political and economic ideas of the ruling liberal élite. Argentina's Liberals were an urban-based clique of bureaucrats and merchants who believed Buenos Aires should be the bastion from which the civilization of Argentina could proceed (Burns 1980).

Table 2.1 Estimated population growth, Buenos Aires, 1580–1880

Year	Population	Year	Population	Year	Population
1580	300	1712	8000	1826	60 000
1617	1000	1753	15 000	1854	90 000
1638	2000	1786	30 000	1869	171 000
1667	4000	1810	45 000	1880	300 000

Source: After Sargent (1974).

From the civilized capital, European technology and culture – the tools of modernization and progress – would serve to develop Argentina in the image of both Europe and Buenos Aires. As David Rock (1987, p. 121) argued, from the Liberals' perspective:

> the port-city would enjoy complete political and economic primacy, using the provinces as markets, a source of exportables or local food supplies, essentially as tributaries to be exploited or ignored at will.

Thus, absolute political control over the republic was central to the plans of the *porteño* élite.

Buenos Aires finally prevailed in its struggle for political hegemony over the nation, although the city lost its position as capital of wealthy Buenos Aires province. The seeds for political dominance had been sown in the 1853 Constitution, which provided for a strong central government and free internal trade. By nature of its location, economic power, and institutional strength, Buenos Aires would become a federal district. However, political maneuvering, internal dissent, and an exhausting war with Paraguay delayed the process for 27 years. Not until 1880 did Buenos Aires become a federal district and the official capital of the Republic of Argentina. The major portions of two *partidos* (counties) and a small portion of a third were combined with the city of Buenos Aires to create the Federal District, with territorial limits of 18 800 hectares (Figure 2.4).

With the political struggles behind them, *porteño* civic leaders now could concentrate on remodeling Buenos Aires into a progressive, modern city. Buenos Aires underwent a dramatic physical, cultural, and social transformation between 1880 and 1920, evolving from *La Gran Aldea* (the big village) into the showplace of Latin America. The federal capital's urban facade began to take on its present form, shaped by a growing cosmopolitan population, renovated architecture, European ethnic groups and their likes and habits, an active and expanding port, and the beginning of a modern industrial base driven by railroads,

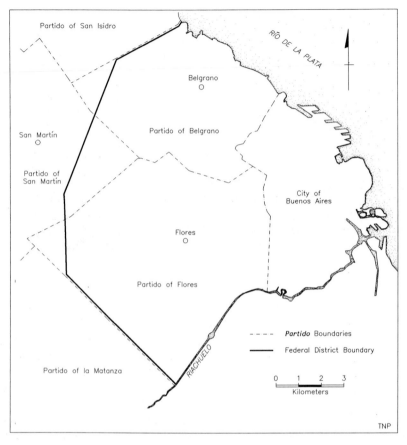

Figure 2.4   The boundaries of the Federal District of Buenos Aires, 1880. *Source:* After Sargent (1974)

streetcars, and printing factories (Romero 1984). In addition, national infrastructural and economic development clearly favored Buenos Aires. As a major port, the focus of the country's dendritic railroad network, and the principal source of finance capital, Buenos Aires prospered from its increasing articulation with the world economy. In contrast, the interior slipped deeper into poverty, disease, isolation, and underdevelopment. The bifurcation of Argentina into a wealthy coastal region and an impoverished interior would have profound implications for Buenos Aires during the latter half of the twentieth century.

Baron Georges Haussmann's late nineteenth century Parisian designs provided a template for urban renovation in Buenos Aires. *Porteños* expressed their admiration for French culture and society by attempting to give the Hispanic colonial city a more Parisian feel. The two plazas

Figure 2.5   Parisian-style architecture in the Buenos Aires city center

adjacent to the cathedral that functioned as the traditional center of power and prestige in the city were reunited to form the present-day Plaza de Mayo. Architects and planners cast aside Juan de Garay's original street plan and widened many streets into broad, paved avenues replete with Jacaranda trees, sidewalks of Swedish marble, and Parisian-style cafés. Many sections of the downtown core were leveled to create four parallel avenues: Santa Fe, Córdoba, Corrientes, and Avenida de Mayo. Inaugurated in 1894, Avenida de Mayo became the major spine linking the Casa Rosada (Presidential Palace) to the new Congress complex 2 kilometers west, as well as the dividing line between the city's northern and southern *barrios*. This grand avenue, the "Champs-Élysées" of Buenos Aires, saw the city's first automobiles (1890s), first elevator (1898), first omnibus (1904), and its first underground railroad (1913) (Sargent 1975). The *La Prensa* newspaper building, the Gothic–Roman Pasaje Barolo, and the myriad hotels, cafés, bookshops, carnivals, and theaters that lined Avenida de Mayo all exuded Parisian style and ambience. Throughout the downtown core, impressive public and private buildings constructed in the Parisian mold began to replace traditional colonial architecture (Figure 2.5). Bois de Boulogne in Paris served as a model for the cultivated gardens and promenades of remodeled Palermo Park, while the Champs-Élysées provided a blueprint for wide Avenida 9 de Julio. The contours of contemporary Buenos Aires now were defined clearly.

British railroad companies showed some resistance to the *porteños'* boundless admiration for French style. Euston station in London and

Liverpool's Lime Street, not the Gare du Nord in Paris, served as models for Buenos Aires' two major railroad terminals, Constitución and Retiro. The terminals became the southern and northern limits, respectively, of commercial activity in the city. The area around Retiro functioned as an important industrial center, while agro-industrial processes concentrated behind Constitución, along the Riachuelo, and southward (Walter 1993). Centers of industry and population also grew in the suburbs of Quilmes, Avellaneda, Barracas, Merlo, Ensenada, Tigre, and Moreno, mostly beyond the boundaries of the Federal District. By the early 1900s, nearly 25 percent of Argentina's manufacturing establishments, over 30 percent of all persons employed in industrial activities, and over 50 percent of total industrial investments were located in and around the city of Buenos Aires (Walter 1982, Schvarzer 1983). However, despite rapid areal expansion, much of the original federal territory still remained under agriculture in 1914, especially along the western and south-western corridors.

Central to the modernization of Buenos Aires and its incorporation more fully into the regional and international economies was the development of adequate port facilities. Buenos Aires long had suffered from major inefficiencies in the loading and unloading of cargo and passengers, with obvious financial impacts on shippers, retailers, and consumers. The advent of larger and faster steamships and refrigerated vessels also placed great stress on the city's cargo-handling capabilities. Plans for building a new port provoked long and bitter debates over construction methods and location (Scobie 1971). A site on the mud flats directly east of the civic center finally won approval, and construction on Puerto Madero began in 1887. New port facilities (Puerto Nuevo) were added north of Madero near Retiro in 1914. Locating the city's port facilities near the Plaza de Mayo reinforced the importance of the civic center and encouraged commercial development north of the Plaza rather than south. Throughout the early decades of the twentieth century, wholesale and retail outlets, warehouses, transportation facilities, and real estate interests focused primarily on the *barrios* west and north of the Plaza. This pattern of growth solidified the power, prestige, and wealth of the *porteño* élite who concentrated north of the civic center.

Economic, political, and commercial growth stimulated demographic change, and vice versa. Between 1869 and 1930, the population of Buenos Aires increased 14-fold. Over 3 million people, approximately 30 percent of Argentina's total population, lived in or close to the Federal District as the decade of the 1930s dawned. European migrants especially flocked to Argentina during the first decades of the twentieth century. Precluded from buying farms on the Pampas by the small, tight-knit group of families who controlled land ownership, most immigrants ended up in Buenos Aires. More than any other urban center, the capital provided labor opportunities for newcomers in the meat-packing plants, railroad and service industries, and small factories that ringed the urban core. The more successful immigrants became shopkeepers, teachers, bureaucrats, bank clerks, and small business owners, forming a new urban middle class in the process.

Several clearly demarcated zones divided pre-World War II Buenos Aires. The *gente bien* (well-to-do) inhabited the mansions of Barrio Norte, Palermo, and the northern suburb of Belgrano. Beyond lay the suburban *quintas* (estates) of San Isidro, Vicente López, and Olivos, dotted along the Río de la Plata shoreline north toward Tigre. Middle-class neighborhoods were located in the center and westward to Flores and beyond. To the south lay the industrial, manufacturing, and working-class areas of Nueva Pompeya, Barracas, Avellaneda, and La Boca. Housing proved to be a persistent problem in Buenos Aires. Wealthy and poor *porteños* lived side-by-side in the inner-city *barrios*, where *conventillos* (tenements) remained interspersed with wealthy mansions. Nearly 80 percent of all working-class families lived in one-room households. One dwelling may have been occupied by as many as 12 families. Skilled industrial workers and middle-income white collar workers built up much of the suburban areas. Initially, however, entire suburban *barrios* were subdivided without basic facilities. Paved streets, sanitation, street lights, and piped water were not part of the developer's mission. No zoning existed, so any piece of land could be used for any purpose, whatever the environmental implications.

During the 1920s and 1930s, *porteños* and others considered Buenos Aires to be the cultural mecca of Latin America. Opera and ballet presented in the Teatro Colón rivaled performances in Milan and Berlin. The tango emerged from the brothels, bars, and *conventillos* (tenements) of the city's southern *barrios* to achieve respectability in France and subsequent worldwide renown. Intellectuals, writers, and students huddled over endless cups of coffee in the trendiest cafés and restaurants, discussing the latest fads and fashions from Paris and London. Art galleries, literary magazines, bookstores, and newspapers found a ready and almost insatiable audience. Buenos Aires enjoyed its most glorious days. However, although growth and change in Buenos Aires continued apace throughout the 1930s and early 1940s, the city's golden age of development was drawing inexorably to a close. The onset of a national political crisis, combined with the 1929 Wall Street crash, the ensuing global economic depression, the introduction of import-substitution policies in Argentina, and World War II began to change the dynamics of urban evolution in Buenos Aires.

Emerging world city, 1946–1990

Although the roots of the city's contemporary condition stretch back to the sixteenth century, perhaps the most profound changes in Buenos Aires have occurred since the end of World War II. [Over the past 50 years Buenos Aires has emerged as one of the world's 10 great megalopolises, exerting control over a region with tremendous natural and human resources. Several clear spatial patterns emerged during this most recent stage of Buenos Aires' geohistorical evolution (Sargent 1993). First, the peripheral areas of the city expanded and infilled at a rapid pace, accentuating the need for a reappraisal of the territorial definition of Greater Buenos Aires (GBA). Second, steady and high core-area densities continued to characterize the Federal District. Third, densities increased in upper-income *barrios* as high-rise apartments and condominiums replaced older mansions, especially north of the downtown core. Fourth, population rates began to stagnate in the industrial lowlands. Fifth, massive migration from the interior provinces led to the large-scale development of *villas de emergencia* (shantytowns) around the urban periphery and in selected *barrios* of the Federal District. The Municipal Housing Commission embarked on an ambitious construction program to deal with the influx of migrants. But population growth and suburban expansion outpaced the ability of the government to build houses, maintain adequate employment opportunities, and to provide health and education facilities. Finally, the spatial dynamics of mobility in Buenos Aires changed as automobiles, roads, and freeways replaced the tramways and trolley buses.]

Institutional and social changes played a critical role in the post-World War II reshaping of Buenos Aires. Perhaps the most enduring legacy from this period is Juan Domingo Perón's development of the social state. Perón nationalized much of Argentina's transport system, public utilities, and major industries, and led the drive toward domestic industrialization and economic independence (Rock 1993). In theory, disarticulation from a world economy that drew primary exports from Argentina and returned goods manufactured in the North Atlantic countries would allow Argentina to develop its own national economic and social identity. A more equitable process of regional development would result from such a strategy. Import substitution programs primarily benefited the Buenos Aires metropolis, however, as the major industries concentrated along the Río Paraná and Río de la Plata from San Nicolás in the north to Ensenada south of the capital. Development strategists headquartered in Buenos Aires gave little recognition to social, economic, political, and cultural diversity in the interior provinces. They pursued a homogeneous approach to national planning driven by the idea that the rest of Argentina should be like Buenos Aires. Perón's administration, argued James Scobie (1971, p. 235), "deliberately depreciated rural occupations and promised bread and circuses for the urban masses." The national capital thus became the employment heart of Argentina, and even more people flooded in from the countryside and from neighboring states.

Perónist domestic policies, dubbed *Justicialismo* (social justice), reshaped Buenos Aires society by improving social benefits, housing, and jobs in the public sector, and by institutionalizing lucrative fringe benefits for many workers. A belief that the state should provide became embedded quickly in the ideology of both the working and middle classes. However, participation and pride in local government institutions eroded as fraud, inefficiency, and corruption reached new heights. Massive featherbedding in state-run businesses became the norm, the number of *ñoquis* (people who received a paycheck but never turned up for work) proliferated, and a general malaise in entrepreneurial spirit settled over Buenos Aires. Between 1943 and 1963, the cost of living index in the capital multiplied by a factor of 60. Using 100 as a base index in 1960, by the end of the decade the index had risen to 687. Unfortunately, neither wages nor the value of Argentina's currency kept pace with inflation. The rich got richer, while the working and middle classes suffered a severe erosion in buying power and standard of living. Both city and nation fell into a period of political and economic crisis, culminating in military repression, the "Dirty War" (1976–1982), massive foreign debt, and a dramatic deterioration in the quality of life for the urban masses.

Rural–urban migration flows during the immediate postwar period were spurred, in part, by government policies that encouraged industry over agriculture and allowed interior transport facilities to deteriorate. Jobs and rising standards of living became available only in the major urban centers, primarily the capital. Between 1947 and 1951 alone, nearly 200 000 people annually migrated from the interior to GBA. Profound demographic changes in Buenos Aires have continued to this day. The metropolitan population swelled between 1947 and 1991 from just under five million to nearly 13 million, with growth occurring almost entirely in the city's suburbs. Only 11 percent of the national population resided after World War II in the 19 *partidos* surrounding the Federal District. By 1991, this number had grown to 25 percent. In contrast, the number of people living in the Federal District has declined slightly since 1947, when 18.8 percent of Argentina's total population resided there. Now the Federal District accounts for approximately 9 percent of the country's population. However, since 1970, the overall rate of demographic increase in the Buenos Aires agglomeration compared with the national level has shown signs of decline. This coincides with the general perception by potential migrants that the comparative advantages provided by Buenos Aires in past decades, whether real or perceived, are not as available in the 1990s (Ainstein 1992). Nonetheless, Buenos Aires continues to attract substantial flows of migrants.

Reflecting the post-1945 reorganization of the world economy and growing disenchantment with Perónist economic policies, direct foreign investment from the United States poured into Buenos Aires during the late 1950s and early 1960s. The United States now accounted for over 50 percent of the foreign investment capital circulating in Argentina, signaling a dramatic change in the country's global economic linkages. Traditional ties to Europe were being augmented by strong relationships with the United States. Multinational capital focused particularly on the petrochemical, metallurgical, mechanical, pharmaceutical, and electronics industries. New industrial plants in Buenos Aires created a second industrial belt within a radius of 40 kilometers from the urban core. These industries grew along the principal axes of communication, especially to the south (Berazategui and Ensenada), the southwest (Isidro Casanova and San Justo), the west (Merlo), and to the north along the Pan-American Highway (General Pacheco, Garín, and Pilar). Yet despite the construction of new factories and plants beyond the Federal District, management and administrative functions were carried out from offices in the central city. The concentration of service, financial, and tourist activities in the downtown area encouraged the densification and northward expansion of Buenos Aires' commercial–bureaucratic core. It also motivated the municipal government to develop the Catalinas Norte office complex opposite Retiro station, deactivate the docks of Puerto Madero, and push back the shoreline of the Río de la Plata with landfill and reclamation projects (Ludueña 1993).

Intensification of Buenos Aires' commercial–bureaucratic functions increased the diurnal flow of traffic to and from the downtown area. A steady increase in the use of private automobiles, coupled with ongoing congestion along the city's major arterials, influenced the construction during the 1970s of a series of urban freeways. Traffic planners drew heavily from North American interstate highway ideology, arguing that direct freeway access into the downtown core would stimulate economic development, address traffic flow problems, and ease congestion on urban arterials. As with several freeway projects in cities around the world, however, construction has been suspended on many of the freeways because of financial difficulties and environmental opposition. Moreover, increased economic development and a reduction in urban traffic congestion proved elusive goals for Buenos Aires' transport planners. Cynics argued that urban freeways in Buenos Aires had become nothing more than the shortest link between two traffic jams (Meyer and Gomez-Ibáñez 1981).

Buenos Aires has experienced further morphological changes since the 1989 election of President Carlos Menem. Unfortunately, holes in the downtown sidewalks are not evidence of new construction. They are more indicative of general urban decline and infrastructural collapse. The Menem government's policy of "disappearing the state" through privatization, deregulation, and globalization strategies has encouraged an influx of speculative capital into Buenos Aires. Yet globalizing the city's economy has not stimulated the development of high-rise office towers, high-tech factories, or urban infrastructure. Problems of inadequate housing, sewage facilities, electricity, and transportation throughout the metropolitan area remain subjects of rhetoric not political action. Instead, glitzy megamalls, trendy sports clubs in élite *barrios*, and upscale shopping centers have sprung up around Buenos Aires. The speculative real estate boom also has spurred the construction of high-rise, luxury condominiums and apartment complexes in the wealthier neighborhoods.

As the decade of the 1990s unfolds, Buenos Aires faces many local crises as the government pursues the dream of world city status and global economic involvement. Institutional, individual, and community responses to the dynamic tensions that stem from the convergence of local and global forces are forging new spatial and temporal patterns in the modern metropolis. In the following chapter, we shift from a broad historical overview of urban development to an intimate and detailed analysis of Buenos Aires' contemporary urban landscapes.

3

The visible city: contemporary urban landscapes

Defining the exact areal extent of contemporary Buenos Aires is an important first step in examining the city's urban landscapes. What are the boundaries of the metropolitan area? Traditionally, metropolitan Buenos Aires has comprised the Federal District and 19 *partidos* or counties that surround the core. Data published by Argentina's National Census Institute (INDEC) long have relied on this definition of metropolitan Buenos Aires. During the 1970s and 1980s, planners and others began to include Greater La Plata and six other *partidos* (the Middle Ring) when defining the areal extent of Greater Buenos Aires (GBA). As early as 1978, however, strategies outlined by the Department of Planning and Development (SEPLADE) for the modernization of Buenos Aires defined the metropolitan axis as including the 23 counties that form the city's Outer Ring (SEPLADE 1978) (Figure 3.1). The boundary of urbanized and semi-urbanized territory considered by SEPLADE coincides with the course of the Río Salado, southwest of Buenos Aires, and with the Río Paraná to the north.

In the 1990s, a consensus is being reached by geographers, planners, and others that the framework for analyzing urban processes in Buenos Aires ought to be the metropolitan axis defined by SEPLADE. This definition of Buenos Aires makes sense for several reasons. First, it acknowledges that the dynamics of growth and change in the city have spatial implications beyond the boundaries of the Federal District and its adjacent *partidos*. Second, it provides a sound basis for an integrated, territorial strategy to address the spatial distribution of growth in the metropolitan region. Third, it recognizes the urban interdependencies,

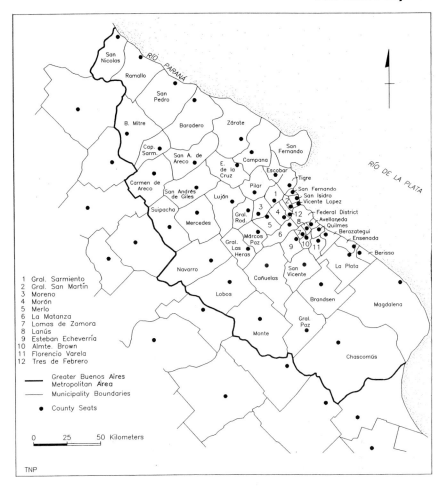

Figure 3.1 The Greater Buenos Aires Metropolitan Area, 1994

interlinked associations of establishments, and transport flows that shape functional relationships in the Buenos Aires region. Finally, it lays the foundation for a coordinated approach to confronting the political, economic, and social tensions resulting from Buenos Aires' involvement in the world economy and the world city system.

Unlike Tokyo, Paris, New York, or Sydney, there are no observation towers or centrally placed high-rise buildings in Buenos Aires from which the general public may enjoy a panoramic vista of the city. Nor are there physical landmarks, other than the Río de la Plata, to help develop a sense of orientation, as in Río de Janeiro, San Francisco, or Hong Kong. Buenos Aires' flat, urbanized landscape seems to stretch to

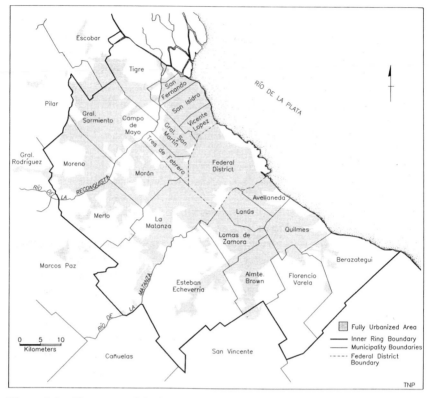

Figure 3.2 The extent of the fully urbanized area of Buenos Aires, 1994. *Source:* After Jones (1993)

infinity. From the air, the metropolitan area exhibits the characteristics of a city with tentacles, with the intensity of urban use decreasing from the center of Buenos Aires and also away from the communication axes (Ludueña 1993). Buenos Aires is characterized spatially by four primary development axes that splay out northwest, west, southwest, and south from the Federal District. The expansion of the city's built-up area historically has taken place along these corridors. Cities and towns dotted along the corridors form chains of urban axes along which has spread the development impetus of Buenos Aires' economic dynamism. Figure 3.2 highlights the totally urbanized area of Buenos Aires, most of which is contained within the Federal District and the suburban Inner Ring. Approximately 45 percent of the territory of Buenos Aires is under continual urbanization. Large industrial facilities account for 6 percent, forests, parks, and natural reserves cover 15 percent of the territory, and non-urban, agricultural, and transitional uses account for the remaining 34 percent.

The most practical way of exploring and explicating the modern city is through a neighborhood survey. Buenos Aires, as with every world city, is best understood and appreciated by seeing, feeling, sensing, smelling, and tasting the essence of life in the *barrios*. Cultural geographer Jan Broek (1965, p. 72) argued that "each society in each era perceives and interprets its physical surroundings and its relations to other [places] through the prism of its own way of life." Impressions and images of the urban environment help to shape people's attitudes toward their surroundings, and many urbanists have attempted to measure and understand people's perceptions of the urban landscape. Kevin Lynch (1960), an urban designer, suggested that five important elements can be found in the mental maps of urbanites. First, "pathways" such as streets, transit corridors, and freeways are routes of frequent travel that circumscribe zones of activity. Second, "edges" are the boundaries between areas. Rivers, shorelines, freeways, and other neighborhoods commonly function as edges. Third, "nodes" are strategic junction points where important pathways intersect. Fourth, "districts" such as *barrios* (neighborhoods), ethnic areas, and functional zones are small areas with common identities. Finally, "landmarks" are reference points that help people develop context and sense of place. Historic buildings, cultural icons, frequently visited stores, and neighborhood cafés all provide legibility to the urban landscape. These elements provide an important frame of reference as we read and interpret the urban landscape of Buenos Aires.

Although this chapter is primarily descriptive in nature, designed to give spatial context and meaning to the analysis of later chapters, a thematic–spatial approach provides a framework for understanding the city. Four central themes shape our examination of the various municipalities and neighborhoods in Buenos Aires. Each area's changing population characteristics, industrial activities, and major transport arterials or "pathways" help to define a district's basic geographic qualities. The location of important physical and cultural reference points or "landmarks" helps to distinguish each "district" as separate and distinct components of the urban system. Various "edges" and "nodes" characterize each area's position and function within the metropolitan region and give it context in the urban system. Finally, changes in settlement patterns give some indication of the city's ongoing socioeconomic transformation.

The study's primary focus is on change in the *barrios* of the Federal District and the *partidos* of the Inner Ring. However, the municipalities that comprise Buenos Aires' Middle and Outer Rings merit attention as they are vital components of the metropolitan system. Thus, from a spatial perspective, first we examine the principal urban centers located along the four primary corridors of the Outer Ring. Second, Greater La Plata and the growing *partidos* of the Middle Ring are discussed and analyzed. Third, we explore the mix of country clubs, middle-class suburbs, industrial centers, suburban farms, and *villas de emergencia* that define the 19 *partidos* of the Inner Ring. Finally, the focus shifts to the 47 *barrios* of the Federal District, beginning with the neighborhoods that form the inner-city periphery and ending at the heart of contemporary Buenos Aires, the Plaza de Mayo.

The Outer Ring

Twenty-three municipalities, stretching from San Nicolás near the boundary between Buenos Aires and Sante Fé provinces in the northwest, to Chascomús in the south, comprise the Outer Ring of metropolitan Buenos Aires (Figure 3.3). With a total population exceeding 800 000, and a growth rate of 16 percent between 1980 and 1991 (Table 3.1), these satellite urban and rural areas have become crucial components of the city's functional relationships. Several important towns and industrial zones are located along the four major corridors that fan out from Buenos Aires and serve as principal pathways in the Outer Ring. The most significant corridor runs northwest from Buenos Aires through the six *partidos* contiguous to the Río Paraná: San Nicolás, Ramallo, San Pedro, Baradero, Zárate, and Campana. A broad-gauge line of the General Mitre railroad and the Pan-American Highway (National Route 9) function as the corridor's two major pathways, linking Buenos Aires with Rosario (Argentina's third largest city) and providing vital transport services to the cities of San Nicolás, Zárate, and Campana. The corridor also includes the *partidos* of Bartólome Mitre, Capitán Sarmiento, Exaltación de la Cruz, and San Antonio de Areco. Many factories, industrial complexes, and commercial centers have located along this growth axis in recent decades, spurring a steady growth in population. Since the 1980 census, for example, San Nicolás has recorded a 16.9 percent growth rate, Zárate 17.6 percent, and Campana has registered a 23.4 percent growth.

The city of San Nicolás is an important industrial center, with a population of 100 000. One of Argentina's largest industrial complexes, the General Savio steel plant, is located here, along with other important manufacturing plants. San Nicolás functions as an edge or boundary, the outermost node of the Greater Buenos Aires metropolitan area (GBAMA), and as a vital component of the region's premier economic development axis. Zárate, the second major town and the most important node of the northwestern corridor, sits on the banks of the Río Paraná approximately 90 kilometers from Buenos Aires. The town functions as

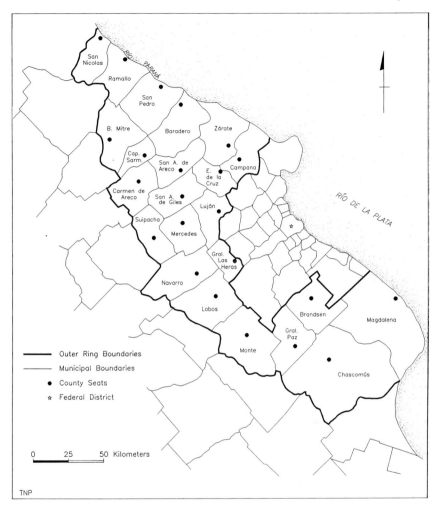

Figure 3.3 The municipalities and county seats of the suburban Outer Ring, 1994.
Source: República Argentina (1991)

the northwest terminal of Buenos Aires' suburban railroad system and as an important interchange point for traffic crossing the Paraná delta via the Brazo Largo bridge complex. Increased trade with Brazil and Uruguay as a result of the Common Market of the Southern Cone (MERCOSUR) agreements has increased the flow of traffic to and from Buenos Aires, much of which utilizes the Brazo Largo bridge. Services, factories, and other infrastructure have sprung up along the northwest axis since 1990 in response to this new regional economic dynamism.

The western corridor encompasses the seven *partidos* of Carmen de

Table 3.1   Population growth in the Outer Ring of Greater Buenos Aires, 1970–1991

Corridor/ municipality	Population 1970	Population 1980	1991	Area (km²)	Density (population/km²)
Northwestern					
Baradero	21 390	26 041	28 493	1514	25.0[a]
Bartóleme Mitre	20 466	22 012	24 576	1183	20.8
Campana	44 297	57 839	71 360	982	235.5[a]
Capitán Sarmiento	9479	10 326	11 474	617	18.6
Exaltación de la Cruz	10 630	12 859	17 041	662	25.7
Ramallo	18 339	22 704	27 023	1040	26.0
San Antonio de Areco	14 255	16 370	18 872	852	22.2
San Nicolás	82 925	114 241	133 503	680	196.3
San Pedro	34 350	41 049	48 650	1322	36.8
Zárate	61 546	78 046	91 820	1202	150.5[a]
Western					
Carmen de Areco	9900	11 031	12 603	1080	11.7
General Las Heras	7480	9371	11 007	760	14.5
Luján	58 909	68 689	80 712	800	100.9
Mercedes	47 073	51 207	55 685	1050	53.0
Navarro	12 472	12 197	13 842	1630	8.5
San Andrés de Giles	15 433	16 353	18 260	1135	16.1
Suipacha	7245	7275	8031	950	8.5
Southwestern					
Lobos	26 022	27 753	30 815	1740	17.7
Monte	11 165	12 883	15 495	1890	8.2
Southern					
Chascomús	25 927	29 936	34 980	4225	8.3
Brandsen	12 568	15 361	18 452	1130	16.3
General Paz	8444	8979	9271	1240	7.5
Magdalena	20 248	21 710	22 416	3490	6.4
Total	580 563	694 232	804 381	31 174	25.8

Source: República Argentina (1980, 1991).
[a] Excluding the area of the Río Paraná islands.

Areco, General Las Heras, Luján, Mercedes, Navarro, San Andrés de Giles, and Suipacha. Population growth continues at a steady pace in this zone, although not at the rate experienced by the northwestern counties. Luján, the most populated *partido* of the western Outer Ring, and General Las Heras grew rapidly during the 1980s, each recording a 17.5 percent increase in population (see Table 3.1). The remaining *partidos* have retained their rural character, with urban development concentrated primarily along the main highways and railroad lines that slice through the heart of the corridor. Mercedes functions as the major node of the western axis, and suburban railroad services terminate here.

Much of the land in the western zone is given over to rural activities. Cattle raising, suburban truck farms, and some large-scale commercial agriculture dominate the landscape. Two of the three major streams of the GBA area, the Río Luján and the Río Reconquista, rise in the flat western farmland of the Outer Ring and run east, eventually spilling into the Río de la Plata estuary. Flooding is a perennial problem along the rivers' courses.

Along the southwestern corridor sit the *partidos* of Lobos and Monte, perhaps the most rural of the Outer Ring's 23 counties. The towns of Lobos and San Miguel de Monte were founded in the late eighteenth century as forts for the defense of Buenos Aires against marauding indigenous groups. Today the towns play host to urbanites who escape the noisy and polluted central city to enjoy water sports, fishing, and hunting. Camp grounds, barbecues areas, restaurants, bars, and hotels have flourished on and around the area's lakes, woods, and streams. Although Monte recorded a population increase of over 20 percent during the 1980s, much of the growth occurred in San Miguel de Monte, the county seat and only urban center. Suburban railroad service extends only to Lobos, the larger of the two urban centers in the Outer Ring's southwestern zone.

The southern development axis of the Outer Ring incorporates the *partidos* of Chascomús, Brandsen, General Paz, and Magdalena. Much of this corridor remains under small-scale agriculture and cattle ranching, with little evidence of suburbanization processes extending along the General Roca railroad line or along National Highway 2. Only Chascomús and Brandsen have experienced significant population growth in recent decades (see Table 3.1). The town of Chascomús lies 125 kilometers from the Plaza de Mayo on the shore of one of the region's most important lakes and near the Parque de los Libres del Sur, a museum complex extending over some 20 hectares of woodland. Also in Chascomús can be found the Chapel of the Negroes, one of the few remaining references to African culture in the GBA region. At the beginning of the nineteenth century, many liberated slaves joined the *Hermandad de los Morenos* (the Colored Brotherhood) and mingled with the so-called "lost people" living on the outer fringes of the city. The chapel is now a National Historical Monument and serves as a reminder of the important role African-Argentines played in the development of the city's culture and economy.

Buenos Aires' Outer Ring remains predominantly semirural in form and function. Suburbanization processes are occurring primarily along the northwestern corridor and in satellite towns such as Luján, Mercedes, and Lobos. Inadequate public transport infrastructure and services in the Outer Ring have inhibited urban expansion in recent decades, although many of the Outer Ring's residents commute daily into the city by private automobile. Land and property prices have not experienced the rapid increases of central Buenos Aires, although some evidence of property speculation can be found around the outskirts of these satellite towns. In contrast to most North American cities, large-scale suburban subdivisions and semi-urban housing estates have yet to reach the Outer Ring.

The Middle Ring

Buenos Aires' rapidly growing Middle Ring contains the six *partidos* that were incorporated into the official Buenos Aires Statistical Region in 1991, plus the three *partidos* of the Greater La Plata region (Figure 3.4). With the exception of Greater La Plata along the southern axis, the *partidos* of the Middle Ring have experienced the most dramatic population increases of the entire GBAMA over the past two decades. With much of the Federal District and Inner Ring completely urbanized and densely settled, suburban expansion during the 1980s and 1990s has occurred primarily in the Middle Ring along the northwestern axis and to the southwest (Table 3.2). For example, a comparison of population growth rates between 1980 and 1991 in the GBAMA reveals the highest rates of increase in Escobar, Pilar, Marcos Paz, and General Rodríguez (Figure 3.5). Pilar, Escobar, and General Rodríguez experienced over 50 percent growth between 1980 and 1991, growth stimulated in part by the expansion of business and industry along the northwest corridor. Urban expansion has occurred particularly around the towns of Escobar, Garín, Pilar, Savio, and Maschwitz, and along the Sarmiento railroad line toward Luján and Mercedes.

A phenomenon of suburban development in the Middle Ring during the 1980s was the transformation of *quintas* or weekend homes into "country clubs" for permanent residence. Easy access to the downtown core by private automobile encouraged the élite to move out to the suburbs, and country clubs sprang up quickly along the two main highways linking Escobar and Pilar to the Federal District. With access controlled by gatekeepers, walls, and fences, the country clubs quickly became suburban enclaves for the wealthy. Individual houses inside the grounds of the clubs are spaced among beautifully manicured gardens, open grounds for sports and recreation, and often a nine- or 18-hole golf course (Figure 3.6). The availability of basic services such as telephones, water, and sewers inside the country clubs stands in stark contrast to the thousands of surrounding houses that have no municipal services at all.

To the west, the *partidos* of Cañuelas and Marcos Paz are infilling

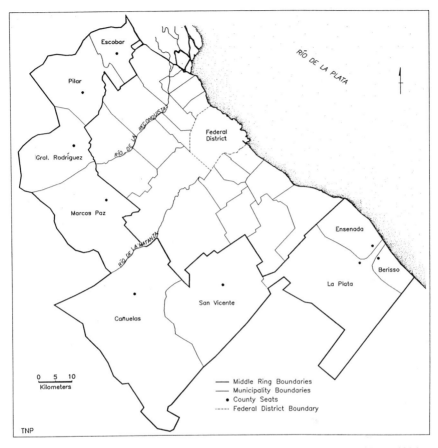

Figure 3.4 The municipalities and county seats of the suburban Middle Ring, 1994.
Source: República Argentina (1991)

slowly but steadily, with towns and villages along both railroad and road corridors starting to coalesce east toward the Federal District. Suburban bus and rail services extend to the major settlements of these municipalities, which encourages daily commuting to the factories of the Inner Ring or the offices of the downtown core. To the southwest, country clubs also are springing up beyond Ezeiza international airport and toward San Vicente. It is not unusual on a Saturday morning to see red-coated horse riders with hounds in tow preparing themselves for the weekend hunt in true English country style. The gentrification of several of the outer suburbs is changing the complexity of suburban life in Buenos Aires and forcing rapid increases in both land and housing costs. Although property developers rarely take an interest in the open, low-lying areas along suburban streams and rivers (the traditional location

Table 3.2 Population growth in the Middle Ring of Greater Buenos Aires, 1970–1991

Corridor/ municipality	Population 1970	Population 1980	1991	Area (km^2)	Density (population/km^2)
Northwestern					
Escobar	46 150	81 385	128 651	277	556.9[a]
General Rodríguez	23 596	32 035	48 358	360	134.3
Pilar	47 739	84 429	130 177	352	369.8
Western					
Cañuelas	21 430	25 391	31 012	1200	25.8
Marcos Paz	15 070	20 225	29 101	470	61.9
Southwestern					
San Vicente	39 187	55 803	74 890	740	101.2
Southern					
Berisso	58 833	66 152	74 012	135	548.2
Ensenada	39 154	41 323	48 524	101	480.4
La Plata	408 300	477 175	542 567	926	585.9
Total	699 459	883 918	1 107 292	4561	242.8

Source: República Argentina (1980, 1991).

[a] Excluding the area of the Río Paraná delta islands.

for *villas de emergencia* or shantytowns), any vacant land in the periphery now is viewed as a potential site for a country club, private golf course, or suburban housing estate. Some *partidos* of the Middle Ring are beginning to experience the type of suburban expansion that characterized North American cities during the 1950s.

At the southern end of the Middle Ring sits the Greater La Plata urban area. Encompassing three *partidos*, Greater La Plata is home to nearly 700 000 people and extends over 1162 square kilometers (see Table 3.2). The city of La Plata, capital of the province of Buenos Aires and located 56 kilometers southeast of the Federal District, has a conventional grid pattern design with superimposed diagonals that connect numerous plazas (Figure 3.7). As with the development of Buenos Aires in the late nineteenth century, many of La Plata's public buildings were influenced heavily by European architecture and style. On the southwest edge of the Plaza Moreno sits the unfinished neo-Gothic cathedral, similar in appearance to the medieval cathedrals of Cologne and Amiens in Europe. The Municipal Palace on the opposite side of the Plaza followed the German Renaissance style, and Flemish Renaissance architecture influenced the construction of the Casa de Gobierno (government house).

In addition to La Plata's important role as provincial capital, the city also functions as a major industrial center and international port. The central docks are situated in the *partido* of Ensenada with access to

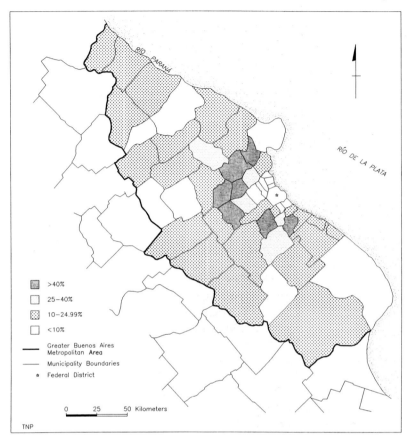

Figure 3.5 A comparison of population growth rates in Buenos Aires, 1980–1991.
Source: República Argentina (1991)

the Río de la Plata via the channelized Río Santiago. Long controlled by the Federal Port Authority in Buenos Aires, the La Plata docks complex has been returned to provincial government control and is slated for privatization. It provides an alternative to the port of Buenos Aires, and provincial authorities envision a more dynamic role for La Plata's port complex in the global maritime system. Clustered around the docks are petrochemical, iron, and steel works, oil refineries, military establishments, and a host of smaller industrial facilities.

La Plata today is practically and perceptually part of the GBAMA, despite the attempts of local bureaucrats and boosters to carve out a separate and distinct identity for the city. Probably its greatest handicap as a provincial capital is its proximity to downtown Buenos Aires. Provincial officials find it difficult to prevent the continued development

Figure 3.6 A golf course and country club estate in the suburban Middle Ring, reproduced with permission from Juan A. Roccatagliata

Figure 3.7 Aerial view of the La Plata city center, reproduced with permission from Juan A. Roccatagliata

of suburban Buenos Aires from overwhelming other provincial needs. Moreover, deindustrialization processes in the urban economy have forced many of the people once employed in the factories and industries of La Plata to seek work in the Federal District's growing service sector. The daily flow of traffic between Greater La Plata and central Buenos Aires has increased dramatically in recent years, despite poor railroad service and an unfinished freeway project.

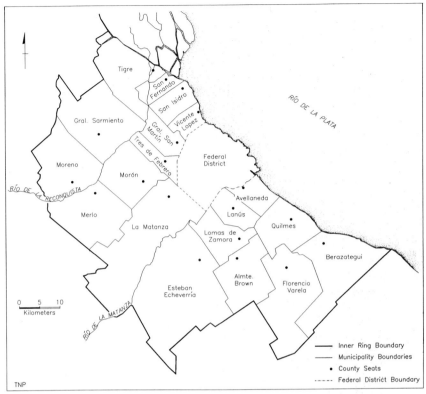

Figure 3.8   The municipalities and county seats of the suburban Inner Ring, 1994.
Source: República Argentina (1991)

The Inner Ring

The 19 *partidos* of the Inner Ring comprise the original suburban area of GBA (Figure 3.8). Thirteen of the 19 municipalities are either highly or totally urbanized, with population densities exceeding 3000 inhabitants per square kilometer (Table 3.3). The remaining six *partidos* have population densities under 3000 per square kilometer and still have substantial tracts of land given over to ranching, intensive agriculture, or leisure activities. With the exception of Lanús and Vicente López, which experienced a slight population decline during the 1980s, growth rates continue to be significant in the Inner Ring. In the northwestern sector, Moreno recorded a 47.7 percent population growth between 1980 and 1991. Esteban Echeverría to the west grew by 46 percent, as did Florencio Varela along the southern axis. The remaining *partidos* had population growth rates that ranged from 35 percent (Almirante Brown) to just over

Table 3.3 Population growth in the Inner Ring of Greater Buenos Aires, 1970–1991

Corridor/ municipality	Population 1970	Population 1980	1991	Area (km²)	Density (population/km²)
Northwestern					
General San Martín	360 573	385 625	407 506	56	7276.9
General Sarmiento	315 457	502 926	646 891	196	3300.5
Merlo	188 868	292 587	390 031	170	2294.3
Moreno	114 041	195 440	287 188	180	1595.5
Morón	485 983	598 420	641 541	131	4897.3
San Fernando	119 565	133 624	144 761	924	6294.0[a]
San Isidro	250 008	289 170	299 022	48	6229.6
Tigre	152 335	206 349	256 005	360	1730.0[a]
Tres de Febrero	313 460	345 424	349 221	46	7591.8
Vicente López	285 178	290 072	289 142	39	7413.9
Western					
Esteban Echeverría	111 150	188 923	276 017	377	732.1
La Matanza	659 193	949 566	1 121 164	323	3471.1
Southwestern					
Almirante Brown	245 017	331 919	449 105	122	3681.2
Lanús	449 824	466 980	466 755	45	10 372.3
Lomas de Zamora	410 806	510 130	572 769	89	6435.6
Southern					
Avellaneda	337 538	334 145	346 620	55	6302.2
Berazategui	127 740	201 862	243 690	188	1296.2
Florencio Varela	98 446	173 452	253 554	206	1230.8
Quilmes	355 265	446 587	509 445	125	4075.6
Total	5 380 447	6 843 201	7 950 427	3680	2160.0

Source: República Argentina (1980, 1991).

[a] Excluding the area of the Río Paraná delta islands.

1 percent (Tres de Febrero). Population densities are the highest in the *partidos* clustered around the Federal District boundary.

Expansion along the northwestern corridor

Vicente López, San Isidro, San Fernando, and Tigre are perhaps the wealthiest areas of the Inner Ring. Most of the middle-class and élite urban expansion in the post-World War II period has occurred in these *partidos* bordering the Río de la Plata. The quality of housing along the north shore is probably the highest of any *partido* outside the Federal District (Figure 3.9). The Pan-American Highway slices through the northern suburbs from the Federal District and bifurcates near the San

Figure 3.9 A typical suburban home along the north shore of the Río de la Plata

Isidro Golf Club, one branch running to Tigre and the other heading north for the outer suburbs. Myriad factories are clustered near the highway, including Fiat, Atanor, the Everready battery factory, the Fate tire plant, the Belgrano railroad workshops, several military installations, and other industrial sites. Large tracts of open land are given over to the Hipódromo San Isidro, the Jockey Club, a polo ground, and several golf clubs. Although the traditional grid pattern dominates the street layout of the north shore *barrios*, many of the wealthier suburbs have curvilinear, circular, and random pattern streets. San Fernando and Tigre also have many industries associated with maritime activities. Along the Río Luján shoreline are shipyards, boat storage facilities, yacht clubs, rowing clubs, and other maritime services.

Housing quality begins to change noticeably north of San Isidro, with more working-class districts and several *villas de emergencia*. Most of the area's self-help housing (dwellings built with scavenged materials) can be found along the banks of *arroyos*, on vacant land, and in abandoned factories. In 1993, several immigrant families had taken over the abandoned Delta railroad station at the junction of the Tigre and Luján rivers. Other open land or unused buildings in the area have been similarly commandeered. Tigre attracts a great deal of traffic during the weekend, as the delta area is one of the city's major recreational zones. In recent years, real estate on the many islands that comprise the delta has become a valuable commodity. Thousands of homes ranging from modest shacks to elaborate 10-room mansions, as well as hotels and restaurants, have sprung up along the canals and waterways of Tigre.

At the boundary between the *partidos* of Tigre and Sarmiento, the northern freeway bifurcates again into National Highways 8 and 9. The land here is mixed in use, with commercial activities found along the service roads that parallel the freeways and also along the major arterials that feed traffic to and from the surrounding *barrios*. One of the corridor's most important industrial plants is the Ford Motor Argentina factory wedged between Route 9, the Mitre railroad, and Avenida Henry Ford near *barrio* López Camelo. Other manufacturing and industrial activities are scattered among houses and apartment complexes in no discernible pattern. Zoning or land-use controls are clearly absent or extremely weak along the northwest corridor.

Near the southeast corner of General Sarmiento municipality sits the Campo de Mayo, a huge expanse of open space controlled by the military and through which runs the Río Reconquista. Part of the planned *Cinturón Ecológico* (green belt), much of the low-lying land around the river is subject to constant flooding. However, many *villas de emergencia* have taken advantage of the open space and self-help housing has become a dominant feature of the landscape. Apart from the available open land, the area is attractive to many migrants for its excellent road, bus, and railroad services to both the Federal District and the nearby factories and businesses. Since 1970, the population of General Sarmiento has doubled, and the *partido* is projected to exceed 750 000 inhabitants by the end of the century. In comparison, population growth in the *partidos* of Morón, San Martín, and Tres de Febrero has slowed considerably in recent years as these suburbs have reached a state of almost total urbanization (Figure 3.10). At the northern edge of Morón is the Río Reconquista Green Belt zone and the Camino del Buen Ayre, a ring road that provides east–west links between the Pan-American and the Western freeways. In the *barrio* of Rubén Dario one finds the Hurlingham Club, one of Buenos Aires' more exclusive country clubs and home to the game of polo. The Goodyear factory, Eternit cement works, and Armco, among others, provide industrial employment in Morón.

The peripheral *partidos* of the Inner Ring's northwest corridor, Merlo and Moreno, also have experienced rapid population growth in recent decades as urbanization continues along and between the major transport arterials. The electrified suburban railroad line that links Merlo and Moreno to downtown Buenos Aires has become one of the most heavily used routes in the suburban network in recent years. Much of the urban expansion has been residential in nature, with commercial activities concentrated along the major roads that connect each *barrio* and on either side of the Western freeway. *Villas de emergencia* have sprung up primarily along the banks of the Río Reconquista. Much of the open land in the western section of Merlo and the northeastern section of

Figure 3.10 Intensive urbanization along the western corridor toward Morón, reproduced with permission from Juan A. Roccatagliata

Moreno is being slowly subdivided for residential use. Individual home construction and subcontracting appear to be the typical building method, as few North American-style suburban estates are evident on the landscape. Although examples of large and very expensive houses are found throughout the area, most housing is working- or middle-class in style and quality. Few major industries have located in this area, Olivetti and the Platense Tire factory are exceptions, and many of the area's residents commute to jobs in the city.

Rural–urban fringes in the western corridor

Straddling the Río Matanza along the western corridor are the *partidos* of Esteban Echeverría and La Matanza. The northern side of the Río Matanza is heavily urbanized, with over 1 million people concentrated in the lower eastern half of La Matanza municipality. The western section of La Matanza is sparsely populated in comparison, with substantial tracts of open land. In recent years, horticultural activities, suburban truck farming, and biological food production projects have sprung up along the western corridor and have become a vital component of the Buenos Aires' food supply system (Flood 1991). At least 15 000 hectares are utilized specifically for horticultural activities in the suburban *partidos* and over 6000 square kilometers are available for truck farming (Gutman et al. 1987). Industrial expansion in La Matanza has occurred primarily along the highway that runs southwest from the Federal District toward Cañuelas. Mercedes Benz Argentina, for example, has opened a plant 45 kilometers from the Plaza de Mayo near the boundary with Marcos Paz.

Much of the densely populated eastern half of La Matanza has developed on the basic grid pattern, although variations on the grid theme abound throughout the area. Most neighborhoods had their genesis around the railroad stations and grew outwards to eventually coalesce with adjacent areas. Predominantly middle- to working-class in social composition, many residents of La Matanza work in the downtown financial district or in the surrounding service economy. Industrial employment has declined in recent years, although several major industrial plants and hundreds of small manufacturing facilities are clustered close to the Federal District boundary. Volkswagen Argentina has a large production facility in Barrio San Justo, and several textile factories are located between Río Matanza and National Highway 3, as are distilleries, refineries, and gas production plants. The Central Market of Buenos Aires for wholesale agricultural products occupies several city blocks in Barrio La Salada.

South of the Río Matanza in Esteban Echeverría, a development pattern similar to La Matanza is encountered. Much of the land surrounding the Ezeiza International Airport is open woodland or swamp utilized by sporting clubs, swimming pools, and golf clubs. Most urban development has occurred near the boundary with the *partido* of Lomas de Zamorra and along highway 205 leading to Cañuelas. The electrified section of the Roca suburban railroad network terminates at Ezeiza station. Several up-scale country clubs are located in Canning near the inactive Belgrano railroad line and just south of provincial highway 58. Little major industrial activity is located in Esteban Echeverría.

Peripheral urban expansion along the southwestern corridor

Along the southwest axis, the *partidos* of Almirante Brown, Lanús, and Lomas de Zamora each have close to half a million inhabitants. Lanús is completely urbanized and experienced no change in population during the 1980s. Almirante Brown grew by 35 percent and Lomas de Zamora by 12 percent between 1980 and 1991, with urban expansion occurring primarily along the General Roca railroad line and either side of Route 210. Lanús is moderately industrialized, with several factory complexes near the channelized Riachuelo and in Barrio Monte Chingolo. Few open green spaces are found and the street plan is totally inorganic, representing the unplanned and often spontaneous nature of suburban development in Buenos Aires. The southern corner of Almirante Brown remains largely undeveloped, although in recent years urbanization has begun to creep slowly toward the open areas. Electrified rail service extends only as far as Glew, which has tended to concentrate housing construction to the north toward the Federal District. Undeveloped private land and abandoned buildings continue to attract self-help housing to the predominantly working-class residential neighborhoods.

The industrial southern corridor

The southern axis of the Inner Ring includes the four *partidos* of Avellaneda, Berazategui, Florencio Varela, and Quilmes. Avellaneda, the smallest of the southern municipalities at 55 square kilometers, is located across from the Federal District along the southern bank of the Riachuelo. Almost totally urbanized, the *partido* comprises densely populated working-class residential neighborhoods interspersed with plots of vacant land, industries, and commercial centers. A substantial number of immigrants live in temporary housing set up on vacant land along and around Dock Sud in the northeastern corner. The Esso, Shell, and YPF (Yacimientos Petroliferos Fiscales) oil storage complexes line the shore of the Río de la Plata. Railroad lines and freight marshalling yards occupy much of the land between Avellaneda, Bullrich, and Gerli railroad stations near the Federal District boundary. Construction on the Buenos Aires–La Plata freeway has cut a swath through the Dock Sud neighborhood extending southeast toward Quilmes.

Quilmes is approximately twice the land area of Avellaneda and has a population over 500 000. Urbanization began in earnest during the 1950s with the construction of factories that attracted a large work force. Rapid population growth during the 1960s and 1970s placed tremendous stress on public services, and today Quilmes remains one of the poorest *partidos* of suburban Buenos Aires. Construction on the La Plata freeway and on the planned southeastern freeway has swallowed up many working-class houses and disrupted traffic flows in Quilmes. Estimates of the number of people living in *villas de emergencia* or temporary housing in Quilmes range from 40 000 to 50 000 people, perhaps as high

Figure 3.11 Poor quality housing along the southern corridor of the suburban Inner Ring

as 10 percent of the total population. Quilmes long has been a favored location for self-help settlements due to its proximity to the Federal District and to industrial plants.

Florencio Varela and Berazategui both have experienced rapid population growth in recent decades as urbanization continues to extend southward toward La Plata. Plans to electrify a branch of the General Roca railroad that passes through both *partidos* certainly encouraged some property speculation during the 1980s. As in all the other *partidos* of GBA, urbanization remains focused primarily around the railroad lines and major roads. Housing construction is spreading out into Barrio La Carolina, the undeveloped southern portion of Florencio Varela, and along Provincial Route 53 that runs through the *partido's* extreme southwest corner. However, much of the housing stock along the southern corridor is of poor quality and residents suffer from a lack of access to basic services (Figure 3.11). Suburban truck farming also remains important in this area.

The Federal District

Forty-seven *barrios* comprise the 200-square kilometer Federal District of Buenos Aires (Figure 3.12). Within these neighborhoods dozens of other smaller *barrios*, essentially clusters of high-rise government apartments, have clearly defined identities. The population of the Federal District has

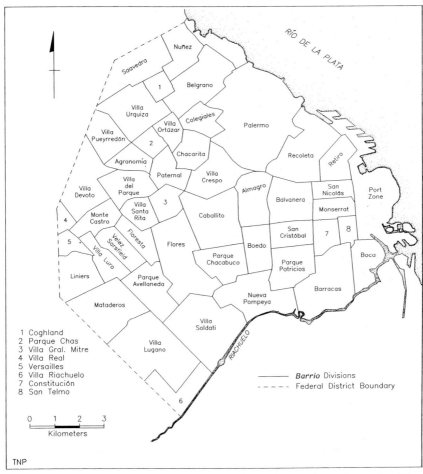

Figure 3.12 The 47 *barrios* of the Federal District of Buenos Aires. *Source*: República Argentina (1991)

remained relatively stable since World War II. From an official peak of 2 981 000 in 1947, the population declined by 15 000 during the 1950s and increased by 6000 during the 1970s. Census inadequacies in Buenos Aires, however, long have cast doubt on the accuracy of the population count. Illegal immigrants, squatters, and shantytown residents often are not included correctly in the census data. Charles Sargent (1974) suggested that the Federal District's true population in 1970 was closer to 3.3 million. The population declined by 50 000 during the 1970s, in part because of the government's attempt to eradicate the *villas de emergencia* located inside the Federal District. By 1991, however, the population had recovered almost to the 1970 level, with just over 2.96

Table 3.4   Population change in the Federal District, 1980–1991

Corridor/ census district	Population 1980	Population 1991	% change (1980/1991)	Area (km^2)	Density (population/km^2)
Northwestern					
1	296 850	279 338	−5.9	14.5	19 264.7
2	258 275	261 426	1.2	7.6	34 398.2
9	254 674	261 220	2.6	17.0	15 365.9
10	215 218	232 071	7.8	14.9	15 575.2
14	102 678	101 669	−1.0	9.1	11 172.4
15	104 110	108 013	3.7	8.2	13 172.3
16	89 671	87 997	−1.9	7.7	11 428.2
Western					
7	160 944	170 744	6.1	7.2	23 714.4
11	107 435	109 075	1.5	7.1	15 362.7
12	116 130	115 799	−0.3	6.2	18 677.3
13	107 113	115 097	7.5	10.7	10 756.7
17	128 988	131 986	2.3	9.3	14 192.0
18	105 325	104 371	−0.9	8.8	11 860.3
20	91 732	91 994	0.3	9.0	10 221.6
Southwestern					
6	155 729	158 978	2.1	4.9	32 444.5
8	143 599	148 534	3.4	6.2	23 957.1
19	55 588	58 166	4.6	8.2	7093.4
21	82 441	92 074	11.7	15.3	6017.9
Southern					
3	150 110	140 087	−6.7	6.0	23 347.8
4	99 287	92 889	−6.4	10.5	8846.6
5	96 932	99 448	2.6	11.6	8573.1
Total	2 922 829	2 960 976	1.3	200.0	14 804.9

Source: República Argentina, INDEC (1980, 1991).

million people living in the Federal District (Table 3.4). Despite inaccuracies in the census data, population numbers have remained relatively constant in the Federal District for nearly 50 years, although significant shifts in population distribution have occurred. During the 1980s, for example, southern census districts 3 and 4 registered more than a 6 percent decline in population. Contrast census district 21 along the southwestern corridor, which recorded a population increase of nearly 12 percent or about 10 000 people. Before examining growth and change in the Federal District, some basic data about land use in the central city area might help to set the scene. Streets and avenues cover about 20 percent (4350 hectares) of the Federal District's territory. Ports (500 hectares), railroads (700 hectares), and the Jorge Newbery airport (375 hectares) account for a further 7 percent. Green spaces cover a little over 850 hectares or 4 percent of the Federal District, while the remaining 69 percent (14 000 hectares) of territory is given over to residences, businesses, and other commercial activities (Valdes 1991).

The wealthy northwestern barrios

The northwest corridor encompasses the 12 *barrios* of Belgrano, Chacarita, Coghland, Colegiales, Nuñez, Palermo, Parque Chas, Recoleta, Saavedra, Villa Ortúzar, Villa Pueyrredón, and Villa Urquiza. Although the census district boundaries do not correspond to the boundaries of the *barrios* (Figure 3.13), data for the northwestern corridor give an indication of population densities and intercensal changes. Census district 1 incorporating Retiro, Recoleta, and a small part of Palermo lost 17 512 residents between 1980 and 1991. To the north, census district 10, which includes Nuñez, Belgrano, Coghland, Colegiales, and parts of Palermo and Saavedra, gained 16 853 residents, an increase of 7.5 percent over 1980. The replacement of single-family homes and small apartment complexes with multistory apartment towers along the northwestern corridor accounts for part of this population shift. Another contributing factor is the continued expansion of the financial district into the northern *barrios*. New office towers in the Retiro area, especially along Avenida del Libertador and around the 9 de Julio interchange, coupled with attempts to address the problem of squatters and *villa de emergencia* residents, have contributed to population adjustments in census district 1.

Much of the northern shoreline of the Río de la Plata has been built up as a commercial and recreational area. Although high-rise apartment complexes line the major arterials leading toward Avenida General Paz, the interior streets of *barrios* such as Saavedra are dominated by a mix of middle-class high-rise apartments, single-family houses, and duplexes. Straddling census districts 10 and 15, Saavedra is densely settled, it has a ratio of 85 males to every 100 females, and is predominantly white-collar middle class in socioeconomic composition. Avenida General Paz is the official boundary between the Federal District and the suburbs. It functions as a powerful perceptual edge, separating the classic Europeanized downtown from the "less civilized" suburbs. One can sense a palpable change in attitude upon entering the Federal District, as well as observe a very different cultural and economic landscape.

Many of the northwestern *barrios* are similar in form and function. Commercial activities cluster around the railroad stations and along the major avenues. Above most of the ground-level shops are apartments

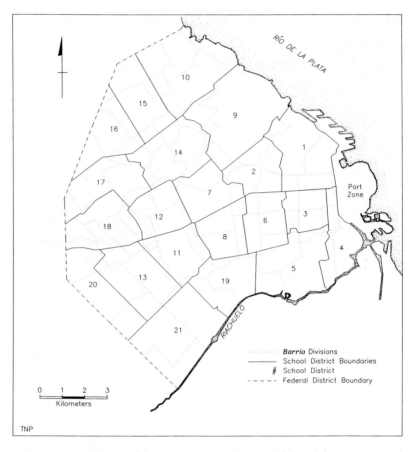

Figure 3.13 The relationship between census district and *barrio* boundaries in the Federal District of Buenos Aires, 1994. *Source:* República Argentina (1991)

and a few professional offices. These wealthy *barrios* have an ample supply of doctors, lawyers, dentists, accountants, consultants, and other professional services. In recent years, high-rise apartment complexes have sprung up throughout the area in no discernible pattern. Whereas most of the pre-1980s apartment towers are concentrated along the major roads, construction recently has been occurring on just about any available piece of vacant land. Large-scale industrial activities are not commonplace in the northern *barrios*, although small manufacturing plants, factories, and warehouses can be found on and around the major arterials, especially near railroad lines. On the east side of Colegiales railroad yard, for example, are several small industrial facilities and raw material outlets.

Figure 3.14 The high-rise skyline of Belgrano in the Federal District, reproduced with permission from Juan A. Roccatagliata

Chacarita functions as an important transportation node for the northwest corridor. The standard-gauge Urquiza railroad operates from Federico Lacroze terminal and there are constant flows of passengers between the railroad and subway systems. Passengers traveling by train to and from Paraguay, Uruguay, Brazil, the Mesopotamian provinces, and the tourist centers of Misiones (Iguazu Falls and the Jesuit mission ruins) passed through Lacroze in the days when the rail service still operated. Today, the ambience is more suburban than international, but the area still generates a substantial daily flow of people. The triangle of roads in front of the station is an important center for *colectivos*. Over 20 bus lines converge here from all over the Federal District and from the outer suburbs.

The most important *barrios* of the Federal District in terms of status and cultural symbolism are Belgrano, Palermo, and Recoleta. Home to the majority of the Federal District's wealthy élite and upper middle classes, these *barrios* have undergone subtle yet important changes in recent years. All three are bounded to the east by the Río de la Plata. A forest of high-rise apartments stands clustered around the Barrancas de Belgrano, a ravine that separates higher ground to the west from lower ground near the Plata shoreline. The apartment towers stretch out in all directions from Belgrano's main railroad station (Figure 3.14). Although some single-family houses and duplexes still can be found in the western section of Belgrano, it seems as if every block has been swept by the tide of property speculation and high-rise construction. The wealthy northern *barrios* are well endowed with plazas, green spaces, and

Figure 3.15 Monumental stadium in the *barrio* of Belgrano, reproduced with permission from Juan A. Roccatagliata

recreational areas, especially toward the river. In the northwest corner of Belgrano stands Monumental Stadium, a landmark of significant cultural importance (Figure 3.15). Home to one of Buenos Aires' most famous and successful soccer clubs, River Plate, the stadium played host to the 1978 soccer World Cup championships, which the Argentine national team won.

Palermo is the largest *barrio* in the Federal District by hectares and, according to Argentine writer Martínez Estrada, it is the most poetic spot in Buenos Aires (del Pino 1991). Jorge Luis Borges, a Palermo native and arguably the most internationally famous of Argentina's writers and poets, certainly gained inspiration from the *barrio's* Italianate villas, creviced and cobbled streets, recreational facilities, and leafy parks. His works are imbued with commentary about the frayed expectations of the city and dreams of what might have been for Buenos Aires. Yet poverty and squalid living conditions are not unknown in this wealthy area. Squatter families recently took over a cluster of government-owned warehouses and buildings along the San Martín railroad just west of Palermo station. Other abandoned or unused buildings, both residential and industrial, scattered around the *barrio* also have been occupied temporarily by homeless families.

Palermo Chico, a neighborhood within a neighborhood, is home to the rich and famous of Buenos Aires. Built up after the 1880 federalization of the city, Palermo Chico's web of curvilinear side streets and thoroughfares host some of Buenos Aires' most elegant turn-of-the-century French-style mansions, replete with prim gardens and ostentatious ornamentation. Armed guards, doberman dogs, electronic surveillance cameras, and imposing entrance gates symbolize the existence of a world not experienced by most of the city's 13 million residents. Although economic hardship in recent years has forced many property owners to sell their estates, many of which have been turned into foreign embassies and ambassadorial residences, brand-new mansions continue to be built. Late twentieth century rock stars, television personalities, sports heroes, and successful entrepreneurs have left their imprint on the landscape in the form of sprawling (at least by Buenos Aires standards) Southern California-style estates. Evidence from mailbox names throughout Belgrano, Palermo and Recoleta, and from the author's personal inquiries, suggests that property ownership, or at least property tenancy, is becoming much more international in profile. North American, Japanese, German, British, and Brazilian investment in real estate along the northwest corridor is a clear indication of globalization forces at work both in the local economy and on the urban landscape.

A new center of activity in the northern *barrios* is the Alto Palermo shopping center on Avenida Santa Fé (Figure 3.16). With two cinemas, a large parking garage, restaurants, cafés, and many retail outlets purveying the finest goods from New York, London, Paris, and Tokyo, Alto Palermo has become a significant economic landmark attracting people from all over Buenos Aires. Security guards patrol the entrances to monitor access and to lend an air of exclusivity to the property. *Ambulantes* (itinerant sales people) and poor street children, selling everything from chewing gum to religious articles, routinely are denied access. Several merchants have argued that shoplifting is a growing problem, with a hint of racism evident in suggestions that the perpetrators generally were recent Bolivian, Peruvian, or Paraguayan immigrants. Other new shopping centers, arcades, retail warehouses, and giant department stores are slowly appearing on the landscape of the northern *barrios*.

The neighborhood of Recoleta, popularly known as Barrio Norte, has the most Parisian feel of all the Federal District *barrios*. From humble origins as home to a large slaughterhouse, swampy lowlands, slave quarters, and open garbage pits, Barrio Norte has evolved into an upscale area. Replete with expensive restaurants, beautiful mansions, trendy bars and night clubs, luxury apartments, and the famous Recoleta Cemetery, the *barrio* is an important focal point for both *porteños* and visitors. As with Palermo, most of Recoleta's open spaces and cultural landmarks are situated near the river, between the Retiro railroad yards and Avenida General Las Heras. A pedestrian bridge linking the red-columned Museum of Fine Arts to the Greco-Roman edifice that houses the University of Buenos Aires Law School provides

Figure 3.16 Alto Palermo shopping center on Avenida Santa Fé

an exceptional view of Avenida Libertador to the south. With its multiple lanes clogged with cars, trucks, motorcycles, taxis, and *colectivos* all jockeying for position, Libertador reminds you of an out-of-control Roman chariot race (Figure 3.17). The avenue is lined with high-rise apartments and office buildings that stretch as far as the eye can see toward Retiro and the city center.

The western barrios

Eighteen *barrios* comprise the western corridor of the Federal District. Coinciding approximately with the seven census districts that cluster either side of Avenida Rivadavia, the major western arterial through the Federal District, these *barrios* have not experienced dramatic population changes in recent decades. Census districts 12 and 18, which include parts of Flores, Floresta, Velez Sarsfield, Versailles, and Villa Luro, registered a small decline in population between 1980 and 1991 (see

Figure 3.17 Traffic congestion near Recoleta

Table 3.4). Only census districts 7 and 13 recorded any substantial population growth, with 6.1 and 7.5 percent increases, respectively. The most densely populated census district (7) is also the closest to the central city, and it includes parts of Almagro, Caballito, and Villa Crespo. District 7 also has the lowest index of masculinity in the western corridor, with only 82 males for every 100 females. Average household sizes in the western *barrios* range from 2.42 to 2.94 inhabitants per dwelling.

Liniers, Versailles, Villa Devoto, and Villa Real are bordered to the west by Avenida General Paz. Villa Devoto has the highest overall elevation in the Federal District, giving it a unique microclimate, and it is often called the "Garden of the City." Plaza Arenales with its abundant supply of trees provides open space for local residents. Many turn-of-the-century French-style mansions were located on the blocks surrounding the plaza, although most of the mansions have since been demolished, replaced by new chalets and apartment houses. Vacant lots in Villa Devoto are in high demand and carry a price tag of 100 000 dollars and upwards. High land prices have encouraged the development of duplexes and three- to four-story apartments, especially toward Avenida San Martín. High-rise buildings are actively discouraged, as the neighborhood council limits apartment complexes to a maximum of four floors. Villa Devoto is not a commercial neighborhood. Most of the area's commercial activities are focused on and around Plaza Arenales. Tree-lined streets, affordable single-family homes, and good city services make the *barrio* a solidly middle-class neighborhood.

A distinct characteristic of Liniers is the elevated Perito Moreno freeway that cuts through the *barrio* east to west parallel to the Sarmiento railroad. Space underneath the freeway has been converted into parking lots, paddle-tennis courts, and junk storage yards. Some of the vacant areas under the freeway have been taken over by migrants and turned into mini *villas de emergencia*. These self-help settlements are very similar in form and function to the types of temporary facilities set up by homeless people under freeway overpasses in cities such as Atlanta, Houston, and Los Angeles in the United States. On the north side of the freeway is the Velez Sarsfield soccer club and stadium. The stadium is the favorite venue for large-scale rock music concerts, and most of the international popular music groups that visit Buenos Aires perform here. Velez Sarsfield's bread and butter, however, is soccer. On Saturday afternoons or evenings during fall and winter, Velez Sarsfield stadium is jammed to the rafters with supporters of whatever teams are matched that day. South of the freeway, the Liniers railroad workshops stretch for seven blocks parallel to Avenida Rivadavia. During its heyday, the Liniers site employed thousands of railroad workers and kept the suburban commuter lines functioning. Lack of infrastructural investment and privatization policies have cut the work force dramatically in recent years. Today, the workshops look more like abandoned buildings than productive facilities. The remainder of Liniers south of the Sarmiento railroad is predominantly low income in socioeconomic status and infrastructure. Some high-rise apartment buildings are clustered around the Liniers railroad and along Avenida Rivadavia, and municipal housing complexes can be found near Avenida General Paz.

The 25 de Mayo freeway functions as an important "edge" in the western corridor and divides several *barrios* into two very distinct zones. Northwest of the freeway, one finds a solidly white-collar, middle-class, single-family home neighborhood centered on Plaza Pueyrredón and the Flores railroad station. Flores is the outermost *barrio* of the Federal District to have subway service. Immediately adjacent to the elevated freeway and to its southeast, land use is split between residential, industrial, recreational, and other activities. Although the Cinturón Ecológico company has a garbage transfer station in southeast Flores, much of the open ground in the area suffers from illegal garbage dumping which has created terrible eyesores on the landscape (Figure 3.18).

Villa Crespo is one of two major Jewish neighborhoods in the Federal District. Jewish culture clearly is evident along Avenida Corrientes that bifurcates the *barrio* southeast to northwest. Those in search of fresh bagels, challah bread, and kosher foods can easily

Figure 3.18   An illegal garbage dump near the Plaza de los Virreyes in Flores

satisfy their needs in the many Jewish delicatessens of Villa Crespo. The *barrio* of Balvanera functions as a transition zone between central city and residential activities. Avenues such as Rivadavia, Corrientes, and Córdoba that run due west through the *barrio* are major shopping thoroughfares, and retail functions account for nearly 100 percent of street-level activities. Plaza Misserere and the railroad terminus of Once de Septiembre form a major transport node in the west central part of Balvanera. Once is the terminal for the Sarmiento railroad that serves suburbs along the western and northwestern corridors. Passenger interchanges between the suburban railroad, subway Line A, and the many *colectivo* routes that converge on Plaza Misserere make the Once area an extremely busy and active zone. Two subway routes also pass through Balvanera, giving the *barrio* excellent connectivity to the downtown core.

The nine or 10 blocks between Avenidas Callao and Pueyrredón are dedicated to commercial activities. Also known as Once, the area is the second of the city's two major Jewish neighborhoods and is also a concentration point for Korean immigrants. Buenos Aires' garment district is located here, with street after street lined with fabric shops offering material to both wholesale and retail customers. Local gourmands are very familiar with the plethora of meat markets, rotiserías, pastry shops, and fishmongers concentrated in the *barrio*. Just across from the Faculty of Economic Sciences in Once stood the DAIA headquarters, an important local landmark which brought together under one roof many of Argentina's Jewish associations. The building was destroyed in July 1994 by a terrorist bomb aimed at the Jewish people.

Inner-city transition in the southwestern barrios

Ten *barrios* comprise the southwest corridor of the Federal District: Boedo, Mataderos, Nueva Pompeya, Parque Avellaneda, Parque Chacabuco, Parque Patricios, San Cristobal, Villa Lugano, Villa Riachuelo, and Villa Soldati. Apart from census district 21, population growth has been relatively slow in this zone since 1980. The highest densities in the southwest corridor are found in census district 6, which includes the *barrios* of Parque Patricios and San Cristobal. At 32 444 people per square kilometer, this census zone has the second highest density in the Federal District. The southwest corner was the last area in the Federal District to be developed and urbanized. Census district 21, for example, recorded the Federal District's largest increase in population between 1980 and 1991 at 11.7 percent. There still remains a tremendous amount of vacant land in the southwest corner, especially around Almirante Brown park. Although this census district contained only 93 000 people in 1994, with the lowest population density of all the inner-city *barrios*, the construction of high-rise municipal housing complexes and illegal *villas de emergencia* continues to attract people to the underdeveloped portions of the district.

Buenos Aires' light-rail system, the Premetro, serves a recently constructed municipal housing complex (Barrio Savio and Barrio Mascias) at the southwest corner of Almirante Brown park (Figure 3.19), but transport services overall are quite poor in the southwest corridor. Several *villas de emergencia* were located in Almirante Brown park during the 1960s and 1970s, but nearly all of them were eradicated by the military government between 1976 and 1979. A large and well-established *villa* remains on Avenida Costa, occupying several city blocks east of the Parque Zoofitogeográfico. The five southwest corridor *barrios* closest to the downtown core also function as transition zones. Although primarily working-class in socioeconomic composition in the southern half, housing quality improves substantially toward Avenida Independencia and the north. Commercial and light industrial activities line Avenidas Caseros and Juan de Garay to the east.

The historic southern barrios

Barracas, Boca, Constitución, and San Telmo comprise the southern corridor of the Federal District. The three southern census districts,

Figure 3.19 Barrio Savio, a government housing complex in the southwest corner of the Federal District

which include most of the city center, accounted for 11.2 percent of the Federal District's total population in 1991, down from 11.8 percent in 1980. Nearly 14 000 people moved away from the southern area during the 1980s. While there are many factors influencing changing population dynamics, certainly an important contributor to declining populations is the steady expansion of the financial and administrative core to the south and west. Globalization of the economy has encouraged property speculation in and around the financial district, pushing land values and rental prices up. Many middle-class and low-income residents of the southern corridor have been squeezed by rising prices and falling incomes and are leaving the city center for other inner-city *barrios* or for the suburbs. Census district 4, which includes La Boca, San Telmo, and parts of Montserrat and San Nicolás, lost 6.4 percent of its population between 1980 and 1991. Both census districts 4 and 5 have relatively low population densities compared with the rest of the Federal District, an indication of settlement patterns in the area. Most of the houses are three- or four-story apartments or duplexes, subdivided former mansions, and some eight- to 12-floor high rises. In the traditional working-class *barrios* of La Boca and southern San Telmo, two-story single-family row houses are the norm, with few high rises on the landscape (Figure 3.20). Despite low population densities per square kilometer, the average household size of 3.04 persons in census district 4 is high compared with other districts.

La Boca and Barracas are highly industrialized *barrios*, especially

Figure 3.20 Typical row houses in La Boca

around the southern docks and the railroad yards. The Sola freight yards of the Roca railroad and Buenos Aires station on the narrow-gauge Belgrano line occupy much of the northwest corner of Barracas. Self-help housing is dotted along the banks of the Riachuelo stream. For example, several hundred people occupy makeshift housing where the Roca railroad crosses over into the suburbs, and over 20 000 squatters inhabit Villa de Emergencia 21–24, which sits astride the railroad tracks dividing the *barrios* of Barracas and Nueva Pompeya. The 9 de Julio freeway cuts through the eastern third of Barracas, effectively separating the western from the eastern section.

La Boca is a traditional Italian immigrant neighborhood and port area. Much of its past economic dynamism focused on the southern port complex as well as on the small factories and warehouses clustered around both the docks and the railroad. The *barrio* has deteriorated physically in recent decades, with factories, port infrastructure, and railroad facilities bearing the brunt of a shift in economic activities to the northern and western areas of Buenos Aires. Most of the railroad tracks that formed the Playa de Maniobras or marshalling yards in the shadow of Boca Juniors soccer stadium have been removed and the land given over to recreational use. Predominantly working-class in structure, La Boca has become an important part of the urban tourist economy. Its local artists, artisans, and immigrant backgrounds have been commodified and mythologized as representative of the more bohemian side of life in Buenos Aires. Some historic preservation is taking place in La Boca and there is evidence on the landscape of gentrification forces at work.

The heart of Buenos Aires

The financial, administrative, cultural, and perceptual heart of Buenos Aires stretches from Plaza Constitución to Retiro terminal and incorporates the barrios of Monserrat, Retiro, and San Nicolas, as well as the port zone. Tens of thousands of people live in the central city, yet its form and function is primarily economic and governmental in nature. Downtown Buenos Aires has no discernible characteristic skyline. Although small clusters of high-rise office and apartment towers can be identified near the Retiro railroad terminal, adjacent to the Plaza de Mayo, and along Avenida Libertador, generally buildings are dotted about the landscape in quite a haphazard fashion. An important controlling factor in Buenos Aires' morphology is the layout of the city's streets. Diagonals and broad avenues have been superimposed on the classic Spanish grid pattern that focused on plazas and major buildings. From the air, two features stand out: the shoreline of the Río de la Plata, with its jumble of port buildings, open spaces, and industrial complexes; and the Avenida 9 de Julio, which cuts a wide swath through the heart of the city from Retiro south to Constitución and the Riachuelo (Figure 3.21). In general, though, the heart of Buenos Aires is a hodgepodge of building sizes, shapes, and functions, open spaces, wide avenues meeting narrow streets, and humble two-story residences sitting in the shadow of modern skyscrapers.

Within the downtown core, four specific edges or nodes define the boundaries of the central city. The first node is the area focused on the Retiro transportation complex to the northwest of the downtown core. Retiro is the main transport hub of the Federal District, and the suburban rail services of the Mitre, Belgrano, and San Martín lines terminate here. Most of the major national and international bus companies are located in the long-distance bus station, which sits between the railroad terminal and the port complex. One of the downtown area's major squatter settlements is located in the Retiro railyards, where hundreds of people occupy the buildings previously used by Fabricaciones Militares. The currently active docks are not officially part of any *barrio* but comprise a district of their own. Much of the port area has been the focus recently of rehabilitation plans.

Three of the city's most utilized plazas – San Martín, Fuerza Aérea Argentina (known as Plaza Gran Bretaña before the Malvinas/Falklands debacle in 1982), and Canadá – are located adjacent to Retiro and function as important physical and cultural reference points in the city. An important concentration of commercial high rises can be found scattered around these plazas. Several office towers containing the headquarters of major multinational corporations are located in the area

Figure 3.21   Avenida 9 de Julio looking south toward Constitución

Figure 3.22   The Catalinas office complex between Retiro and Puerto Madero, reproduced with permission from Juan A. Roccatagliata

known as Catalinas Norte, adjacent to the Retiro complex (Figure 3.22). The corporate logos of IBM Argentina, ICI Argentina, and Dupont, for example, feature prominently on these buildings. The Sheraton Hotel sits on the corner of San Martín and Libertador overlooking a replica of London's Big Ben (el Torre de los Ingleses) and the Retiro railroad terminal (Figure 3.23). Several major office towers also are located

Figure 3.23   Retiro Station and the Plaza de la Fuerza Aérea Argentina, reproduced with permission from Juan A. Roccatagliata

Figure 3.24   Bullrich Shopping Center near the Retiro Transportation Complex

around the Plaza San Martín and along Avenida Libertador. The upscale Bullrich shopping center serves as an important pole of attraction just off Avenida Libertador and is located within walking distance of several international hotels (Figure 3.24).

The second major node of the downtown core encompasses the area between the Palace of Justice on Plaza Lavalle and the National

Figure 3.25 Avenida 9 de Julio and the Obelisk

Congress complex on the Plaza del Congreso. In this approximately 70 square-block area, much of Argentina's federal government, judicial, and academic business is conducted. Avenida 9 de Julio, claimed to be the world's widest avenue at 140 meters, separates this section of the city both practically and perceptually from the more commercial area to the east. Although the *barrios* of Monserrat and San Nicolas officially contain the central city, with western boundaries along Avenidas Entre Ríos and Callao, the wide Avenida 9 de Julio functions as an important north–south axis and a practical boundary between the downtown core and the rest of the city. Important cultural landmarks such as the Colón and San Martín theaters are found in this western corner of the downtown core. The famous Obelisk, built in 1936 to commemorate the 400th anniversary of the first founding of Buenos Aires, sits in the Plaza de la República in the middle of Avenida 9 de Julio (Figure 3.25). Many *porteños* joke that the Obelisk serves as an obscene cultural metaphor, a giant phallic symbol indicating local attitudes toward the rest of the country and the world at large.

Figure 3.26 The Plaza de Mayo and the *Cabildo Antiguo*

To the southwest sits Plaza Constitución and the Constitución railroad terminal, the third major node or edge in the heart of Buenos Aires. Constitución is another of the city's major transport nodes, providing train and bus connections to the southern and southwestern suburbs. This is the least attractive of the four major downtown zones, a gritty, grimy, and bustling congregation of shops, *colectivos*, hustlers, petty thieves, flower sellers, truant students, and suburban workers. In many ways, Plaza Constitución is a microcosm of Buenos Aires society, where silk suits mingle with workers' dungarees and middle-class office workers vie with underemployed *ambulantes* (itinerant salespeople) for seats on the trains and buses that link the suburbs to the commercial center.

At the very heart of Buenos Aires sits the Plaza de Mayo, the city's traditional focus of activity and the fourth of the downtown area's major nodes (Figure 3.26). The Plaza sits at the east end of the Avenida de Mayo, which is the important practical and perceptual dividing line between the southern *barrios* and *el microcentro*, the commercial and administrative district of Buenos Aires. Most federal and city government administrative activity takes place in the several blocks around the Plaza de Mayo. The Casa Rosada (presidential palace), Cabildo (old council chamber), various federal government departments, the City of Buenos Aires municipal government offices, banks, and Argentina's Stock Exchange all surround the Plaza. Many of the city's major commercial and entertainment activities also are focused on *el microcentro* (see Chapter 8).

To continue the theater-play analogy, in this chapter we have explored in some detail the context, setting, and scenery that define the contemporary urban landscape of Buenos Aires. The stage now is set for a detailed examination and analysis of the institutions and individuals that bring the theater to life and that constantly are changing the physical and cultural context within which the play of life in Buenos Aires takes place. Chapter 4 explores politics, planning, and housing in Buenos Aires and examines their role in shaping growth and change in the city.

4

The institutional city: politics, planning, and housing

The institutions and people of Buenos Aires are the principal actors in the daily drama of life played out in the city. Bureaucrats, politicians, planners, policy makers, and community leaders all work to structure the physical and social environment through which the citizenry of Buenos Aires move and interact. This chapter focuses on certain aspects of politics, planning, and housing in the city. First, the political framework of Buenos Aires is examined and several jurisdictional problems are highlighted. Of particular importance is the idea of relocating federal government functions to an interior city. Second, the role of city and regional planning in mediating growth and change in the Greater Buenos Aires Metropolitan Area (GBAMA) is discussed, with examples from past and present management strategies. Contemporary urban planners in Buenos Aires must cope not only with the constant struggle to provide adequate housing for immigrants, but also with a desperate need for some type of historic preservation. Finally, we look at the basic characteristics of residential accommodation in the *barrios* and explore the various housing options available to the people of Buenos Aires.

The political framework of urban management

Argentina is a federal state, divided into 23 provinces and a federal district, with separate executive, judicial, and legislative branches. Administrative functions are shared between the national, provincial, and municipal governments, although the latter two have extremely weak powers. Jurisdiction over the GBAMA is divided between national, provincial, and local bureaucracies, an interjurisdictional body, and several quasi-governmental organizations. Herein lies the root of Buenos Aires' urban management problems.

The federal government has jurisdiction over the Federal District and has operational power over interjurisdictional matters. A legislative body in the Federal District is elected directly by city residents, but is controlled politically by the national legislature. Thus, a situation often exists whereby the mayor, appointed by the President, often comes from a political party different from the dominant forces in the legislative body. This situation frequently seriously complicates the administrative process within the Federal District. Exacerbating the management problem is the absence of any functional administrative territorial subdivisions, zones, or regions to govern the three million people who live in the district's 47 diverse and varied *barrios*. The Federal District is divided into 28 electoral districts or *circunscripciones* for voting purposes (Mouchet 1972) (Figure 4.1). The District is divided further into 21 school or census districts, 52 police districts, and a host of other territorial divisions for public safety, telephone, and postal services. As a comparison of Figures 3.13 and 4.1 reveals, the boundaries of these various districts overlap. Yet there are few formal or functional relationships between any of these territorial divisions, which makes urban management difficult.

Argentina's 1949 Constitution granted all power over the Federal District of Buenos Aires to the President. The *intendente* (mayor) of the district is appointed by the President, with no input from the electorate. As part of the Menem government's restructuring program, a plan has been devised to allow for direct election of the mayor beginning after 1995. Moreover, after 1995 the Federal District could be divided into 11 administrative zones, similar to the *mairies* of Paris, each with approximately 250 000 inhabitants. Every new zone would have an elected submayor. The city council would be reduced from 60 to 33 seats, and the present 127 *consejeros vecinales* (neighborhood councillors) posts would be eliminated. The program also calls for the reduction of the city's bureaucracy from 100 000 to 70 000. Presently, nearly 90 percent of the Buenos Aires City Council budget is spent on salaries and allowances for councillors. As city mayor Saúl Bouer observed in April 1993, Buenos Aires has 10 municipal workers for each block in the Federal District, and of the US$180 million collected by the municipality each month over US$120 million is spent on salaries (*Buenos Aires Herald*, April 24, 1993).

The government of the Province of Buenos Aires administers the *partidos* that comprise Greater Buenos Aires (GBA). To make matters

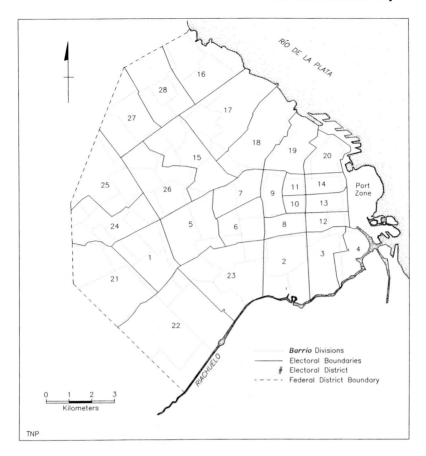

Figure 4.1   The relationship between electoral and *barrio* boundaries in the Federal District of Buenos Aires, 1994. *Source*: Rebública Argentina (1991)

more complicated, the provincial government is headquartered in La Plata, which essentially is part of the Buenos Aires metropolitan continuum. Each of the municipalities that constitute Greater Buenos Aires (GBA) has an elected mayor and a legislative body. The same problem occurs in the *partidos* as in the Federal District, with clashes between mayors and legislative bodies from opposing political parties. Since 1987, the National Commission of the Buenos Aires Metropolitan Area (CONAMBA) has attempted to coordinate interjurisdictional relationships between the Municipality of the City of Buenos Aires and the Province of Buenos Aires. However, CONAMBA lacks political power and has been unable to promote any meaningful common policies among the different bureaucracies involved in managing the city. For example, public enterprises that administer infrastructural services (energy, transportation, sanitation, etc.) have been controlled primarily by the federal government, although both provincial and local governments have input into the process. However, the physical and contextual jurisdictions of these enterprises rarely have corresponded, and the result has been massive operating inefficiencies and inequities. In 1994, uncoordinated government-run public services were being replaced by uncoordinated privately run public services. Ownership may have changed but service inefficiencies and infrastructural problems remain. Moreover, although privatization and deregulation policies have resulted in new and clearly defined operating arenas for public services, regulatory power still rests with either federal, provincial, or local governments, none of whom have any clearly enunciated or coordinated regulatory policies.

In 1994, no clear, integrated, urban management system existed in contemporary Buenos Aires. Bureaucratic relationships between the different territorial units that comprise the GBAMA are fraught with petty jealousies, territorial rivalries, ideological differences, rampant corruption, and a lack of long-term urban planning goals. As most planners and policy makers agree, a city of over 13 million people cannot be managed in such a piecemeal manner (Pesci and Ibáñez 1992). Desperately needed is a management strategy that treats the entire metropolitan region as a single, integrated political unit. However, city and regional planning is not well developed in Argentina and little progress in recent years has been made toward developing a sound, long-term, coordinated urban management system.

A new federal capital?

One of the problems that can hinder the development of urban management strategies is the frequently unbalanced relationship between a world city (often the political capital and primary urban center) and its national hinterland. When the national government is located in a world city, as in Buenos Aires, it often becomes extremely difficult to separate national planning goals from local urban issues. In addition, the physical presence of the national government in a world city often gives that city an advantage, which can lead to dominance over the political, economic, social, and cultural life of the country. Buenos Aires and Argentina long have suffered from such a problem, with Buenos Aires frequently described as a Goliath standing on the shoulders of an impoverished and dwarfed interior. Several countries have attempted to solve the undue influence of a primary city by relocating federal functions to a new capital city or by decentralizing government activities (for example, Abuja, Brasilia, Canberra, Dodoma, Islamabad, and Yamoussoukro). Other countries have attempted to split national government functions between two locations (Cape Town and Pretoria, or Santiago and Valparaíso). Even the European Community has divided administrative activities between Brussels, Strasbourg, and other urban centers. However, many world cities are not important government administrative centers (for example, New York, Melbourne, and Osaka), while most others have not really considered the possibility of relocating national or federal government functions elsewhere. Only Lagos in Nigeria has experienced the relocation process recently, and preliminary evidence suggests that the overwhelming national dominance of Lagos has not been ameliorated by the new federal capital in Abuja (Peil 1991).

In Argentina, the idea of either devolving federal government functions from Buenos Aires to an interior city or building a new capital has its roots in the nineteenth century battle between unitarists and federalists. Unitarists supported a strong national capital in Buenos Aires, whereas federalists were concerned with the dominance Buenos Aires exerted over the entire country. When the government federalized Buenos Aires in 1880, it acknowledged that debate about the location of Argentina's capital would continue. Indeed, serious plans to separate the decision-making power of the federal government from Buenos Aires' economic and political power began to surface in the early 1960s (Aguirre 1983, 1987). After years of debate and inaction, in April 1986, the Argentine government announced the construction of a new national capital in the Patagonian city of Viedma. Situated on the Río Negro, which forms the boundary between the Pampas and Patagonia, Viedma would serve as a gateway city and give impetus to policies designed to develop the resources of the south. A new federal capital would help develop a much needed Patagonian growth pole and reduce the influence of Buenos Aires over the nation. Moreover, relocating the capital would allow the government to shed thousands of needless bureaucratic jobs in Buenos Aires. Construction of a new federal capital also had a social aim. Supporters of the new city argued that the unlimited growth of Buenos Aires had "perverted social concord, increased criminality, and greatly disturbed family structures" (Scovazzi 1993, p. 524). A new city in Patagonia could help to reverse the unmanageable growth of Buenos Aires and lead to a more harmonious and balanced urban system.

Although initial support for the project proved strong, historical inertia, entrenched political and economic interests, and a debilitating recession combined to kill the plan. Officially still a viable project, the relocation of Argentina's federal capital to Viedma or any other interior city is unlikely in the near future. Argentina's contemporary urban planners, economists, and bureaucrats generally do not see either relocation or devolution as a viable strategy for reducing the influence of Buenos Aires over the nation or for spreading the city's economic impetus to the hinterland. Moreover, the estimated price tag of building a new federal capital – ranging anywhere from US$300 billion to US$5 trillion depending on the source – makes it a fiscal impossibility for most governments.

Buenos Aires' continued influence over Argentina and its role as an economic and social pole of attraction, however, continue to be topics for serious debate. At present, five scenarios remain on the planning agenda. First, move the federal government functions to an interior city. This is unlikely to happen given the lack of political will and public support for devolution. The second scenario would be to define a small area in the city center along Avenida de Mayo between the Congress and the Casa Rosada, relocate all federal government functions there, and designate the area exclusively a federal zone. Again, this idea does not excite planners because of the problems of land ownership and commercial activities within the potential zone. Third, relocate the provincial government to Bahía Blanca and create a new federal district in La Plata for all the federal government functions. Scenario three is unlikely because of the cost of relocating two government structures and because the provincial government has strong cultural and economic ties to La Plata.

The fourth scenario would be to create a new metropolitan government for the entire Buenos Aires urban area. Federal government functions would remain in Buenos Aires, but a new elected political body would govern the city and suburbs that today comprise the territory of the GBAMA. However, under this scenario, problems would arise with the status of La Plata, the capital of the province of Buenos Aires. Would provincial government functions remain in La Plata under the jurisdiction of a metropolitan government? Unofficial attitudes suggest that La Plata would not wish to become a functional component of a politically reconstituted GBAMA. The final scenario would be to do nothing. Given the history of urban planning in Buenos Aires and the powerful historical inertia working against urban territorial reorganization, this scenario appears the most likely to occur. Most urban planners and policy makers in Buenos Aires do favor some type of territorial reorganization along the lines suggested in scenario four. However, from a pragmatic perspective, restructuring the spatial dynamics of Buenos Aires would require a level of urban management and long-range planning that does not yet exist in the city.

City and regional planning

The term "urban management" often is considered an oxymoron in Buenos Aires. Public officials and private citizens alike long have bemoaned the ills of unrestrained growth, the lack of land-use controls, air pollution, shantytowns, and inadequate public services. Yet, as Alan Gilbert (1994) so cogently observed, despite urban management weaknesses, cities like Buenos Aires have absorbed millions of people in recent decades without suffering a major disaster or social revolution. Buenos Aires has suffered, of course, from incredible waste, rampant corruption, and often total incompetence in the urban management arena. Nonetheless, urban managers, planners, and policy makers in Buenos Aires generally have coped reasonably well with growth and change. The real problem is the political, economic, and social context within which urban management takes place (Gilbert 1994). A lack of resources, training, funding, and political will to contain and manage urban growth consistently has stymied the policies of Buenos Aires' managers. Moreover, a failure to define clearly the spatial limits and components of the GBAMA has encouraged a fragmented approach to urban management issues.

Over 20 years ago, Jorge Hardoy (1972) argued that the structured growth of Buenos Aires is a national problem that requires planning and policy making within a broad national context. However, a lack of planning for orderly urban growth in Buenos Aires has plagued both city and nation throughout the twentieth century. Although city plans have been around since the 1900s, generally they have been unconnected, ineffective, and often completely ignored. Zoning or land-use planning laws are either weak or non-existent, and a hodgepodge of buildings, functions, and services can be found in almost any part of the metropolitan area. A lack of continuity exists in planning and policy matters, which is exacerbated by public disinterest in urban management issues. Moreover, jurisdictional problems between the national, provincial, and municipal governments have hindered any attempts at integrated planning (Prévôt-Schapira 1993). As a result, the unbridled expansion of GBAMA since the 1940s has resulted in an urban management crisis of astounding proportions.

The evolution of planning

The roots of Argentina's urban development policies can be traced to the early nineteenth century when political independence movements flowered from the seeds planted by the collapse of Spain's American empire. European models of progress and modernization nourished to maturity the political and economic ideas of Buenos Aires' ruling élite. According to the development blueprint of the city's liberal intellectuals, Buenos Aires would serve as the center of progress and modernization for the entire nation. Paris, France, served as the structural model for urban development in Argentina and, between the 1880s and 1920s, the ruling élite proceeded to reshape Buenos Aires in the Parisian mold.

Although a tradition of land-use control had been inherited from the Spanish, in practice city regulations extended mostly to height limitations for buildings, use of construction materials, and other superficial restrictions (Sargent 1974). Other than the desire to recreate a Parisian environment in Buenos Aires, organized urban design did not exist. Unrestrained growth in the Buenos Aires region during the first decades of the twentieth century, spurred by the addition of over 2 million new residents, encouraged the municipal government to consider adopting an urban master plan. Between 1925 and 1937, various attempts were made to introduce zoning regulations, land-use controls, and restrictions on urban growth (Table 4.1). After a 1929 visit to Buenos Aires, Le Corbusier (1947), the eminent French urban planner, suggested that the city be contained areally by establishing a green belt, designating satellite cities, and setting definite limits to urban expansion. Speculative "chaos" in the metropolitan area, argued Le Corbusier, would be overcome only by strong and enforceable land-use and development laws.

In 1944, the federal government introduced a new *Código de Edificación* (Building Code) that established regulations for land use, construction volumes and practices, and the location of certain activities. However, continued rapid growth in the *partidos* of GBA after 1945 overwhelmed the federal and provincial governments and led to a deficit in housing and public services. Juan Perón's first 5-year national development plan (1947–1951), which placed primary emphasis on industrial expansion, accentuated the preexisting trend of concentrating labor opportunities in the metropolitan region. Thus, in addition to the new wave of postwar Spanish and Italian immigrants, over 200 000 interior residents annually moved to GBA during the late 1940s and early 1950s. Lack of adequate housing for immigrants encouraged the development of squatter settlements both in the Federal District and in the suburbs (Radrizzani de Enríquez 1989). Although the government made the highest investment in history in the construction of public housing between 1950 and 1952, the *villas de emergencia* continued to spring up everywhere.

Responding to unrestrained urban growth, Perón's 1952 *Ley de Propiedad Horizontal* (High-rise Property Law) encouraged property ownership and new investment in high-rise buildings primarily in the

Table 4.1   Urban planning in Buenos Aires, 1925–1994

Year	Plan
1925	First urban plan developed for the Municipality
1932	Development plan for the rapidly expanding Greater Buenos Aires Metropolitan Area
1934	Zoning regulations introduced for Greater Buenos Aires
1938	Le Corbusier's plan for urban development published
1944	Zoning regulations established by the federal government for the metropolitan area
1949	The Municipality of Buenos Aires and Buenos Aires Province sign an agreement to implement aspects of Le Corbusier's plan
1958	The Governing Plan of Buenos Aires is introduced
1960	Another agreement is signed between the Province and the Federal District to coordinate urban planning
1962	The Buenos Aires Development Plan is published
1965	The federal government proposes the establishment of Greater Buenos Aires as one of eight national development regions
1970	Preventive zoning introduced for the *partidos* of Greater Buenos Aires, including Greater La Plata
1972	A transport study for the metropolitan area is initiated
1972	The municipality of Buenos Aires creates the Urban Planning Council
1974	The federal government, Province of Buenos Aires, and the city of Buenos Aires agree to a new definition of the Greater Buenos Aires metropolitan region
1977	The Urban Planning Code is introduced in the Federal District to regulate the use, occupation, and development of urban land
1977	Federal Law 8912 controlling land use in the provincial municipalities is introduced
1977	The ecological greenbelt (*Cinturón Ecológico*) for the metropolitan area is created
1984	A new Central Market of Buenos Aires is inaugurated in an agreement between the federal, provincial, and municipal governments
1987	Creation of the National Commission for the Greater Buenos Aires Metropolitan Area (CONAMBA)
1989	Publication of CONAMBA's urban development plan "Proyecto 90"
1990	Creation of the Permanent Interjurisdictional Commission (CIPOS) to address transport, sanitation, land use, and housing issues in the metropolitan area
1994	Project 2000 initiated by CONAMBA and others

Source: CONAMBA (1989), Ludueña (1993).

urban core and in secondary centers with good accessibility and high socioeconomic standing (for example, Belgrano, Barrio Norte, and Palermo). This law stimulated a period of profound urban renovation and restructuring in Buenos Aires that played a significant role in configuring the contemporary urban physical structure. Older single-family dwellings in the better *barrios* were replaced with apartment towers.

Perón's government also initiated several high-rise complexes designed for the working class and urban poor, many of which were built on the fringes of the Federal District.

During the early 1960s, the Buenos Aires city government introduced an urban plan based on the regional concept of development. The Regulating Plan of the Municipality of the City of Buenos Aires (OPRBA) proposed a scheme of regional microdecentralization designed to absorb future growth. The government encouraged many of the factories and industrial plants scattered around the Federal District to relocate to specially designated sites just outside the downtown core in the *partidos* of the suburban Inner Ring. Industrial expansion along the northwest corridor and in the *barrios* south of the Riachuelo attracted new residents to the Inner Ring and fueled the rapid urbanization of areas such as Morón, San Martín, Quilmes, and Lanús. The development and relocation of industry to the Inner Ring from the Federal District also reinforced the commercial–bureaucratic nature of the downtown core, which in turn changed the dynamics of transportation flows to, from, and within the city center. Continued growth beyond the Federal District put added pressure on an already inefficient and ailing urban transport network.

Cognizant of Buenos Aires' increasing economic dominance over the nation and the plight of many poor interior provinces, in 1965 Argentina's federal government established eight development regions designed to stimulate growth beyond the core metropolitan zone (República Argentina 1965). As arguably the most important of the eight regions, the Metropolitan Development Zone played a central role in national planning. In 1966, the Consejo Nacional de Desarrollo, Argentina's federal planning agency, developed its *Plan Esquema 2000* with four clearly enunciated goals for the GBAMA. First, specific functions would be identified and assigned to the GBAMA for its role in the national development context. Second, the occupation, use, and development of land throughout the GBAMA would be strictly regulated. Third, interregional and urban accessibility for urbanized nuclei and preferred axes of development would be improved and reorganized. Finally, political jurisdictions at the national, provincial, and local levels would be coordinated to develop an integrated urban management strategy. Despite clear goals, the *Plan Esquema 2000* did little more than gather dust on the desks of city planners and bureaucrats.

A series of plans, schemes, and stopgap measures were introduced during the early 1970s to try to curb runaway growth in Buenos Aires. However, political instability and economic chaos left little energy for urban planning. When the military took over the federal government once again in 1976, it introduced the *Proceso de Reorganización Nacional* designed to reform the bloated state sector, stabilize the economy, eliminate corruption, and control the unrestrained growth of Buenos Aires. Urban planning during the *Proceso* had two central objectives: decentralize industrial and manufacturing activities to satellite towns and develop an integrated urban freeway network. At the same time, planners recognized a need to control the chaotic growth of Buenos Aires brought about in part by migration from the interior.

In 1977, the military government introduced its new Urban Planning Code and embarked on a program to eradicate the *villas de emergencia* that had sprung up all over the Federal District. Forced relocation of the inner-city poor would not only "clean up" much of the inner city, it also would satisfy the government's desire to show Buenos Aires' best urban face to the world as 1978 host for the quadrennial soccer World Cup. Rental policies were liberalized, which the government hoped would stimulate the construction of private dwellings in the suburbs. Traffic congestion in the downtown core would be alleviated by an integrated system of urban freeways. A program of land expropriation along the planned freeway construction routes began in 1978, displacing primarily low-income groups. To ease congestion on city streets and to eliminate the problem of illegal parking, underground lots sprang up around the city center, and open space along the wide Avenida 9 de Julio became parking lots. Aestheticians moaned that the beautiful avenue had been turned into a giant used car yard. Other stated urban planning goals of the military government were to remodel and reequip the city's public spaces, cope with the crises of unsatisfied basic needs, address the lack of public safety in the suburbs, and devise a workable strategy to reverse a deteriorating urban environment.

The lofty urban planning goals of the *Proceso* did not materialize into concrete and productive changes in Buenos Aires. Only two of the projected freeways were constructed, traffic flow and congestion in the city center remained horrendous, economic deterioration inhibited industrial relocation, and the city's physical environment continued to worsen. However, despite an overall lack of success in reinvigorating the urban environment, there were a few bright spots for Buenos Aires during the late 1970s. The *Cinturón Ecológico* (urban green belt) project initiated in 1977 succeeded in ridding the city of many of its festering and disease-ridden open garbage dumps. The industrial and residential dumps that littered the southwest corner of the Federal District underwent intensive rehabilitation. Much of the reclaimed area was landscaped into a municipal golf course, two major parks (Almirante Brown and Presidente Roca), an amusement center, and a boating lagoon. Plots of land also were set aside for three new elementary schools, a commercial center, and a new municipal housing complex, as well as 6 hectares for the Jumbo supermarket complex on the corner of Avenidas Escalada and Cruz in Villa Lugano.

In addition, despite frequent harrassment and brutal police oppression, low-income groups in both *villas de emergencia* and established *barrios* in the Federal District gained a stronger political voice in urban planning. The strengthening and empowering of *juntas vecinales* (neighborhood councils) and *sociedades de fomento* (neighborhood organizations) contributed to the reconstitution of territorially based urban organizations after the restoration of democracy in 1983 (Silva and Schuurman 1989). At the very least, lip-service now was being paid to the rights of low-income groups in self-help housing projects.

Contemporary urban planning

After the Falklands/Malvinas military debacle in 1982 and the subsequent restoration of participatory democracy in 1983, fresh attempts were made to address the problem of unrestrained urban growth in Buenos Aires. City and regional planning moved to the forefront of the urban management agenda. One of the first major development projects of the contemporary period was a scheme designed to create a new administrative mini-city on reclaimed land in the Río de la Plata estuary. Land shortages around the city center encouraged the government to look toward the river for additional development space, and work began during the early 1980s to reclaim approximately 300 hectares of the Río de la Plata shoreline east of the Puerto Madero docks. The loss of this traditional recreational area dealt a serious blow to the city's fledgling environmental movement, which foresaw serious ecological damage to the harbor zone's plant and animal life. As with many grand schemes in Buenos Aires, however, financial problems forced the project to the bottom of the priority list. Finally, in 1987, the government abandoned the idea of an administrative mini-city and instead turned the area into an ecological reserve using much of the reclaimed land beyond the Puerto Madero docks.

Serious attempts were made to integrate planning throughout the metropolitan area. In 1983, the new provincial government of Buenos Aires created the Buenos Aires Conurbation Directorate to coordinate planning between the 19 *partidos* of the suburban Inner Ring, various public and private institutions, and the provincial legislature. One year later, in November 1984, the provincial government and the Municipality of the City of Buenos Aires reached an agreement to create a territorial entity known as the Area Metropolitana de Buenos Aires (AMBA). Planners and policy makers argued that defining an interjurisdictional territory would enable the respective governments to coordinate a holistic and interdisciplinary approach to city and regional planning. In the first positive move toward a workable interjurisdictional body in Buenos Aires, the federal government endorsed the 1987 establishment of the CONAMBA. Charged with designing and implementing a coordinated urban management strategy, CONAMBA released its preliminary development plan titled *Proyecto 90* in late 1989 (CONAMBA 1989).

Proyecto 90 set out three groups of territorially based strategies designed to work interactively. The first group of strategies focused on the decentralization of decision-making processes, the deconcentration of economic activities, the strengthening of municipal powers, and the promotion of local planning initiatives. In the second group of strategies, the objective was to improve levels of employment and economic profitability in specially designated sectors of the city. Potential urban growth poles, research and technology parks, and relocated industrial centers were identified primarily in the inner and middle suburban rings of Buenos Aires. The third group of strategies focused on enhancing quality of life in Buenos Aires. This would be achieved by preserving the city's natural resources, improving the provision of social services, and by containing urban expansion in the periphery. These strategies were developed against the backdrop of a political system that supported strong government involvement in all aspects of the economy and society. Unfortunately, although CONAMBA had developed a workable urban management plan, it fell victim to bad timing, as government ideologies began to change.

Carlos Menem and the Justicialista (Peronist) Party came to power in late 1989 in the midst of arguably Argentina's worst economic crisis in history. Rampant inflation, capital flight, declining standards of living, and incredible inefficiencies in the provision of public services had pushed both city and nation to the brink of collapse. Menem's government struggled through its first 12 months coping with one dire emergency after another. It even took a first step toward implementing the CONAMBA plan by supporting the newly established Permanent Interjurisdictional Commission (CIPOS). Created in 1990 by an agreement between the Buenos Aires provincial government and the Municipality of the City of Buenos Aires, the Commission's task was to address transport, sanitation, land use, and housing issues in the metropolitan area. CIPOS proposed the transfer of land to its control in order to facilitate the development of urban policies and the construction of new government housing (Ludueña 1993).

Faced with growing social and economic chaos, the Menem government in 1991 turned completely and unreservedly to globalization strategies. Abandoning the policies of the past, Menem opened up

Figure 4.2   Billboard advertisement for the city ombudsman

Argentina's economy to free-market forces, stabilized the currency with the Convertibility Plan (the plan pegged Argentina's currency to the US dollar), aggressively pursued the privatization and deregulation of all public services, and began to disengage the state from the domestic economy. These dramatic changes in economic ideology, however, pushed government-led urban management strategies into the background. Certainly there was a great deal of rhetoric about managed urban growth, free-market stabilization and control of public services, and environmental issues, but no concrete, interjurisdictional, enforceable, or implementable urban management plan emerged.

At the local level, the municipal government of the Federal District has introduced programs to deal with some of the more important social issues, particularly problems with housing, public transport, and utilities. For example, the city ombudsman project is designed to help *porteños* deal with bureaucratic red tape and to address the problem of rampant corruption at all levels of government (Figure 4.2). However, the general populace still has little confidence in the government's ability to address seriously the city's management problems. According to information provided by officials at CONAMBA and CIPOS and by urban planners, during 1994 work was underway on a "Buenos Aires 2000" plan designed to take the city forward to the twenty-first century. At present, however, most physical and structural planning in Buenos Aires is coming from the private sector in the form of property speculation, expansion of the service economy, and the growth of so-called "niche" market opportunities in the housing and retail sectors.

There still exists little functional land-use control in Buenos Aires, no practical interjurisdictional management, no functional zoning of activities, and little evidence of a serious commitment to addressing the severe environmental problems faced by the city.

Historic preservation

The globalization of Buenos Aires' economy has encouraged property speculation and some privately funded urban renovation schemes. Unfortunately, little attention has been focused on the alarming loss of the city's architectural heritage, especially the urban degradation that has occurred south of Avenida de Mayo. Almost 40 percent of the land between Avenidas de Mayo, México, Colón, and 9 de Julio comprised vacant lots, empty and dilapidated buildings, and abandoned areas in 1991. Buenos Aires' rich colonial and post-colonial past is an important part of the political and social lives of its residents. San Telmo, for example, long has functioned as the historic center of Buenos Aires, even though the *barrio* has not been the locus of traditional services since the early nineteenth century. As an important tourist landscape, San Telmo is marketed as the representative neighborhood of colonial Buenos Aires, where visitors and residents alike can experience the material and physical heritage of the city. Constructive management of the area's historic buildings, monuments, habits, customs, and rituals is vital to maintaining both "sense of place" and community. As Jorge Hardoy and Margarita Gutman (1991, p. 108) observed in their overview of historic preservation in Latin American cities, the role of the municipal government "as the constant articulator of social, administrative, and economic life is irreplaceable." Yet defending the heritage of Buenos Aires traditionally has not received much support from either the municipal or federal government, nor has it provoked much response from the economic and cultural élites.

Renovation, rehabilitation, and preservation projects in Buenos Aires have been piecemeal and mostly the result of private enterprise. Attempts to transform collapsing warehouses, broken-down apartments, and old mansions in the southern *barrios* into upscale lofts and condominiums began in the 1980s, yet have had little long-term success. Lack of finance capital, poor public safety, and embedded attitudes about the perceived lower socioeconomic status of the area have hindered gentrification processes. Historic preservation projects have transformed certain important tourist sites in San Telmo such as Plaza Dorrego, but many buildings in the southern *barrios* remain dilapidated and unkempt. Other privately funded building restoration or rehabilitation

Figure 4.3   Building rehabilitation near Plaza Lavalle in the Federal District

projects are occurring throughout the downtown area. Generally, the exteriors of late nineteenth century buildings are kept and restored, while the interior is completely gutted and rebuilt. In many cases, a completely new building is constructed around a preserved portion of an older building (Figure 4.3).

In the old port district of Puerto Madero, private investors are attempting to preserve warehouses and dock buildings by converting them into condominiums and office buildings. Competition from the more technologically advanced Puerto Nuevo after the 1920s left Puerto Madero with little traffic and no real urban identity. Plans designed to incorporate Puerto Madero more fully into the urban system have been on the drawing board ever since. In 1925, the French urban planner J.C.N. Forestier developed the Southern Riverside concept and envisioned a recreational and residential zone in the dock area. The same concept was put forward again in 1969 in the city's "Plan Esquema 2000." An agreement between Buenos Aires and the Barcelona City Council in 1985 proposed a harbor redevelopment scheme, but a lack of funding and political will to carry the project forward scuttled the scheme. In 1991, the Buenos Aires city municipal government and the Central Society of Architects organized a "National Ideas Contest" to elicit feasibility studies for the rehabilitation and preservation of the port zone. A city ordinance approved the designation of the area in May 1992 as the "Old Madero Port Hereditary Protection Area," and restoration work began thereafter under the auspices of the newly formed private Corporación Antiguo Puerto Madero.

Figure 4.4 Rehabilitation of warehouses in the Puerto Madero Area

Figure 4.5 The City Port Project in Puerto Madero

The first stage of the "City Port" project is the restoration and conversion of the red brick warehouses facing Avenidas Huergo and Madero (Figure 4.4). These buildings are being converted into office suites and apartments. The Argentine Catholic University has signed an agreement to establish a Higher Learning Institute in the City Port complex, and other tenants are being actively sought by the project's promoters (Figure 4.5). During 1992, in recognition of the 500th anniversary of Christopher

Figure 4.6 Puerto Madero and the Exhibition of the Americas site, 1992, reproduced with permission from David Cutting

Columbus' voyage to the western hemisphere, the area around the grain elevators on the east side of the docks became the temporary site of the Exhibition of the Americas (Figure 4.6). The number of visitors to the exhibition bolstered claims by the City Port promoters that the docks area could play a major role in urban revitalization. Supporters of the City Port project argue that, as the biggest urban renewal undertaking in Buenos Aires in over a quarter of a century, success of the project is vital to reestablishing the vitality of the central city area and to restoring the balance between the northern and southern *barrios*.

The only major government-sponsored renovation project in recent years has been the Avenida de Mayo Revitalization Program (PRAM) inaugurated in November 1990. Also in honor of the 500th anniversary of Columbus' voyage to the Americas, a Spanish group and the Buenos Aires city municipal government established PRAM to rehabilitate the avenue and to bring about a renaissance in urban redevelopment. Avenida de Mayo long has functioned as an edge or frontier between the poorer southern *barrios* and the financial center and élite residential *barrios* of the north. It became a symbol of progress and modernization when constructed in the 1880s, a boulevard showcasing European Beaux Arts structures, mansard roofs, marble sidewalks, and cafés. Fourteen blocks long and connecting the Congress complex to the presidential palace, Avenida de Mayo also was home to the world's first motorized bus line and Latin America's first subway system. As Argentina slipped deeper into an economic and political malaise after the 1950s, Avenida de Mayo began to show signs of serious decay. By the end of the 1980s, holes in the sidewalks, boarded-up buildings and windows, homeless people, wild dogs, rats, broken street lamps, and accumulated garbage had turned the avenue into a landscape of fear. Tourists were warned about walking the area alone at night. Avenida de Mayo had gone from being a symbol of economic growth to that of urban collapse in barely a century (Goldman 1993).

The PRAM project incorporates 104 parcels of land along the Avenue, of which 86 are eligible for renovation funding. Nearly 43 buildings already had been fully or partially renovated by 1993. The famous Teatro Avenida, close to collapse in 1988, has undergone a US$5 million facelift, and the municipal government agreed to spend US$700 000 on *faroles* or old-fashioned streetlights to attract more people during the evening. Although budget problems, contract disputes, and disagreements over payment have marred the project in recent years, most business owners and residents of Avenida de Mayo agree that urban renewal must proceed. The president of the Friends of the Avenida de Mayo Association, Manuel Perez Amigo, points out that "the idea of recovering traditional structures in a Latin American city is almost unheard of. . . . For Argentina, a country with a history of partially done projects, completion is critical" (Goldman 1993, p. 46). Historic preservation and urban renewal projects in the Puerto Madero, Monserrat, San Telmo, and Retiro districts and along Avenida de Mayo are seen as important models for future redevelopment in Buenos Aires. Although progess has been disappointing to date, the idea of recapturing the elegance of past eras and of transforming Buenos Aires into a world city showcase has captured the imagination of many in both government and private realms.

Accommodating urban growth

A major issue for both institutions and individuals in Buenos Aires since the 1940s has been a lack of sufficient and adequate housing. In 1960, according to a report by the Regional Office of Metropolitan Area Development, only 1.6 million residential units were available in the metropolitan area to accommodate 2 million families (República Argentina 1969). Moreover, in the southern *barrios* of the Federal District (La Boca, San Telmo), and in the southern and western industrial suburbs (Avellaneda, Lanús, La Matanza, Tres de Febrero, and General San Martín), much of the housing stock was assessed as old, dilapidated, deteriorating, and without adequate services (D'Angelo 1963). The same assessment could be made of these neighborhoods today. In 1972, the federal government created the National Housing Fund (FONAVI) under the supervision of the Ministry of Social Welfare. Funding for FONAVI would be provided by a tax of between 2.5 and 5 percent on gross wages paid in the city. The funds are used to construct low-rent apartments for the urban poor, although low-income status does not guarantee preferential treatment on the apartment waiting lists. Moreover, since its inception, FONAVI has struggled to maintain compliance of the wage-tax payment. Many employers, including the federal government, do not collect or remit the wage tax and FONAVI remains constantly short of funds. Although other government-sponsored public housing programs have been in existence since 1915, they have not met growing demands and at best have been sporadic and ineffective. Inflation, land speculation, land scarcity in the inner suburbs, and government inaction continue to affect negatively public housing construction programs, forcing migrants and others to seek alternative housing solutions.

Jorge Mochkowsky (1991) argued that the government's failure to address deteriorating housing conditions in the Federal District is part of a new free-market economic philosophy. Increased land rent values and property speculation are playing key roles in urban restructuring as Buenos Aires' economy opens up to global forces. The theory is that globalization of the Buenos Aires economy will encourage land and property speculation around the downtown core, thus raising the value of land. Increased land values, in turn, will lead to new privately funded office, shopping, and apartment complexes. *Barrios* close to the financial and institutional center of Buenos Aires such as San Telmo and Montserrat are the primary targets for property speculation and urban renewal, with neighborhoods such as Balvanera, Constitución, and Retiro a close second. Expulsion of the poor and the working class from the downtown core thus becomes essential to the successful restructuring and modification of land use in the city center.

Globalization of the Buenos Aires economy also is helping to create a situation in the urban housing market whereby several conflicting forces are coming into play. The economically disadvantaged population of the Federal District is being forced out to the suburbs through increasing rents, property speculation, restrictions on illegal building occupation (squatting), and a lack of low-income housing construction. However, the loss of industrial employment in the suburbs and continued inefficiencies in public transport are forcing many from the lower income sectors of society to seek jobs and housing in the Federal District. Jobs in services and administration are more readily available in the financial center than in the suburbs. Thus, the economically disadvantaged are caught in a vicious circle, with no apparent short-term solution. Many wealthier middle-class urbanites are buying property and joining country clubs in the outer suburbs because cheaper automobiles and better urban highways allow for rapid commuting to the city center. On the other hand, the continued lack of basic public services, increased crime, and massive traffic jams are encouraging some *porteños* to reconsider the suburban lifestyle and to purchase or rent one of the new luxury apartments under construction in the Federal District's northern *barrios*. Thus, two circular patterns of movement within the GBAMA are at work, each creating friction with the other. Poor urbanites are forced out to the suburbs but need to move into the Federal District to find suitable employment, and many wealthier suburbanites are moving back to the Federal District while their potential neighbors are moving out to exclusive neighborhoods in the suburbs. As a result, throughout Buenos Aires we see luxury high-rise apartments and suburban estates juxtaposed against rudimentary forms of shelter lacking any basic services, and squatter families living next to the scions of *porteño* society.

The most visible and oft-discussed aspect of urban growth throughout Latin America is the existence of shantytowns or self-help settlements known variously as *villas de emergencia*, *villas miserias*, *favelas*, or *barriadas*. There has been much debate over the terminology used to describe self-help housing and about the actual living conditions and time of tenure in these settlements. However, most planners agree that the distinguishing characteristic of self-help housing is that it "always begins as a rudimentary form of shelter lacking all kinds of services and is developed on land which either lacks planning permission or which has been invaded" (Gilbert 1994, p. 80). A popular belief is that self-help housing exists only in the peripheral zones of Latin American urban centers. While it is true that large self-help settlements ring the outer areas of many Latin American cities, they also are found in the inner city. In Buenos Aires, self-help housing ranging from isolated squatter settlements to larger *villas de emergencia* can be found not only in the outer suburbs and on the fringes of the Federal District along low-lying areas, but also in the downtown core within walking distance of the Plaza de Mayo (Figure 4.7). Self-help housing has proliferated in Buenos Aires since the 1940s quite simply because the poor have had no alternative. Thus, any available piece of unoccupied land, vacant building, or suitable structure that can be used for temporary accommodation is sought out by the poor. Shacks on vacant land are constructed with whatever material is available: corrugated metal, wood, cardboard, stone, masonry rubble, and rubber tires. The majority of these dwellings lack any type of basic public service, such as water, sewerage, electricity, transportation, or telephone.

As Alan Gilbert (1994) points out, improvements in suburban public transport, the benign attitude of the government toward informal land occupation, and the spreading net of services and infrastructure

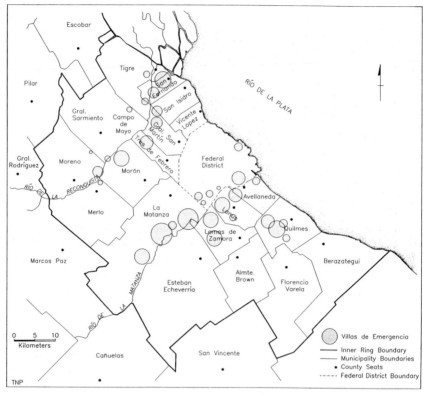

Figure 4.7   The location of *villas de emergencia* in Buenos Aires, 1994. *Source*: República Argentina (1991); Torres (1993)

throughout Buenos Aires have encouraged the spatial dispersion of self-help housing. In Buenos Aires, self-help housing is found in multiple jurisdictions and has diffused over a broad expanse of urban territory, which makes coordination and management extremely complicated. For example, tenants' rights groups have had tremendous problems trying to coordinate political and social action in the myriad self-help settlements. In the GBAMA, official and private estimates of the number of people living in hundreds of different self-help housing environments range anywhere from 500 000 to over 1.5 million. Regardless of the correct number, a huge sector of Buenos Aires' society lives in what can only be described as incredibly miserable housing conditions.

An analysis of housing patterns in Buenos Aires revealed six general types of accommodations, three informal and three formal. Informal housing comprised: (i) *inquilinatos* (tenement houses) and family hotels; (ii) *conventillos* (subdivided former mansions) and *casas tomadas* (abandoned or vacant buildings illegally occupied by squatters); and (iii) *villas de emergencia* (shantytowns) and *asentamientos* (formal land invasions). Formal housing included: (iv) municipal high-rise apartments and single-family urban and suburban houses; (v) private high-rise apartment buildings and duplexes; and (vi) luxury condominiums, *quintas* (country houses), and wealthy estates. Although one can find examples of each housing type throughout the GBAMA, there is a general spatial pattern to the distribution of these different types of accommodations.

Inquilinatos and family hotels

Inquilinatos developed initially in La Boca and Avellaneda around the docks and catered primarily to immigrants. Mostly constructed of wood and sheetmetal, many of the buildings still in use today are between 50 and 100 years old. Later buildings in other parts of the city were more solidly constructed, often with brick and/or rough-stone masonry. Research in Buenos Aires by Programa Habitat (PROHA), in cooperation with an urban tenants' organization (Coordinadora de Inquilinos de Buenos Aires or CIBA), has established that hotels and *inquilinatos* catering mostly to low-income families now are located primarily in a small northeast corner of the *partido* of Avellaneda around Dock Sud and Maciel and in the Federal District *barrios* of La Boca, Almagro, Barracas, San Telmo, Monserrat, San Cristóbal, Villa Crespo, and Once (Gazzoli 1991). A large concentration of family hotels also is found in Flores, just west of the downtown core. In census district 4, which incorporates San Telmo and La Boca, 23 percent of the total population in 1980 lived in *inquilinato* rooms. By contrast, less than 1 percent of the total population along the northwestern and western corridors of the Federal District in 1980 lived in rooms. Census districts 3, 4, and 6 south of the city center also had the highest proportion of *inquilinato* rooms to total accommodations in the entire metropolitan area (Cuenya 1988).

Demand for cheap rental accommodation in the Federal District since 1990 has forced rents sharply upward and the average apartment size downward. The average rental size of low-income, inner-city apartments has dropped from three rooms to one over the past decade (Mochkowsky 1991). It is commonplace for families who can no longer afford to rent a private apartment to move to a family hotel, pensión, or *inquilinato*. Seventy-five percent of *inquilinato* families live in one room, with densities frequently over three people per room. In the family hotels, it is not atypical for five or more families to share a communal kitchen and bathroom. Moreover, many of the inner-city *inquilinatos* and hotels do not accept families with children under 10 or 12 years of age. Noise is strictly prohibited and children are forced to play out in the frequently dangerous streets because there are few open spaces for recreation in the low-income, inner-city *barrios*.

In 1984, Rubén Gazzoli, architect Néstor Jeifetz, and sociologist Silvia Agostinis formed PROHA to address the problems of the city's poor tenants. One of PROHA's first tasks involved surveying the residents of the *inquilinatos* and family hotels in order to identify dominant social characteristics and to prioritize the tenants' problems. According to the surveys, 70 percent of the tenants in these establishments were under 35 years old (Gazzoli 1991). A higher proportion of young people concentrated in this type of housing than in any other housing type across the Federal District. Moreover, the surveys revealed significant differences in migrant backgrounds. The majority of people living in the *inquilinatos* and family hotels were from neighboring countries (primarily Bolivia and Paraguay), whereas the foreign population of the Federal District in general comprises migrants from Europe, Asia, and other non-neighboring regions. Sixty-three percent of those who lived in *inquilinatos* and family hotels worked in the service sector, compared with only 22 percent who found employment in industry and manufacturing. In La Boca and Avellaneda, however, more people worked in industry because of the proximity of industrial activities. Major problems for the tenants ranged from inadequate facilities, high rents, unscrupulous landlords, and a lack of regular maintenance, to overcrowding, safety hazards, and little privacy. Loss of employment further exacerbates the accommodation problem and forces many families to seek shelter where they do not have to pay a regular monthly rent. Shelter usually is found in squatter settlements, *villas de emergencia*, or in one of the mini-shantytowns that have formed under the elevated freeway that cuts through the southern section of the Federal District.

In 1980, approximately 11 percent of the Federal District's population, or 300 000 people, lived in rooms. By the end of the decade the number had risen to over 400 000 people, 14 percent of the Federal District's total population. In 1994, authorities estimated that somewhere between 200 000 and 250 000 people in the Federal District occupy single rooms in substandard housing. Another 50 000 people live in *conventillos*, 60 000 in family hotels, and over 100 000 people illegally occupy houses, factories, and other abandoned buildings. Indeed, the squatter group has been the fastest growing sector in recent years in Buenos Aires.

Conventillos and casas tomadas

Throughout the GBAMA, abandoned factories and residential buildings have become an important component of the urban accommodation supply system. *Conventillos*, which essentially are abandoned or vacant houses and former mansions, are found primarily in San Telmo, Monserrat, and Constitución close to the commercial center. These buildings frequently are subdivided into rooms and occupied illegally by squatters. Half a block from the Plaza de Mayo, for example, 40 families lived in what was once a mansion that belonged to the widow of an Argentine president (Welna 1988, Martin 1992). The building had no bathroom or windows, it was rat-infested, and it had only a communal latrine and a closet for a kitchen. Many of the buildings or *casas tomadas* occupied by squatters belong to the municipal or federal government. Abandoned state-owned factory buildings scattered around the Federal District in *barrios* such as Retiro, Palermo, and Barracas generally provide homes for several squatter families. In the upscale Palermo neighborhood, several immigrant families have occupied factory buildings alongside the San Martín railroad just one block west of Palermo station. Abandoned industrial facilities in the suburbs of Avellaneda, Quilmes, Tigre, and San Fernando also have been taken over by squatter groups.

Several unused government buildings in the city center have become *casas tomadas* in recent years. Squatters reason that the political scandal from trying to evict them would be too embarrassing and would be an admission that the government is incapable of providing adequate housing for its citizens. Some of the houses expropriated by the government along the route of the planned U3 freeway in the northwestern *barrios* also have been taken over by squatters. Construction on the coastal freeway has been delayed for many years and the government has tried to rent many of the expropriated houses. However, illegal occupation of some of these houses poses a difficult problem for the government. Many people do not want to rent next to an illegally occupied house. Moreover, the growth of the drug trade in recent years and the possible use of some of these houses as drug distribution points seriously inhibits both rental and resale opportunities. Abandoned railroad carriages also are used by squatters as temporary residences. Around the city's many railroad yards, some families have occupied railroad carriages for over 6 months without access to basic services of any kind. Often the nearest water or toilet facility is a 10-minute walk over dangerous terrain.

Despite official estimates of over 100 000 unoccupied housing units in the Federal District alone, the Buenos Aires housing market continues to be bleak for low-income groups. Recent immigrants from Argentina's interior or from neighboring countries frequently turn to illegally occupying a building because obtaining rental accommodations can be impossible for the urban poor. A powerful element of racism often is found in barriers to renting. Many landlords will not rent to migrants from Bolivia and Paraguay, who are described frequently by the derogatory term of *cabecitas negritas* (little black heads). Obtaining a valid lease usually entails providing proof of employment, finding a co-signer who owns property in the city, and paying the equivalent of 5–6 months advance rent for lease commissions, damage deposits, and the first month's rent. Little wonder, then, that family hotels, squatting, or *villas de emergencia* often are the only accommodations available to the urban poor.

Villas de emergencia and asentamientos

Few urban shantytowns, the archetypal symbol of modern Latin American housing, were found in Buenos Aires prior to the 1940s (Gilbert 1994). Those settlements that did exist generally were small and located relatively close to the city center. Between the 1950s and the 1990s, the population living in shantytowns or *villas de emergencia* in Buenos Aires exploded from less than 100 000 to over 1 million. Today, about 10 percent of the urban population lives in some form of self-help housing. In 1994, over 51 000 people lived in *villas de emergencia* inside the Federal District, occupying some 12 000 houses that covered approximately 1.38 square kilometers. Nobody knows exactly how many people live in substandard housing conditions throughout the GBAMA, but the best estimates from INDEC, CONAMBA, and private researchers put the number at well over 1 million (Tobar 1972). Most of the self-help settlements in GBA are clustered along the banks of the Río de la Reconquista and the Río de la Matanza, and in the *partido* of Quilmes (see Figure 4.7). Riparian land is the primary target of self-help settlers because it is almost always undeveloped, it often has little commercial value, and because the various government bodies in Buenos Aires have little motivation to enforce land-use controls.

Villas de emergencia are very different in form and function from *asentamientos* or organized land invasions. *Villas* generally have no regular form, do not recognize the legal landowner, nor do they divide the plot into parcels or lots. In contrast, since the 1980s *asentamientos* have been the preferred form of illegal land occupation in the GBAMA. From their genesis, the *asentamientos* are divided formally into lots and parcels in an attempt to assist authorities in granting future legal status and in providing basic services. Unlike with the *villas de emergencia*, the policies of the State and of the *asentamientos* are directed toward the regularization of land use. The *asentamientos* have become the only process that gives recognizable form to the suburbanization of lower income groups.

Many processes have contributed to the genesis and growth of *villas de emergencia* and *asentamientos* in Buenos Aires. However, government legislation, planning practices, and economic policies have played perhaps the most decisive roles in shaping the dynamics of self-help housing in the metropolitan area. Legislation and planning policies up until the mid-1970s generally attempted to cope with the rapid and uncontrolled growth of suburban Buenos Aires by supporting municipal housing projects and rent controls, and by giving tacit approval to illegal land and building occupation. A dramatic change in official policy came in 1976, when the military seized control of the government. One of the first major urban policies of the military focused on the liberalization of rent controls. Housing rents in Buenos Aires had been fixed since 1943 with only minor adjustments based loosely on inflation rates. Abolishing rent control, argued the government, would stimulate private investment in rental housing. Yet few low-cost housing units were built during the military period by either private companies or municipal governments. Increased rents, coupled with a drastic fall in real wages for much of the city's work force, precipitated a 30 percent decline in the number of renters between 1976 and 1978. Former renters frequently had little option but to move into already established slum settlements, to form new settlements through *asentamientos*, or to find accommodations in one of the multitude of slummified turn-of-the-century mansions that now operated as hotels, *pensiones*, or *conventillos* (Silva and Schuurman 1989).

Following hard on the heels of increased rents, in 1977 the military government introduced the *Ley de Erradicación* which banned all *villas de emergencia* from the Federal District. Some 280 000 people lived in 31 *villas de emergencia* scattered across the Federal District in *barrios* such as Retiro, Villa Lugano, and Barracas. Estimates are that nearly 200 000 inhabitants were evicted from the slums in the Federal District during the late 1970s and physically denied access to the urban center. Some of the largest *villas* were located in and around Almirante Brown park in the southwestern corner of the Federal District. Villa del Bajo Flores, for example, had 6230 houses accommodating 6710 families in 1976. By 1980, only 494 families remained in 455 houses. Many of the expelled residents moved to Barrio Luján, an *asentamiento* in the western *partido* of La Matanza. Families from the Villa #20 de Emergencia de Lugano that occupied a large tract of land between Avenidas Larrazabal, Escalada, and Fernandez de la Cruz in Almirante Brown park moved out to Barrio 5 de Noviembre in the *partido* of Florencio Varela. Other evicted families from the southwestern neighborhoods moved to Barrio San José Obrero in the *partido* of Merlo (Cuenya et al. 1984).

The military government's eradication policy had racial overtones. Bolivians and Paraguayans especially were targets for expulsion and many were taken by train to the Argentine border and told not to return. However, most found their way back to the city within a few months. Buenos Aires' international image also played an important role in the eradication of the shantytowns. As host to the 1978 soccer World Cup Championships, Buenos Aires would be seen by hundreds of thousands of visitors, as well as on television by millions around the world. The military government wanted to ensure that Buenos Aires' status as the "Paris of Latin America" would not be tarnished by the existence of inner-city slums and poor people on the downtown streets. Another major component of the military government's new urban modernization policies focused on redesigning the city's transportation network and involved the construction of nine freeways that would dissect the Federal District. Over 15 000 houses were scheduled for demolition along the planned freeway routes, and many houses in low-income neighborhoods were quickly destroyed. Although only two of the freeways were actually built, the majority of the residents along the construction routes were displaced. Construction of the freeways physically divided neighborhoods along the southwestern corridor, and today the freeways act as both perceptual and practical edges or boundaries.

The government's 1981 socioeconomic census of *villas de emergencia* recorded 287 000 people living in "temporary" housing conditions in the 19 *partidos* of the suburban Inner Ring, as well as another 30 000 people who still resided inside the Federal District (República Argentina 1981). Forty-six percent of the nearly 200 000 residents forcibly evicted from the Federal District ended up living about 30 kilometers from the city center. Thirty-five percent lived up to 40 kilometers away, and the remaining 19 percent found themselves over 45 kilometers from the city center. With the restoration of participatory democracy in 1983 and the reconstitution of territorially based neighborhood associations, people began moving back to the Federal District. During the 1980s, several small self-help settlements were established under the elevated Perito Moreno freeway along the western and southwestern corridors. Other settlements quickly reestablished themselves near the Retiro railroad yards, along the banks of the Riachuelo, and around Almirante Brown park in the southwest corner of the Federal District. By 1986, approximately 20 000 people lived in 11 major *villas de emergencia* in the downtown area.

Retiro is a prototypical inner-city *villa de emergencia*. Located on land owned by Argentina's major oil company, YPF (Yacimientos Petroliferos Fiscales), the *villa* is sandwiched between the Retiro railroad yards to the west and the harbor to the east. Concrete foundations and pylons from the unfinished Buenos Aires to La Plata coastal freeway begun during the late 1970s still remain on the land. Most of the families who occupied the settlement during the 1960s and 1970s were evicted forcibly by the military government between 1977 and 1979. Only 40 families remained on the site after the purge. The southern portion of the land became the new Buenos Aires national and international bus terminal in the early 1980s, substantially reducing the original size of the settlement.

In January 1984 the municipality of the city of Buenos Aires agreed to a new law that countermanded the *Ley de Erradicación*. Anybody that had been evicted from the Federal District during the period of military rule could return. The municipality even agreed to provide the *villas* with basic public services, although the rhetoric never became reality. By 1986, approximately 800 families had returned to the Retiro site (Silva and Schuurman 1989). Some were new immigrants, while others had been long-time residents of Buenos Aires. There are no sewers in the Retiro *villa*, only a few water taps, no official electrical connections, and no organized distribution of dwellings. Dirt tracks crisscrossing the settlement turn into muddy quagmires after the slightest rain, and flooding regularly damages homes and contributes to severe health problems. Residents of the Retiro site must live with constant insecurity, as the threat of eviction is ever present. The reactivation of the coastal freeway project, coupled with plans to expand the bus terminal and redevelop the railroad yards, mean that residents in the settlement must live from day to day, not knowing if the government will arrive the next morning with eviction orders. Retiro's central location and its role as a major transport node make the site a prime target for property developers. For example, a Canadian consulting firm recently conducted a pilot study on the possible redevelopment of the Retiro area into shopping arcades, offices, condominiums, and retail outlets.

Barrio San Jorge in the northwestern *partido* of San Fernando is a typical suburban *villa de emergencia*. Located on 10 hectares of flat lowlands next to the Río Reconquista in the western corner of San Fernando, the settlement is surrounded by open garbage dumps, rundown factories, vacant lots, and a few isolated houses (Hardoy et al. 1991). The river and two small nearby tributaries are severely polluted with untreated industrial and household wastes. A personal visit to the settlement in 1991 confirmed the reports of other researchers. Stagnant water and untreated garbage created an overpowering stench, and the entire area was overrun with rats, mosquitos, flies, and other insects. Muddy streets and paths made movement difficult and dangerous, and the absence of adequate drainage was evident in the raw sewage pooled at various locations throughout the *villa*. Air pollution from nearby factories added to the assault on both the eyes and the nostrils.

The oldest part of Barrio San Jorge began during the 1960s. The settlement expanded dramatically after 1978 with the arrival of hundreds of families who had been evicted from the Federal District by the military government. A census of the Barrio in December 1990 recorded 2926 residents living in 630 households, an average household density of 4.7 persons (Hardoy et al. 1991). Sixty-one percent of the inhabitants were under 20 years of age, which is quite typical of self-help settlements in Buenos Aires. Only 4 percent of the dwellings in Barrio San Jorge had septic tanks, 57 percent had cesspools, 32 percent used communal latrines, and 7 percent had no method of human waste disposal at all. Residents of the barrio have great difficulty getting police cars, ambulances, fire engines, or sanitation trucks to enter the settlement because of the lack of roads. Although two *colectivo* routes skirt the settlement to the north and west, bus service is very poor at night and outside normal working hours. Moreover, apart from four or five large industries in San Fernando (for example, Everready and Neumaticos Fate), employment opportunities in the secondary sector are limited to comparatively small workshops and manufacturing plants. Service sector employment can be found in the yacht and sports clubs along the Río Luján or in the shops and businesses that cluster around the railroad stations. Several residents of the area commute to service jobs in the downtown core.

Many of the dwellings in Barrio San Jorge are connected illegally to water and electricity, typical of most self-help settlements in Buenos Aires. Clandestine connections to the power grid have created serious problems for governments and power companies alike. As part of Argentina's economic globalization strategies, the government-run electricity system in Buenos Aires has been privatized. Service provision in the metropolitan area has been divided evenly between two companies, Edesur and Edenor, who now provide electricity in southern and northern Buenos Aires, respectively. In June 1993, the two companies began cutting off supply to the estimated 2 million illegal users in Buenos Aires, most of them shantytown residents, causing protests to erupt on the city streets (*Latin American Weekly Report* July 22, 1993). The power companies argued that they were losing over US$250 million annually in revenues. The Secretary of State stepped in and negotiated an agreement whereby the power companies would suspend disconnections while they installed temporary collective meters. In the meantime, the municipalities would pay for the illegally used electricity. The provincial government of Buenos Aires, which administers the *partidos* where most of the illegal connections are located, promptly announced that it had no funds available to pay for shantytown electricity. Argentina's Economic Minister Cavallo then overruled the Secretary of

State and said that there would be no subsidies to the shantytown residents, resulting in a deadlocked situation. Most residents of self-help settlements are willing to pay for electricity and water, but they cannot afford the high rates or the meter installation costs. Meanwhile, the government seems unable to arrive at a solution for the problem, and illegal connections continue to proliferate. *Asentamientos* have fared slightly better than *villas de emergencia* in the provision of basic public services because the territorial organization of the *asentamientos* has been geared toward formal public service provision.

In the southern working-class suburbs of Buenos Aires' Inner Ring, Quilmes provides an excellent example of an *asentamiento*. During the spring of 1981, a period of instability within the military government encouraged the first organized land occupation in Argentina. Nearly 22 000 people invaded 211 hectares of undeveloped private land along the Arroyo San Francisco that straddles the boundary between the *partidos* of Quilmes and Almirante Brown (Cuenya et al. 1990). Many of the participants in the *asentamiento* were *villeros* (shantytown residents) who had been evicted from their homes in the Federal District by the military government. The legal owners of the invaded land had been unable to sell or develop the property because of municipal planning policies, and they generally supported the invasion as it offered the possibility of eventually selling land parcels to the settlers. Unlike the randomly settled *villas*, however, plots in the new *barrios* were carefully measured out at 10×20 meters each, with space set aside for access roads and community facilities.

The military government responded to the land invasion with bulldozers, riot police, and troops. When women, children, and the local priest defiantly stood in front of the bulldozers, the police responded by cordoning off the area with 30 vehicles and 3000 men. Although the land invasion and subsequent siege received wide print media coverage, radio and television largely ignored the story. Beatriz Cuenya et al. (1990, p. 34) described one commentary extremely critical of the lack of television coverage:

> ATC Channel 7 (one of the television channels) sent a team of reporters. They looked around, listened, and then went back to the channel. Nothing ever got on the air. Television, drowning us daily with its irrelevancies, did not consider as worthy of interest the plight of 20,000 persons lacking a roof. Is it that the sight of families living in tents and cardboard shacks would have shown the social failure of a rich and powerful Argentina?

Eventually, the Malvinas/Falklands war that began in April 1982 diverted the military government's attention away from the besieged settlement. The authorities withdrew their men and turned the entire problem over to a court of law.

Six new *barrios* were created in the *asentamiento*. Barrios Santa Rosa, La Paz, and El Tala occupy the west bank of the Arroyo San Francisco in Quilmes, with Barrio Santa Lucía on the east bank. Barrio Monte de los Curas/Dos de Abril straddles the arroyo south of Avenida Donato Alvarez in the *partido* of Almirante Brown. A sixth settlement in Quilmes, Barrio San Martín, also fronts on to Avenida Donato Alvarez and covers 30 hectares of lowland along the arroyo that are prone to flooding. San Martín's urban structure follows the traditional grid pattern and is divided into 20 blocks with streets and sidewalks throughout. Approximately 800 families have homes in Barrio San Martín. Nearly 90 percent of the households surveyed in 1984 suffered from one or more unmet basic need such as water, latrines, inadequate housing, and overcrowding (Cuenya et al. 1990). Conditions in the surrounding district of San Francisco Solano and *partido* of Quilmes were statistically better in 1984, but during the decade since the survey conditions across the entire southern corridor have worsened tremendously.

Collective *asentamientos* also became a popular solution to urban housing problems in Buenos Aires during the 1980s. Thirty-five kilometers from the Plaza de Mayo, the collective settlement known as Barrio Argentino in the *partido* of Merlo has attempted to avoid the chaos of *villas de emergencia* by screening potential residents and organizing cooperative duties. Several families in March 1986 invaded a parcel of land owned by the municipal government not far from the Merlo railroad station. By October 1986 approximately 120 families had moved into Barrio Argentino, many the victims of disastrous floods that had destroyed their homes in other parts of the suburb. The cooperative that runs the *barrio* sees collective land ownership as the only way to avoid individual land speculation (Silva and Schuurman 1989). In many other self-help settlements, land speculation frequently disrupts the stability of the community and heightens the level of mistrust and antagonism among the residents. Similar collective settlements have sprung up on vacant land throughout the suburban Inner Ring.

Formal housing

Although the highly generalized and overused socioeconomic divisions of working, middle, and upper class mask a multitude of variations and interrelationships, they serve a useful purpose in broadly delineating the different types of formal housing found in Buenos Aires. Spatial patterns

Table 4.2 Occupied private housing, households, and population by type of housing in Buenos Aires, 1991

Political division	Total	Houses	Farms/ cabins	Apartments	Tenancy property	Hotel/ boarding- house[a]	Not built as dwelling	Trailers	Other
Federal District									
Housing units	978 330	207 495	11 482	733 619	12 484	(a)	2387	69	10 794
Households[b]	1 023 464	218 898	12 181	747 314	27 220	(a)	2776	73	15 002
Population[b]	2 871 519	726 001	50 269	1 981 060	69 324	(a)	6400	121	38 344
Population % by category[c]	100.00	25.28	1.75	69.00	2.41		0.22	0.00	1.34
Density[d]	2.93	3.50	4.38	2.70	5.55		2.68	1.75	3.55
Greater Buenos Aires[e]									
Housing units	2 083 676	1 540 814	182 812	313 183	5974	638	4892	432	34 931
Households[b]	2 172 716	1 603 198	190 895	321 341	9163	1675	5108	461	40 875
Population[b]	7 924 424	5 936 693	802 173	1 004 431	26 065	3151	12 910	1391	137 610
Population % by category[c]	100.00	74.92	10.12	12.68	0.33	0.04	0.16	0.02	1.73
Density[d]	3.80	3.85	4.39	3.21	4.36	4.94	2.64	3.22	3.94

Source: República Argentina (1993a).

[a] Hotel and boarding house figures are included in other categories because of census-taking difficulties.
[b] Population totals are lower than actual population totals because of census adjustments related to household size.
[c] Population percentage by category is calculated by dividing the total population by the population living in a specific housing type.
[d] Density refers to the average number of people occupying a housing unit in each category and is calculated by dividing the population figure by the number of housing units.
[e] The 19 *partidos* of the suburban Inner Ring.

of housing types also are highly generalized and are used simply to provide a broad overview of housing distribution in the city. For example, in the northwestern *partido* of Moreno, one is likely to find elegant, two-story brick homes on substantial grounds sitting next to modest clapboard houses on tiny lots. Similarly, throughout the peripheral *barrios* of the Federal District, rudimentary shacks can be found huddled in the shadows of middle-class apartment towers. Formal working-class and low-income housing is located primarily along the southern and southwestern corridors, although pockets can be found scattered throughout the *partidos* of the northwestern and western zones. Middle-class housing such as duplexes, better quality single-family homes, and apartments are found mostly along the western and northwestern corridors. Wealthy estates, condominiums, and luxury apartments are clustered primarily in the northern *barrios* and *partidos* adjacent to the Río de la Plata.

Within the Federal District, 69 percent of the population resides in apartments and 25.3 percent resides in single-family houses (Table 4.2). This concentration of people in high-rise apartments accounts for the Federal District's high overall density rate of 14 805 people per square kilometer. Compared with apartments, housing densities are much higher in the non-formal types of accommodation such as cabins, tenancy property, and other dwellings. In the 19 *partidos* of the suburban Inner Ring, housing type occupation statistics show a very different picture. Only 12.7 percent of the total population in the Inner Ring lived in apartments in 1991. Single-family housing accommodated 75 percent of the population, with another 10 percent living in farms and cabins. Population densities per housing unit are much higher in the suburban Inner Ring than in the Federal District, although overall population density in the Inner Ring was only 2160 people per square kilometer. Table 4.2 also highlights the substantial gap between available housing units and total households. The total number of households in the Federal District in 1991 exceeded the number of available housing units by over 45 000. In the suburban Inner Ring, there were 89 000 more households than available housing units in 1991.

Municipal high-rise apartment complexes for low-income urbanites are located primarily in the Federal District. Southeast Flores, for example, has several municipal housing projects. Over 35 apartment towers comprise Barrio Rivadavia near the Parque Chacabuco and Nueva Pompeya boundaries. The huge municipal high-rise apartment complex on Avenida Larrazabal in Villa Lugano is served by Buenos Aires' only light-rail system. Several municipal complexes also are located in *barrios* such as Villa Devoto and Saavedra near the Avenida General Paz ring road. In the suburban *partidos*, municipal and provincial government housing is mostly low-rise apartments and single-family

Figure 4.8 An unpaved road in the suburban Inner Ring

houses. Much of the housing stock along the southern and southwestern corridors is in poor repair, with roads, public services, and other community facilities non-existent or inadequate.

Typical of the formal low-income neighborhoods in suburban Buenos Aires is La Loma. Situated just 15 kilometers from the Plaza de Mayo, the half-finished wood, brick, and cardboard houses and corrugated metal shacks of La Loma stand in stark contrast to the elegant brick and timber homes of wealthier suburbs. Communities such as La Loma frequently lack clean water, paved roads, transport services, health facilities, and sewer systems, and long have borne the brunt of successive urban economic and political restructuring. Only 7 percent of La Loma's residents have running water, 13 percent have no water inside the house, while the remaining 80 percent get their water from wells (Fisher 1993). Many of the wells are self-built and are regularly contaminated by septic tanks and stagnant water. Located on the periphery of the Lomas de Zamora town center along the southwestern corridor, Villa Lamadrid also is typical of low-income communities in the suburban Inner Ring. The entire area is prone to flooding during the frequent summer and autumn storms, and stagnant water collects along the uneven muddy roads that run through the neighborhood. Household wastes frequently drain into the ditches along the dirt roads (Figure 4.8). Cholera can easily spread through the polluted ditches and wells that dot the low-income suburbs of Buenos Aires. Yet local councils have been slow to react to hygiene and sanitation problems in their jurisdictions, despite the recent cholera epidemic in Latin America. In recent years, cholera has seriously affected northwestern Argentina and Bolivia, source of many of the migrants who end up in the poorer suburbs of Buenos Aires.

Modest middle-class housing and better quality apartments, duplexes, and single-family homes are dominant along the western corridor and in most *partidos* of the northwestern area. Since the early 1980s, many young middle-class families in Buenos Aires have found it extremely difficult to buy either land or a house, especially in the Federal District. Land commercialization and the increasing problems of servicing low-density urban sprawl have placed pressures on federal, provincial, and municipal governments to control land use in the urban periphery (Gilbert 1994). Exacerbating the housing problem in Buenos Aires has been the dramatic fall in real incomes over the past decade. Building materials, urban services, and land are much more expensive, while at the same time basic necessities such as food, clothing, and health care take up a larger share of the family budget. In addition, declining levels of public transport service and an increased use of private automobiles are changing the housing dynamics of Buenos Aires. Nonetheless, home ownership rates in Buenos Aires remain relatively high. Sixty-seven percent of the total households in the Federal District own the home in which they live. In the 19 *partidos* of the suburban Inner Ring, home ownership levels have reached 74 percent of the total households, 6 percent higher than the national home ownership rate (República Argentina 1993a).

Toward the latter part of the 1980s, as Argentina sank deeper into economic chaos, housing policies essentially disappeared. Construction stopped and credit for the development of popular housing dried up completely. In every suburb and *barrio* of Buenos Aires, half-finished buildings, empty concrete foundations, aborted additions, and over-grown lots provide visual evidence of the housing market's collapse in 1989 and 1990. Since 1990, available capital has been directed toward the upper-income sector, where the frenzied construction of luxury apartments and condominiums is changing the skyline of the northern *barrios* of the Federal District (Figure 4.9). Especially noticeable in the restructuring of the Buenos Aires housing market has been the proliferation of luxury "country club" estates around the suburban periphery. Activity in this sector is concentrated in the Middle Ring *partidos* of Escobar and Pilar along the northwestern development axis, west of the international airport in the *partido* of Esteban Echeverría, and in the *partido* of San Vicente (Figure 4.10). However, security problems such as burglaries, muggings, and armed robbery in the exclusive residential suburbs (for example, San Isidro, Lomas, and Vicente López) are encouraging relocation back to the city center because the Federal

Figure 4.9 A new high-rise apartment tower in the *barrio* of Palermo

District has a far superior system of public safety. Drug-related crimes have increased dramatically since the late 1980s and police departments in the suburban *partidos* have been unable to cope, in part through inadequate funding, poor training, and a lack of necessary law-enforcement infrastructure. Most Buenos Aires residents perceive the Federal District to be much safer than the suburbs, although official crime statistics suggest otherwise.

The relocation of upper-income families from the northwestern suburbs to the Federal District is contributing to the upward pressure on housing and rental accommodations. Rental and purchase prices for apartments and houses have doubled or tripled in some parts of the Federal District over the past 5 years. For example, a small two-bedroom apartment in Palermo Chico near Recoleta cemetery that rented for US$2000 monthly in 1989 now rents for nearly US$4000 (*La Nación* 1989, 1994). In 1994, small one- and two-bedroomed apartments in the Federal District rented from between US$400 and 600 per month depending on location and amenities (Table 4.3). Rental prices are significantly higher

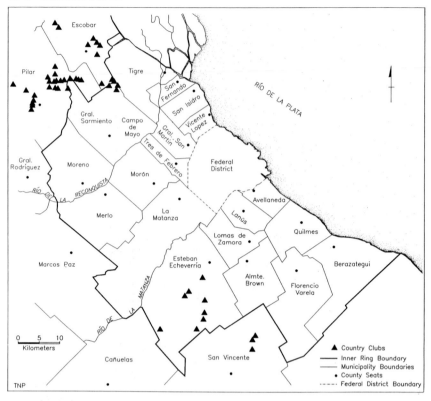

Figure 4.10   Country club estates in suburban Buenos Aires, 1994, *Source:* After Torres (1993)

overall along the northwestern corridor, especially in the *barrios* of Recoleta (Barrio Norte), Palermo, and Belgrano. Average rental costs might seem reasonable when compared with other world cities such as New York, London, and Tokyo, but declining monthly incomes for the middle class in Buenos Aires and the eroding purchasing power of the national currency mean that monthly rents are absorbing an ever-increasing percentage of the household budget. In the suburban *partidos,* housing and rental prices generally decline with distance from the Federal District and from transport nodes, and are much lower along the southern and southwestern corridors compared with the western and northwestern zones (*Revista Mercado Inmobiliario* 1994). For example, prices for an average single-family home in a typical middle-class neighborhood range from US$30 000 to over US$250 000 depending on lot size and location.

The most dynamic aspect of the contemporary Buenos Aires housing market is the construction of luxury high-rise apartment complexes in

Table 4.3   Selected apartment rents in *barrios* of the Federal District, May 1994

Corridor/*barrio*	Base monthly rent (US$)	Number of bedrooms	Location
Northwestern			
Chacarita	300	1	8 blocks from subway
Coghland	750	2	5 blocks from railroad
Nuñez	1200	3	3 blocks from railroad
Palermo	450	1	4 blocks from subway
Barrio Norte	520	1	Next to Bulnes subway
Barrio Norte	1200	2	5 blocks from Retiro
Barrio Norte	3000	3	Next to Plaza de Chile
Barrio Norte	5000	4	Next to the City Zoo
Western			
Liniers	550	2	6 blocks from railroad
Floresta	400	1	3 blocks from railroad
Flores	700	2	8 blocks from subway
Caballito	900	3	3 blocks from subway
Southwestern			
Villa Lugano	400	2	3 blocks from Premetro
Mataderos	380	2	Next to 7 bus routes
San Cristobal	500	2	5 blocks from subway
Southern			
Constitución	400	1	6 blocks from subway
San Nicolás	500	1	City Center (Córdoba)
San Nicolás	1000	2	City Center (Corrientes)
San Nicolás	450	2	City Center (Suipacha)

Source: La Nación May 19, 1994, Sec. 4, 8–9; *Revista Mercado Inmobiliario* May 5, 1994, Año IV(138).

the Federal District. More than 95 percent of all construction activity in Buenos Aires between April 1993 and May 1994 focused on apartment construction. Property speculation spurred by the globalization of the local economy continues to transform the Federal District skyline, particularly along the northwestern corridor. The apartment tower illustrated in Figure 4.9 is under construction in Palermo on Avenida Cerviño behind the US embassy compound. Everyday, local newspapers are full of advertisements for newly constructed or about-to-be-finished apartments. For example, a one-room, 40 meters square (430 square feet) apartment in Edificio Pico, an eight-story complex in northwestern Nuñez just off Avenida Cabildo, cost US$40 600 to purchase in May 1994 (*La Nación* May 12, 1994). One- and two-bedroomed new and refurbished apartments in Recoleta, Palermo, Colegiales, and Belgrano sell from US$100 000 to over US$400 000, and houses along the north shore are equally priced.

Accommodating urban growth remains one of the more serious problems for institutions and individuals alike in Buenos Aires. Much of the city's suburban expansion and related demand for housing since the 1940s have been driven by the perception of Buenos Aires as an employment opportunity center. Traditionally the locus of Argentina's major industrial, manufacturing, and commercial activities, Buenos Aires continues to attract labor and capital which, in turn, fuel urban growth and create demands for housing. In the following chapter we explore the working city of Buenos Aires and examine how changes in the labor and capital markets are restructuring the urban economy and helping to reshape the urban landscape.

5

The working city: labor, capital, and the urban economy

The emergence of Buenos Aires as a world city is inextricably intertwined with the major economic restructuring processes of globalization. Some of the characteristics of the globalization of world city economies include a concentration of international management functions, advanced producer services, and high-technology manufacturing plants that serve specialized markets. World cities also function as basing points for global capital. As Friedmann and Wolff (1982) noted, the primary fact about world cities is:

> the impact which incipient shifts in the structure of their employment will have on the economy and on the social composition of their population. The dynamism of the world city economy results chiefly from the growth of a primary cluster of high-level business services which employs a large number of professionals – the transnational élite – and ancillary staffs of clerical personnel.

Two other growing clusters of employment were identified by Friedmann and Wolff (1982). The second cluster comprises real estate services, construction activities, hotel services, restaurants, luxury shops, entertainment, private police, and domestic services, which grow in concert with the first cluster. International tourism is the third cluster and it is implicitly related to changes in the second cluster of employment. Growth in these three clusters is occurring in Buenos Aires at the expense of manufacturing employment, whose numbers are declining gradually as a percentage of total employment. Other clusters of employment include government services, which are concerned with the maintenance and reproduction of world city processes, and the informal sector. This last cluster of employment has grown rapidly in Buenos Aires in recent years, partly as a result of the government's economic globalization policies.

A key element of economic change in Buenos Aires is the apparent growing polarization of the city's occupational and income structures. Critics of the Argentine government's economic restructuring policies argue that globalization is causing an absolute growth at both the top and bottom ends of occupational and income distribution and a decline in the middle of the distribution. In a scathing commentary on the government's globalization policies, Joe Schneider (1994, p. 10) lambasted the "sham and shame of democracy-by-decree, with quasi-stability camouflaging growing unemployment, a monumental trade deficit, proliferation of school-age dunces, chronic deterioration in health conditions, and unchecked hooliganism in the Boca-River gangs." Economic restructuring in Buenos Aires has allowed the wealthy to increase their share of the city's gross domestic product while millions are pushed deeper into poverty. Saskia Sassen (1991) explored the social polarization thesis recently in New York, London, and Tokyo. She found that polarization in world cities as a result of economic restructuring has precipitated changes in "the organization of work, reflected in a shift in the job supply and polarization in the income distribution and occupational distribution of workers" (Sassen 1991, p. 9).

Supporters of Argentina's economic restructuring policies point out that world city status and incorporation into the world economy could never be achieved with a regulated economy closed to the outside world and with a deficit-ridden government operating in many inappropriate areas. Short-term social polarization and employment redistribution are the price that both Buenos Aires and Argentina must pay for long-term socioeconomic growth and stability (Campbell 1994, *Economist*, February 12, 1994).

The objective of this chapter is to review recent economic changes in Buenos Aires and to discuss their principal features against the background of the social polarization thesis. Beginning with a brief overview of the local economy since the 1880s, first we examine the spatial and sectoral composition of economic restructuring. Labor and capital have interacted in Buenos Aires over time to shape the urban environment in specific ways and in distinctive patterns. Changing global and regional economic linkages also are explored, along with their potential impacts on the local labor and capital markets. Next, the contemporary urban economy is examined, with a particular emphasis on the growing informal sector. How are globalization forces changing the dynamics of economic opportunity within Buenos Aires? Finally, we look briefly at capital formation and development, both intangible and tangible, and examine the impact of capital speculation and monetary reform on the landscape of Buenos Aires. Although stability has returned to the Buenos Aires economy, capital for infrastructural projects remains in short supply.

Spatial and sectoral changes in the urban economy

Buenos Aires experienced its greatest period of urban expansion between the 1880s and 1920s, when wealth generated by the agricultural sector fueled physical growth and change. An exceptionally fertile hinterland yielded huge supplies of grains and animals that provided fabulous profits for the Buenos Aires élite (Johns 1992). Surplus capital from agricultural exports, however, was not invested in industry, manufacturing, or new technologies for Buenos Aires. Although élite demand stimulated the development of a manufactured light wage-goods sector within the Federal District, in general imports satisfied most of the city's industrial demands. Real estate and the consumption of commodities and services absorbed much of the agricultural profit. As a major supplier of raw materials to the world economy, the *porteño* élite were content to reap the profits of the Pampas' bounty without reinvesting in domestic industry.

Major structural changes in the world economy, however, were beginning to transform the economies of the leading industrial powers. Fordist production methods, along with a new mode of corporate capitalism, revolutionized industry in the North Atlantic economies. Despite these radical external changes, little mainstream industrialization occurred in Buenos Aires. The city remained predominantly a proto-industrial, agricultural processing center, with secondary production limited to the basic supplies that help a city to grow: wood products, cement, construction materials, textiles, and basic furnishings. Commercial and administrative functions dominated employment activity in the downtown core, transportation services provided jobs along the major arterials, and retail activities employed thousands in the various neighborhoods and suburbs of the city.

Aftershocks from the 1930s' global economic recession and from domestic political upheaval encouraged the introduction of import-substitution policies designed to increase Argentina's industrial and manufacturing productivity. The international economic crisis of the 1930s altered Buenos Aires' economic position in the world order and created an incentive to develop an urban industrial capacity. Steady profits from agricultural exports no longer were guaranteed for the

Buenos Aires élite, and imported consumer goods had become expensive and difficult to obtain. Focusing industrial development on Buenos Aires made sense because the city controlled the national market, with virtually the entire population of Argentina linked to Buenos Aires through a dendritic transport and communication network. However, although industry and manufacturing in Buenos Aires grew into quite a dynamic sector, employing thousands of people, the majority of production remained oriented toward processing agricultural materials and wage-goods for the urban masses. Food, drink, textiles, and animal products flowed from the factories dotted about the Federal District and surrounding *partidos*, not machinery, steel, or capital goods. As the world economy recovered after the Depression, inexpensive European (primarily British) and North American manufactured goods once again flooded through the port of Buenos Aires, overwhelming local markets and essentially retarding the development of local industry.

Argentina's *oligarquía terrateniente* (landed élite) headquartered in Buenos Aires benefited the most from the robust export economy based on agricultural products. The landed élite strongly resisted any attempt to promote economic diversification in Buenos Aires through industrialization policies. At stake was their way of life and their control over the city's financial, social, and political institutions. In contrast, nationalist forces within Buenos Aires strongly supported industrial mobilization. The diminishing of transatlantic links during the late 1930s and early 1940s spurred several campaigns to increase trade within the Latin American region. Nationalist ideology invoked memories of the Viceroyalty of the Río de la Plata, with a proposed customs union among the Latin American countries under Argentina's leadership. Such a union could establish new markets for exports of manufactured goods, goods produced in the *barrios* of Buenos Aires. More importantly, however, the city of Buenos Aires could become a major entrepôt and the region's undisputed economic hegemon. Unfortunately, historical inertia prevailed in the established economic order and little effort was exerted to broaden the arena of industrialization in Buenos Aires.

Import substitution ideologies were reinforced after World War II with the economic policies of Perónism. Juan Domingo Perón rose to power in the 1940s by drawing on ideas of economic independence based on domestic industrialization. The keys to Perón's idea of a new economic order in Argentina were the urban working class, labor leaders, and conservative nationalists who objected to the powerful role foreign capital played in the national and urban economies. Perón's particular style of *justicialismo* (social justice) included more housing opportunities, jobs in the public sector, social benefits for the working class, and institutionalized fringe benefits. An aggressive nationalization program brought the railroads, public utilities, telephones, ports, and much of Argentina's industrial capacity under state control.

In Buenos Aires, jobs in the public sector grew rapidly, with public expenditures playing a significant role in the social arena. Perón's administration achieved low urban unemployment by allowing the state enterprises to soak up excess, and frequently unneeded, labor. Traditional industrial activities remained concentrated in La Boca, Barracas, and Nueva Pompeya, as well as in other *barrios* of the Federal District. Around the inner-city fringes, *partidos* such as Quilmes, Avellaneda, Lanús, La Matanza, and Tres de Febrero began to grow as industrial and manufacturing plants expanded and absorbed the flow of migrants from interior provinces. The growth of Buenos Aires' industrial capacity in the 1940s and 1950s revealed that both city and nation were quite capable of supplying the national market with sophisticated and technologically advanced capital goods, intermediate, and consumer goods (Ferrer 1992). Unfortunately, for all their good intentions, Perón's economic policies failed to propel the country forward and Perón retreated from Buenos Aires in September 1955 for 18 years of comfortable exile in Spain.

Industrial growth in Buenos Aires, primarily in the agroindustrial and steel sectors, continued apace during the 1960s and early 1970s. The city's position as Argentina's industrial powerhouse, however, had severe development repercussions for the entire country. Rural–urban migration encouraged by the concentration of industrial activity in Buenos Aires stimulated megacephalous growth in the city, especially in the *partidos* of the suburban Inner Ring. At the same time, self-help housing proliferated in the Federal District as migrants flocked in to seek employment in the administrative offices, headquarters, services, and factories of the city center. Social polarization processes clearly were evident throughout this period as migrants competed for jobs, accommodations, and social benefits in the city. Surplus labor and competition for employment widened the wage gap between the poor and the wealthy. A World Bank (1984) report highlighted the unequal distribution of income in Buenos Aires during the early 1970s. The poorest 10 percent of the population received 2 percent of the city's income, earning an average monthly wage of 415 pesos (approximately US$110). In contrast, the wealthiest 9 percent received 28 percent of Buenos Aires' total income and averaged 3167 pesos monthly (US$825), about 7.5 times the income of the poorest sector.

Industrial restructuring and deconcentration

Uncontrolled growth in Buenos Aires, coupled with the economic plight of Argentina's interior provinces, led to the development in 1966 of the

Table 5.1   Industrial sector indicators in Buenos Aires, 1954–1985

Region	Number of establishments			
	1954	1964	1974	1985
Federal District	40 080	30 651	23 838	15 864
Percent	26.4	21.4	18.9	14.5
Greater Buenos Aires[a]	22 580	31 878	30 033	27 904
Percent	14.9	22.3	23.8	25.5
Rest of Argentina	89 168	80 528	72 517	65 608
Percent	58.7	56.3	57.3	60.0
Total	151 828	143 057	126 388	109 376
Percent	100	100	100	100
	Number of industrial workers			
	1954	1964	1974	1985
Federal District	479 436	356 944	338 683	228 854
Percent	33.3	27.0	22.2	16.6
Greater Buenos Aires[a]	358 407	369 495	499 552	424 109
Percent	24.9	28.0	32.8	30.7
Rest of Argentina	601 486	593 681	686 986	728 842
Percent	41.8	45.0	45.0	52.7
Total	1 439 329	1 320 120	1 525 221	1 381 805
Percent	100	100	100	100

Source: República Argentina (1954, 1964, 1974, 1985, 1993a).
[a] The 19 *partidos* of the suburban Inner Ring.

government's *Plan Esquema 2000*. As part of the plan, a concerted effort was made to relocate industrial production out of the Federal District to designated industrial sites in the suburbs of Greater Buenos Aires (GBA) and to other industrial areas around the country. Most industrial companies, however, retained administrative offices in the downtown core, which served only to reinforce the commercial–bureaucratic nature of the city center. At the same time, the discrediting of Perónist ideologies about economic nationalism encouraged an inflow of US capital into Buenos Aires. New factories financed by North American investment to produce pharmaceutical, automotive, and other more specialized manufactured products sprang up outside the Federal District. Between 1954 and 1974, industrial output in the Greater Buenos Aires Metropolitan Area (GBAMA) more than doubled. Moreover, important changes in the location of industrial establishments and workers in Buenos Aires contributed to suburban growth (Table 5.1).

In 1954, over 40 000 industrial plants located inside the Federal District employed nearly 480 000 workers. The Federal District accounted for 26.4 percent of all industrial facilities in Argentina and one-third of the national industrial work force. In the suburbs of Buenos Aires, 22 580 industrial facilities provided work for over 358 000 people. Twenty years later, in 1974, the Federal District hosted only 23 838 industrial establishments, a 40.5 percent decline in the total number of factories. In addition, by 1974 the Federal District had lost over 140 000 industrial jobs, a 29.4 percent decrease in the work force. In contrast, the 19 *partidos* of the suburban Inner Ring gained 7453 industrial establishments between 1954 and 1974, an increase of 33 percent. The number of industrial workers in the suburbs rose by 141 145 or 39.4 percent over the same period. At the national level, the total number of industrial workers increased by approximately 86 000 over the 20-year period, but these jobs were created outside the traditional industrial region of Buenos Aires. This pattern suggests partial success of government policies to decentralize industrial activities away from the GBAMA. Buenos Aires' total number of industrial establishments and workers continued to decline during the 1960s and 1970s, reflecting the international trend toward deindustrialization and economic restructuring in the traditional industrial economies of the world.

Specific government legislation directly affected spatial and sectoral changes in the Buenos Aires economy during the 1970s. The military government that ruled from 1976 to 1983 drastically changed the economic dynamism of Buenos Aires by introducing several new laws and policies. Part of the government's new Urban Planning Code, the 1977 decentralization law expelled several industrial establishments from the Federal District and prohibited the location of new plants in the GBAMA. Claims that the industrial facilities polluted the environment garnered initial popular support for the government's decentralization policy. In addition, a strict monetarist program reduced customs and non-customs tariffs, revalued the rate of exchange, and increased interest rates to control speculation on the US dollar. The government's so-called fiscal austerity policies opened the floodgates to foreign loans and billions of dollars poured into the banks of Buenos Aires. Some of the loan money was used to fund such grandiose but ill-advised public works projects as the Ezeiza toll highway between downtown Buenos Aires and the international airport. While public transport for the city's commuters continued to deteriorate, millions of dollars were lavished on a freeway that served primarily the urban élite, tourists, and transnational corporate employees. Corruption ran at an all-time high in Buenos Aires, reaching all levels of government from federal to local. As imports surged, foreign debt soared, and government ineptitude reached new heights, the Buenos Aires economy began to unravel at the seams.

Buenos Aires' industrial sector underwent a profound transformation as a result of the military government's economic policies. Forward and backward linkages in the urban and national manufacturing sector were broken as imports flooded through the port of Buenos Aires. Petrochemicals, steel, aluminium, and cellulose produced in the suburban factories of Buenos Aires and designed to supply other urban factories that produced consumer goods now were targeted to the export market. The electronics and mechanical industries of Buenos Aires were devastated, and the production of capital goods declined dramatically (Ferrer 1992). Urban unemployment rapidly increased as local industry could not compete effectively against the cheap imports. Especially hard hit were the industrial suburbs of the Inner Ring, where unemployment rates ran to double figures and thousands of people were pushed over the poverty line. Buenos Aires also lost a substantial number of scientists, technicians, and skilled workers to emigration during the military interregnum. This "brain drain" phenomenon had serious consequences for the development of the city after the restoration of democracy in 1983.

Despite the return to a democratically elected government in Argentina, economic instability continued to exacerbate social polarization processes in Buenos Aires. Although migration flows to the capital were beginning to show signs of a slowdown, several hundred people each week arrived in Buenos Aires seeking employment opportunities and housing. The official unemployment rate rose from 3.7 percent of the economically active population in Buenos Aires during 1982 to over 7 percent in 1989. Unemployment figures remained consistently higher in the suburbs than in the Federal District. In 1989, over 8 percent of the economically active population in the suburbs officially were unemployed, compared to only 4.1 percent in the Federal District. The official hourly underemployment rate in Buenos Aires also showed consistently higher figures during the 1980s in the suburbs than in the inner city *barrios* (República Argentina 1993a). Moreover, poorer neighborhoods throughout Buenos Aires experienced faster rates of unemployment growth than did their wealthier counterparts.

Argentina's 1985 Industrial Census affirmed the ongoing decline in Buenos Aires' industrial sector, a decline which exacerbated the lack of employment opportunities for the city's poorer residents. The Federal District hosted only 14.5 percent of Argentina's total number of industrial establishments in 1985, down from 26.4 percent in 1954 (Table 5.1). Nearly 24 000 industrial plants, 60 percent of the 1954 total, closed or relocated from the city center during the 30-year period. Even the Inner-Ring suburbs lost over 1400 establishments between 1974 and 1985, although their share of the country's total industrial facilities rose from

Table 5.2 Changes in the number of industrial establishments in the Inner Ring of Greater Buenos Aires, 1964–1985

Corridor/*partido*	Number of establishments 1964	1985	Percent change	Percent share 1964	1985
Northwestern					
San Martín	4202	3776	−10.1		
Sarmiento	669	741	10.8		
Merlo	464	419	−9.7		
Moreno	307	262	−14.7		
Morón	2110	1835	−13.0		
San Fernando	688	568	−17.4		
San Isidro	1381	975	−29.4		
Tigre	706	793	12.3		
Tres de Febrero	2980	3041	2.0		
Vicente López	2524	2158	−14.5		
Subtotal	16 031	14 568	−9.1	50.3	50.9
Western					
E. Echeverría	490	499	1.8		
La Matanza (west)	1340	3128	133.4		
La Matanza (east)	411	961	133.8		
Subtotal	2241	4588	104.7	7.0	16.0
Southwestern					
Almirante Brown	558	504	−9.7		
Lanús	2792	3055	9.4		
Lomas de Zamora	4042	1492	−63.1		
Subtotal	7392	5051	−31.7	23.2	17.7
Southern					
Avellaneda	3450	2138	−38.0		
Berazategui	396	387	−2.3		
Florencio Varela	270	249	−7.8		
Quilmes	2098	1634	−22.1		
Subtotal	6214	4408	−29.1	19.5	15.4
Total	31 878	28 615	−10.2	100.0	100.0

Source: República Argentina (1985).

15 percent in 1954 to 26.2 percent in 1985. Between 1974 and 1985, the Federal District lost nearly 110 000 industrial workers and the suburban factories lost 75 000 workers, an indication of the impact on Buenos Aires' economy of the anti-industry urban policies of the military government.

Within the 19 *partidos* of the suburban Inner Ring, there were clear winners and losers in the industrial restructuring process (Tables 5.2 and 5.3). Along the northwestern corridor, the number of workers grew by 30.9 percent between 1964 and 1985 despite a 9.1 percent decline in the

Table 5.3 Changes in the number of industrial workers in the Inner Ring of Greater Buenos Aires, 1964–1985

Corridor/*partido*	Number of workers 1964	1985	Percent change	Percent share 1964	1985
Northwestern					
San Martín	41 256	52 702	27.7		
Sarmiento	5727	9355	63.3		
Merlo	5829	6790	16.5		
Moreno	2551	4418	73.2		
Morón	25 196	26 120	3.7		
San Fernando	5415	8375	54.7		
San Isidro	21 051	19 008	−9.7		
Tigre	10 626	23 544	121.6		
Tres de Febrero	20 173	31 455	55.9		
Vicente López	30 580	38 640	26.4		
Subtotal	168 404	220 407	30.9	46.3	52.0
Western					
E. Echeverría	6956	9745	40.1		
La Matanza (west)	13 052	42 947	229.0		
La Matanza (east)	4009	13 193	229.1		
Subtotal	24 017	65 885	174.3	6.6	15.5
Southwestern					
Almirante Brown	3001	5419	80.6		
Lanús	36 073	35 911	−0.4		
Lomas de Zamora	40 303	18 774	−53.4		
Subtotal	79 377	60 104	−24.3	21.8	14.2
Southern					
Avellaneda	49 838	34 742	−30.3		
Berazategui	11 784	10 135	−14.0		
Florencio Varela	4559	7569	66.0		
Quilmes	25 949	25 296	−2.5		
Subtotal	92 130	77 742	−15.6	25.3	18.3
Total	363 928	424 138	16.5	100.0	100.0

Source: República Argentina (1985).

number of industrial establishments. Only San Isidro experienced any significant changes, losing 406 establishments and 2043 workers during the intercensal period. Overall, the *partidos* of the northwestern corridor maintained a 50 percent share of total industrial activity in the Inner Ring of Greater Buenos Aires. The two *partidos* of the western corridor, and particularly the western section of La Matanza, experienced dramatic industrialization between 1964 and 1985. Western La Matanza gained over 29 000 workers and more than doubled its number of industrial establishments, which certainly contributed to the *partido's* rapid population growth during the 1960s and 1970s. Both industrial establishments and workers were lost in the southwestern and southern corridors between 1964 and 1985. Especially hard-hit were the working-class suburbs of Avellaneda and Lomas de Zamora. Lomas lost 21 529 industrial positions over the 21-year period, and industrial establishments declined by 63.1 percent. Many southern-based industries relocated to the northwestern corridor because of better transport services, more readily available land, a deeper pool of specialized and skilled labor, and proximity to urban, national, and international distribution routes.

Despite declining industrial employment opportunities during the late 1970s and early 1980s, however, migrants continued to arrive in GBA from the interior and from neighboring countries. How were these migrants absorbed into the urban work force and which suburbs had the ability to recover from deindustrialization? Buenos Aires' position after 1983 in the rapidly changing global and regional economic environment provides part of the answer.

Urban commercial growth

Argentina's return to democracy in 1983 promised the development of policies geared toward the commercial, financial, and service sectors of the urban economy. The global economic crisis of the early 1980s, the genesis of an identifiable system of world cities, and the beginning of the end of the Cold War marked a new stage of globalization in the capitalist world economy. This stage opened up a potential new role for Buenos Aires in the world economy as the dominant commercial center in the Southern Cone of South America. A key component of globalization in the 1980s was the growth of multinational corporate activity in major cities around the world and the rise of many of these cities as basing points for global capital. World cities also began to function as loci of advanced producer services and as concentration points for new physical and social infrastructure. J.R. Feagin and Michael Smith's (1987) examination of the world's leading financial centers found that of the 17 largest metropolitan areas in 1984, seven contained 96 percent of the headquarters of the top 500 multinational companies (Table 5.4). London, New York, and Tokyo, arguably the dominant centers in the emerging world city system, alone accounted for nearly two-thirds of the headquarter functions of these 500 companies. Buenos Aires had only one multinational headquarters in 1984 but, as Saskia Sassen (1991) pointed out, headquarter functions are not as useful a measure of economic power as they were in the 1960s and 1970s. Although multinational

Table 5.4   The number of headquarters of the top 500 multinational firms in the world's 17 largest metropolitan areas, 1984

City	Number of top 500 headquarters	Population (thousands)
New York	59	17 082
London	37	11 100
Tokyo	34	26 200
Paris	26	9650
Chicago	18	7865
Osaka	15	15 900
Los Angeles	14	10 520
Seoul	4	11 200
México City	1	14 600
Buenos Aires	1	10 700
Bombay	1	9950
Rio de Janeiro	1	9200
São Paulo	0	12 700
Calcutta	0	11 100
Beijing	0	9340
Cairo	0	8500
Shanghai	0	8500

Source: After Feagin and Smith (1987).

corporations continue to rely on the specialized services and financial companies that tend to concentrate in major cities, the changing dynamics of global and regional connectivity mean that headquarter functions are far more "footloose" than in previous decades.

Notwithstanding Buenos Aires' minor role in the growing global and regional financial and service networks, the city's economy did expand into areas other than industry, manufacturing, and agriculture. Many of the migrants to Buenos Aires during the 1970s and 1980s were absorbed into the city's expanding tertiary economy, especially the small business, administrative, and personal services sectors. Between 1964 and 1985, nearly 290 000 additional workers found employment in the commercial sector. However, commercial activities in the 19 *partidos* of the suburban Inner Ring grew at a much faster pace than in the Federal District. Over the 21 year period, the Federal District's share of commercial establishments located in Buenos Aires dropped from 47.6 to 41.3 percent and its share of commercial workers dropped from 65.2 to 58.1 percent (Tables 5.5 and 5.6). In fact, the total number of commercial activities located in the Federal District declined by over 2000 between 1974 and 1985. These data suggest that while the Federal District retains its role as a commercial–bureaucratic center, some commercial decentralization and

Table 5.5   The growth of commercial establishments in Buenos Aires, 1964–1985[a]

Corridor/*partido*	Number of establishments 1964	1985	Percent change	Percent share 1964	1985
Northwestern					
San Martín	8942	9804	9.6		
Sarmiento	4321	9550	121.0		
Merlo	2986	5606	87.7		
Moreno	1815	3688	103.2		
Morón	9540	13 798	44.6		
San Fernando	2736	3531	29.1		
San Isidro	5727	7572	32.2		
Tigre	2565	4400	71.5		
Tres de Febrero	7784	9803	25.9		
Vicente López	7224	8091	12.0		
Subtotal	53 640	75 843	41.4	23.8	28.2
Western					
E. Echeverría	1957	3723	90.2		
La Matanza (west)	9577	16 848	75.9		
La Matanza (east)	2942	5176	75.9		
Subtotal	14 476	25 747	77.9	6.4	9.6
Southwestern					
Almirante Brown	3563	6769	90.0		
Lanús	11 486	11 578	0.8		
Lomas de Zamora	7817	11 396	45.8		
Subtotal	22 866	29 743	30.1	10.2	11.0
Southern					
Avellaneda	10 886	9028	−17.1		
Berazategui	7243	4354	−39.9		
Florencio Varela	1134	3082	171.8		
Quilmes	7707	10 310	33.8		
Subtotal	26 970	26 774	−0.7	12.0	9.9
19 *Partidos*	117 952	158 107	34.0	52.4	58.7
Federal District	107 062	111 029	3.7	47.6	41.3
Grand total	225 014	269 136	19.6	100.0	100.0

Source: República Argentina (1985).

[a] Data are for the 19 *partidos* of the suburban Inner Ring and the Federal District.

growth is occurring in the suburbs. Much of this growth, of course, is in support services such as retail functions for the expanding suburban population.

An analysis of changes in the commercial activities of the 19 Inner-Ring *partidos* reveals several important trends. Avellaneda, along the southern corridor, was the only *partido* to lose both commercial establishments and

Table 5.6 Changes in the number of workers in the commercial sector in Buenos Aires, 1964–1985[a]

Corridor/*partido*	Number of workers 1964	1985	Percent change	Percent share 1964	1985
Northwestern					
San Martín	15 866	23 712	49.5		
Sarmiento	7974	24 243	204.0		
Merlo	4711	9389	99.3		
Moreno	3132	7114	127.1		
Morón	17 312	34 655	100.2		
San Fernando	5453	8742	60.3		
San Isidro	13 097	26 408	101.6		
Tigre	5010	11 933	138.2		
Tres de Febrero	13 187	21 975	66.6		
Vicente López	15 403	27 049	75.6		
Subtotal	101 145	195 220	93.0	16.5	21.7
Western					
E. Echeverría	3656	7908	116.3		
La Matanza (west)	16 161	37 129	129.7		
La Matanza (east)	4964	11 405	129.8		
Subtotal	24 781	56 442	127.8	4.0	6.3
Southwestern					
Almirante Brown	5982	12 964	116.7		
Lanús	19 051	23 801	24.9		
Lomas de Zamora	14 248	26 840	88.4		
Subtotal	39 281	63 605	61.9	6.5	7.0
Southern					
Avellaneda	28 891	23 744	−17.8		
Berazategui	3696	8472	129.2		
Florencio Varela	2021	6408	217.1		
Quilmes	13 133	23 582	79.6		
Subtotal	47 741	62 206	30.3	7.8	6.9
19 *Partidos*	212 948	377 473	77.3	34.8	41.9
Federal District	399 047	523 838	31.3	65.2	58.1
Grand total	611 995	901 311	47.3	100.0	100.0

Source: República Argentina (1985).

[a] Data are for the 19 *partidos* of the suburban Inner Ring and the Federal District.

workers between 1964 and 1985. Coupled with losses in the industrial sector during the same time period, the lack of commercial growth along the southern corridor has been a serious problem for planners and city managers. Unemployment and underemployment rates in Avellaneda are among the highest in the metropolitan area, and the suburb suffers from ongoing social deterioration, with low-income families pushed ever deeper into poverty. Along the northwestern corridor, the wealthier suburbs continued to show robust growth in all sectors of the economy, improving their collective share of the total number of commercial workers in the Inner Ring from 47.5 to 51.7 percent. General Sarmiento especially enjoyed tremendous growth in the commercial sector, which paralleled the *partido's* rapid growth in population between 1970 and 1980. Commercial growth along the western corridor in La Matanza has been spurred by industrial growth and population expansion in the western half of the *partido*.

Data on the gross domestic product (GDP) of Buenos Aires in 1985 support the spatial patterns of industrial and commercial activity described above (República Argentina 1985). Thirty-one percent of the GDP of the Federal District came from the secondary sector, with 69 percent provided by the tertiary sector. In the 19 *partidos* of the suburban Inner Ring, 59.1 percent of the GDP was provided by the industrial and manufacturing sector, 39.7 percent by the tertiary sector, and 1.2 by primary production. Despite employment and plant losses, the southern corridor remained the most industrialized of the Inner-Ring corridors, with 65 percent of its GDP coming from the secondary sector. Primary production continued to be important in the *partidos* of Moreno, Tigre, Esteban Echeverría, and Florencio Varela. These *partidos* still had substantial tracts of land under agriculture during the 1980s.

Throughout the 1980s, Buenos Aires focused increasing resources on improving its position in the global export market. Primary products and agricultural-based manufactures continued to be the mainstay of Argentine exports during the 1980s, ranging from a high share of 82.3 percent of total exports in 1983 to a low of 63.1 percent in 1989. Only beginning in 1989 did manufactures of industrial origin begin to increase as a percentage of total exports. Industrial manufactures accounted for 27.2 percent of total exports in 1990, compared with barely 16 percent in 1981. More importantly to the economic policies of Raúl Alfonsín's middle-class Radical Party government, Argentina maintained a trade surplus during most of the 1980s (Table 5.7). Only after the economic liberalization and globalization policies of Carlos Menem's government were introduced in 1991 did Argentina's trade balance revert to a negative figure. One of the consequences of economic restructuring in Argentina has been a rapid growth in imports, especially in luxury consumer goods. Domestic industries are unable to compete effectively with cheap textiles and shoes from Asia, automobiles from Brazil, and machinery from the North Atlantic economies. As a result, many small manufacturing operations in Buenos Aires have been squeezed out of business by cheap imports.

Table 5.7 Argentina's exports and imports, 1980–1994

| Year | (Millions of current dollars) | | |
	Exports	Imports	Trade balance
1980	8021	10 541	−2520
1981	9143	9430	−287
1982	7625	5337	2288
1983	7836	4504	3332
1984	8107	4585	3522
1985	8396	3814	4582
1986	6852	4724	2128
1987	6360	5818	542
1988	9135	5322	3813
1989	9579	4203	5376
1990	12 353	4077	8276
1991	11 978	8276	3702
1992	12 236	14 872	−2636
1993	13 118	16 783	−3665
1994[a]	15 200	21 200	−6000

Source: República Argentina (1993b), *Latin American Weekly Report* (1994–1995).
[a] Preliminary figures.

Global and regional economic linkages

Direct evidence of Buenos Aires' changing global and regional economic linkages is not readily obtainable. Reliable statistics, for example, on the proportion of Argentina's exports that have value added within the GBAMA do not exist. Neither is it possible to calculate with any degree of accuracy capital flows between Buenos Aires and other world cities. However, ample secondary evidence exists to suggest that Buenos Aires' economic relationships at the global and regional levels are undergoing realignment. Changing transportation and communication routes (see Chapter 6) and international tourism flows (see Chapter 8) intimate increased economic integration with regional neighbors. The growing number of international bank branch offices and representatives in Buenos Aires points toward stronger ties to the dominant global financial centers. In addition, the rapid growth of foreign corporate and multinational activities in Buenos Aires, spurred by privatization and deregulation policies, has opened up the urban economy to global and regional capital circulation and has linked the city more strongly to the major stock markets of the world.

Perhaps the most useful indicators of Buenos Aires' changing external economic relationships are import and export data. Although these data are compiled at the national level, they provide a credible basis for tracking trends in the urban economy. Buenos Aires absorbs a large percentage of the nation's imports and contributes a substantial share of its exports, so trade data at the national level can be reliably extrapolated to indicate the city's external economic links. Barely 11 percent of Argentina's total world trade in 1975 occurred with the countries that now are members of the newly established Common Market of the Southern Cone (MERCOSUR) – Brazil, Paraguay, and Uruguay. North America, Europe, and the Soviet Union absorbed most of Argentina's exports in the 1970s and provided the majority of the country's imports. In 1985, the United States took 12.2 percent of Argentina's exports and Europe purchased 25.4 percent. Twenty-two percent of all exports went to other Latin American countries. A similar pattern of trade could be found in the origin of Argentina's imports in 1985. The United States provided 18.2 percent, Europe 33.1 percent, and other Latin American countries 34.7 percent of the country's total imports. Almost all of these imports came through Buenos Aires, with the majority destined for the local market and the remainder for the much smaller interior market.

By 1992, traditional trading patterns had begun to show signs of realignment as Argentina's economic restructuring policies changed the dynamics of its global and regional economic links. The biggest realignment in trading links involved Argentina's new MERCOSUR partners. Although trade with Brazil particularly had improved steadily since the mid-1980s, rapid growth occurred only after 1990. From a paltry US$358 million in exports to Brazil during 1983, exports reached US$1.7 billion in 1992. Imports from Brazil totaled only US$395 million in 1983, but by 1992 imports had soared to US$3.3 billion. Especially important in the Buenos Aires market are Brazilian automobiles and automotive parts, shoes, textiles, and machinery. Trade with the three MERCOSUR members reached over 20 percent of Argentina's total trade in 1992, and this number is expected to show steady growth during the remainder of the 1990s. Bilateral trade with Chile, not one of the MERCOSUR partners, exceeded US$1.2 billion in 1993, up by 15 percent from 1992 and 12 times the average amount of trade during the 1980s. Improved economic relationships with Chile are forcing a re-evaluation of transport and communication infrastructure between Buenos Aires and Santiago. Transport links traditionally have been relatively poor and they continue to hinder trade growth between the two urban centers.

Although Brazil has become Argentina's primary trading partner, the United States continues to play an important role in the local urban economy. Eleven percent of Argentina's exports and 21.7 percent of its imports were with the United States in 1992. The Buenos Aires economy depends on electrical equipment, mechanical parts, precision instruments, and other advanced technology products from the United States. The so-called "invisible" trade with the United States, which includes professional services, consulting, popular music, soft drink and food franchises, movies, and other aspects of popular culture, is growing daily and it has had a powerful impact on the urban economy and landscape of Buenos Aires in recent years.

Despite the rhetoric of improving Pacific Rim trade and the possible key role of Buenos Aires in a Pacific–Atlantic Rim economic region, imports and exports between Argentina and East Asia have shown little improvement in recent years. East Asia provided 13.8 percent of Argentina's total imports in 1992, up only slightly from 12.6 percent in 1980, and from taking 6.7 percent of Argentina's exports in 1980, East Asia purchased only 9.3 percent of the country's exports in 1992. Poor transport and financial links with Asian markets have hindered the development of Buenos Aires' Pacific Rim relationships in recent years. Moreover, Japanese, Hong Kong, and Singaporean investment capital has not been sought actively by the Buenos Aires economic élite, who have preferred to rely on old established relationships with Europe and the United States.

The contemporary urban economy

When Carlos Menem and the Justicialista Party won Argentina's federal elections in 1989, the economy of both city and nation was in chaos once again. Consumer prices in Buenos Aires rose 20 594 percent between April 1989 and March 1990, and inflation reached nearly 5000 percent annually. Food riots and supermarket looting broke out in May 1989, and mothers reportedly were instructing their hungry children to eat stolen food in the supermarkets and then to run out past the cashiers (*La Nación* 1989). Problems were particularly bad in the *barrios* and suburbs along the southern and southwestern corridors. Nearly 30 percent of the work force had no social security coverage and survived by taking irregular, cash-in-hand work. The urban economy had become smaller in absolute terms than it had been in 1970. By December 1989 the Austral (Argentina's currency) had collapsed from 1 to the US dollar in 1986 to over 1000 to the US dollar. Few other semi-industrial urban centers around the world have experienced an economic collapse as dramatic as that which occurred in Buenos Aires.

Menem's promise of a responsible economic policy oriented toward maintaining stability evaporated in the face of the changing realities of the new global economic order. President Menem withdrew Argentina from the Non-aligned Movement and declared that the country now belonged to a "single world . . . a new juridical, political, social, and economic order" (Gills and Rocamora 1992, p. 515). Moreover, Buenos Aires would play a pivotal role in Argentina's new global strategies as a world city, global gateway, and key financial center in the Southern Cone. Rejecting the working-class Perónist ideologies that had carried his Justicialista Party to electoral success, Menem turned toward *los grupos económicos* (the economic and financial élite) in Buenos Aires and began to woo foreign capital. The doors to Buenos Aires were thrown open to multinational corporations, foreign investors, and Argentina's economic exiles who, Menem believed, could change the face of both society and economy for the better. Progressive economic reforms were abandoned in favor of free-market strategies based on privatization, deregulation, and state disengagement from the domestic economy (Corradi 1992). Globalization became the new economic buzzword in Buenos Aires. Soon both the urban economy and the urban landscape began to respond to globalization policies and practices.

The key to the federal government's globalization strategies was the plan to extricate itself from the public services arena. In Buenos Aires, the subways and suburban railroads, electricity system, water and sewerage network, telephone network, and other public services quickly were sold off to private investors. Privatization, argued the government, would reduce the burden of subsidizing public services and improve their management and efficiency. However, many Argentines complained that privatization was nothing more than a "bargain sale of grandmother's jewelry," a reference to the nationalization of public enterprises by Perón in the late 1940s (Imai 1992, p. 448). Adolfo Canitrot (1993, p. 91) posits that privatization simply is an "all-out effort targeted to eradicate public enterprises completely." For example, rather than broadening the ownership base of public enterprises through share sales to small investors, privatization has concentrated ownership and control in the hands of approximately 10 large Argentine conglomerates headquartered in Buenos Aires (Canitrot 1993). In terms of foreign investors, Italians, Spaniards, Chileans, North Americans, and Brazilians have garnered the largest share of the privatized public enterpises. Although Argentine as well as foreign capital is funding the purchase of these public enterprises, privatization policies have generated much nationalistic rhetoric. Graffiti messages such as "Patria sí, Colonia no" (country yes but colony no) have sprung up around the *barrios* of the Federal District and are clear references to public sentiment about increased foreign investment in Argentina's economy (Figure 5.1).

Figure 5.1   Urban graffiti protesting government privatization policies

As Argentina's federal government disengages itself from the state economy, changes are occurring in the type of private financial services being offered to the public. The most dramatic change in street-level economic activities in Buenos Aires since 1993 has been the proliferation of private pension companies. Brash and boldly decorated offices have sprung up along Avenida Florida, the city's premier shopping and major pedestrian walkway. A major marketing campaign using billboard, radio, cinema, television, and print advertising has attempted to lure prospective customers to these new, North American style, private pension schemes. Other important changes include the proliferation of fast-food outlets in the downtown core, glitzy new shopping centers selling imported luxury goods from Southeast Asia, Europe, and neighboring South American countries, more automobiles on city streets, and a reinvigorated financial district. Privatization, deregulation, and free-trade ideologies also are beginning to affect the structure of Buenos Aires' industrial, manufacturing, and service sectors.

In 1992, 2084 industrial companies employing 30 or more workers were recorded as still operating within the Federal District, although many companies were assigned the jurisdiction of their head office, not the actual location of the factory (República Argentina 1993a). A further 2000 companies were operating in the 19 *partidos* of the city's Inner Ring, with a particular concentration along the northern corridor. Eighty-two percent of all industrial production in Buenos Aires now is concentrated in four sectors: 20 percent in food and beverages, 21 percent in textiles, 18 percent in chemicals, and 23 percent in metal products.

One of the strongest economic performers in Buenos Aires during the early 1990s has been the automobile industry. Argentina's automobile production in 1992 proved to be the highest in over a decade, with much of this growth coming from factories in Buenos Aires. The export coefficient of automobile manufacturers rose to over 10 percent in 1991 from under 5 percent during the 1980s. However, salary costs per unit of automobile production in Buenos Aires still are between 100 and 200 percent higher than comparable costs in Brazil. Yet these costs are less than 50 percent of comparable costs in the United States, so the city's automobile industry retains some competitive wage-labor advantage. Economic restructuring in Buenos Aires also has increased local demand for major products such as refrigerators, stoves, and washing machines. Over half of Argentina's total production of household appliances occurs in the GBA area, although production slowly is shifting to the interior provinces where per unit labor costs can average between 10 and 35 percent lower.

Major changes are occurring in the dynamics of Buenos Aires' labor force. Unfortunately, a serious problem with examining the structural implications for Buenos Aires of globalizing the economy is a lack of basic up-to-date data about labor processes. The federal government conducts an economic census every 10 years, the last held in 1995, although detailed results have yet to be released. Preliminary analysis suggests that job losses persist in the primary and secondary sectors, especially in industry and construction, while employment continues to grow in the tertiary and quaternary sectors (Table 5.8). Opening up the domestic market to foreign capital and investors as part of the government's privatization and deregulation strategies has helped to create new jobs. Recent employment data suggest that many of the jobs lost in industry and through rationalization or downsizing in divested state companies (railroads, telephones, etc.) have been absorbed in the financial sector. Service sector jobs were more readily available in 1994, especially in administration and management. Moreover, the increased circulation of foreign and domestic capital in Buenos Aires has opened up entrepreneurial opportunities in certain niche markets such as financial management, import/export, and entertainment.

The Buenos Aires labor force grew by approximately 295 000 jobs between October 1988 and October 1992. Commercial activities (retail, hotels, and restaurants) expanded by 182 400 jobs, the transport and communication sector expanded by 75 000 jobs, and the social and personal service sector grew by 272 000 jobs. Manufacturing absorbed another 38,500 jobs, while construction lost over 10 000 workers. Employment changes in the finance, insurance, real estate, and corporate services sector have become significant only since 1992; 344 000 people,

Table 5.8 The percentage distribution of the employed population in Buenos Aires by activity category, 1980–1994

Period		Industry[a]	Construction	Commerce[b]	Social and personal services	Other[c]	Total
April	1980	29.5	9.0	18.0	28.5	15.0	100
April	1981	28.2	9.0	19.3	28.6	14.9	100
April	1982	26.1	8.0	19.9	30.7	15.3	100
April	1983	24.9	6.4	19.2	34.2	15.3	100
April	1984	26.2	5.7	17.1	35.0	16.0	100
May	1985	25.4	7.3	17.3	29.1	20.9	100
April	1987	25.8	6.6	19.0	33.7	14.9	100
May	1988	25.1	7.5	19.0	32.2	16.2	100
May	1989	25.0	6.5	18.7	33.3	16.5	100
May	1990	23.3	6.2	19.8	33.5	17.2	100
May	1991	23.8	6.4	20.4	33.4	16.0	100
October	1992	23.6	5.7	21.2	33.3	16.2	100
May	1994[d]	22.0	5.0	22.0	35.0	16.0	100

Source: República Argentina (1991, 1993a).

[a] Industrial and manufacturing employment.
[b] Retail trade, restaurants, and hotels.
[c] Agriculture, quarrying, public services, transportation, and financial services.
[d] Preliminary figures from unpublished working documents at the National Institute of Statistics and Census (INDEC) in Buenos Aires.

7.5 percent of the urban labor force, held jobs in this sector in October 1992, up from 318 000 people or 7.5 percent in October 1988. However, caution is required when interpreting these labor statistics. In 1988, 312 000 jobs could not be categorized adequately and were included in a category called "unknown." Many of these jobs were in the informal sector of the urban economy, especially in the personal services sector. By 1992, the National Institute of Statistics and Census (INDEC) had recategorized many of these jobs, and the number in the unknown category dropped to about 8000. Despite these statistical problems, the structural evolution of Buenos Aires' labor force illustrates an important trend: a steady transition from predominantly secondary sector employment to tertiary and quaternary employment. The economy of Buenos Aires is maturing and becoming more involved in the global information and service networks. This maturation provides support for the argument that Buenos Aires is beginning to exhibit the types of qualities that distinguish world cities from other urban centers. The city is functioning more as a basing point for global, regional, and domestic capital and as a major gateway city for the Southern Cone region, than simply as an overly dominant, internally focused national capital.

Unemployment and the informal economy

Despite the many positive changes in Buenos Aires' labor structure, thousands of people holding unskilled jobs and lower-level administrative positions have not fared so well in the urban restructuring process. As a consequence of nearly 50 years of developing a welfare state, tremendous levels of overemployment existed in the public sector when the Menem government took power in 1989. Railroads, airlines, utilities, ports, industries, and government agencies all had bloated bureaucracies and multiple employees for every position. Moreover, corruption, theft of public monies, and nepotism had become out of control. Policies of privatization, deregulation, and globalization have begun to rectify this situation by shifting surplus and nonproductive labor from the public to the private sector, especially into tertiary and service-oriented activities. In this division and redistribution of the urban labor force, however, the unskilled and poorer sections of Buenos Aires society have suffered more than others. Within the free-market capitalist system, labor is a commodity subject to the laws of supply and demand. Surplus unskilled labor in Buenos Aires has created a situation, particularly among the poorest 20 percent of the urban work force, where average daily wages are forced downward because of intense competition for employment. Exacerbating this process is the continued migration to Buenos Aires of poor, rural Bolivians, Paraguayans, and Argentinians desperate for employment in the urban economy. Thus, since 1989 there has been a significant increase in the number of people categorized as "under-employed" or working in the "gray" informal sector of the urban economy.

Throughout the Federal District and along the major transport routes, thousands of *kioskos*, small mini-shops, have sprung up selling cigarettes, newspapers, candy, and soft drinks. Every day, thousands of *ambulantes* (itinerant salespeople) ride the trains, subways, and buses, or move from café to restaurant and store, selling everything from chewing gum and children's books to kitchen knives, batteries, and ballpoint pens. On one 60-minute train ride from Retiro terminal to Tigre in 1993, I counted 38 *ambulantes* passing through the carriages selling over 50 different items. In addition, young children, many under 10 years old, and mothers with babies in their arms pass through the trains constantly seeking money from passengers. The supplicant generally places a small religious leaflet on the seat or in the passenger's lap and hopes to receive a peso or two in exchange for the leaflet. For many in Buenos Aires, this is the only source of daily income. Although obvious begging is extremely un-common on the streets of Buenos Aires, in recent years many physically disabled and indigent people have become a regular sight on the major pedestrian streets such as Florida and Lavalle in the downtown core.

Buenos Aires' official unemployment rate in May 1991, at the begin-ning of the Menem government's globalization campaign, was 6.4 percent of the economically active population, or about 333 000 people (República Argentina 1993a). The official underemployment rate is calculated from those people working less than 35 hours per week, approximately 390 000 people in May 1991. About 5.2 million *porteños* officially were economically active in May 1991, which equaled about 41 percent of the total urban population. Since the introduction of economic restructuring policies in Argentina, however, Buenos Aires' official unemployment rates have increased steadily. In May 1994, 11.1 percent of the economically active population was unemployed compared with 6.4 percent in May 1991 (Economic Commission for Latin America and the Caribbean 1994). A greater percentage of the total urban population now is underemployed compared with 1991. Over 600 000 *porteños* officially are without permanent employment and a further three-quarters of a million have become part of the growing informal economy. Despite efficiency measures in the industrial and manufacturing sectors, includ-ing privatization and the liberalization of trading policies, real industrial wages in Buenos Aires have not recovered to their 1983 levels, even taking into account changes in the value of currency and the consumer price index.

Table 5.9   The cost of living in the major cities of Latin America compared with New York, December 1994

City	Country	Cost of Living Index
New York	United States	100
Buenos Aires	Argentina	92
Río de Janeiro	Brazil	85
São Paulo	Brazil	83
Mexico City	Mexico	81
Panamá City	Panamá	76
Montevideo	Uruguay	75
Guatemala City	Guatemala	74
Bogotá	Colombia	71
Lima	Peru	70
San José	Costa Rica	68
Santiago	Chile	68
Quito	Ecuador	67
Asunción	Paraguay	64
Caracas	Venezuela	47

Source: Latin American Weekly Report (1995).

Moreover, exacerbating the problem of urban poverty is Buenos Aires' status as the most expensive Latin American city in which to live. When comparing the cost of food, accommodation, transportation, utilities, and other basic necessities in 14 Latin American urban centers, using New York City as a benchmark, Buenos Aires scores 92 out of a possible 100 points (Table 5.9). The high cost of living in Buenos Aires, coupled with downward pressure on the average monthly urban wage, has created a situation where increasing numbers of *porteños* are being pushed ever closer to the poverty line.

Hardest hit in the economic restructuring process have been working-class suburbs along the southern and western corridors, as well as the hundreds of thousands of poor people living in *villas de emergencia*. The middle classes have not fared too well either. Unemployment and underemployment are prevalent particularly in the western *barrios* of the Federal District and in the *partidos* along the north shore. As Table 5.10 indicates, however, the worst effects of the 1989 economic crisis appear to be over. Fewer households in the GBAMA were considered below the poverty line in 1992 compared with 1988, and the indigent household rate has been cut from 6.4 to 2.6 percent of the total number of households. Nonetheless, when national statistics are evaluated, poverty in both city and nation still appears to be increasing (Table 5.11). The richest 10 percent of Argentina's population accounted for 35.3 percent of total income in 1993, up from 30 percent in 1980. Both the poorest 10 percent

Table 5.10   Households below the indigence and poverty lines in Greater Buenos Aires, 1988–1992[a]

| | | (Percentages) | |
| | Indigence | Poverty | |
Period	households	Households	People
May 1988	6.4	22.6	29.9
October 1988	7.8	24.2	32.4
May 1989	6.3	19.7	25.9
October 1989	12.7	38.3	47.4
May 1990	9.1	33.7	42.6
October 1990	5.0	25.3	33.8
May 1991	3.8	21.8	28.8
October 1991	2.4	16.3	21.6
May 1992	2.4	15.1	19.3
October 1992	2.6	13.7	17.8

Source: República Argentina (1993b).

[a] The indigence line is the cost of a basic family food basket. The poverty line is approximately double the indigence line. Data are based on income declared in household surveys carried out by the census bureau. Incomes generally are underestimated by 20 percent. Therefore, percentages are an overestimation and should be treated simply as indicative of trends over time.

Table 5.11   Poverty in Argentina, 1980–1993

Percentages	1980	1989	1993
Poorest 10% of the population – real wages	100	25	58
Share of income (%)			
Poorest 10%	1.9	1.2	1.7
Middle 80%	68.1	58.1	63.0
Richest 10%	30.0	40.7	35.3

Source: Internal World Bank Report (1994) "Un perfil de la emergencia de los pobres en Argentina," in *Latin American Weekly Report* (1994) WR-84-38, p. 450.

and middle 80 percent of the population have lost ground economically since 1980. Indeed, the poorest 10 percent of the population has seen its real wages drop from an index level of 100 in 1980 to 58 in 1993, despite rampant inflation and currency adjustments. The problem is acute particularly in Buenos Aires, where social polarization is far more evident. Unofficial estimates suggest that the richest 10 percent of Buenos Aires' population now controls approximately 40 percent of the gross urban income.

Circuits of capital

Capital, both tangible and intangible, functions as a crucial pillar of the world city and global economic systems. Therefore, as major financial nodes and basing points for the circulation of global capital, world cities develop specific infrastructure to facilitate capital development and management. New office complexes such as Canary Wharf in London or La Défense in Paris, for example, provide the most visual evidence of global capital's impact on the urban environment. However, other equally important but less visible changes are occurring in the provision of educational facilities, support services, investment vehicles, and entrepreneurial opportunities, all of which help to reshape the urban landscape. In Buenos Aires, the rapid expansion and deregulation of international financial transactions, the integration of the stock market into the global financial network, and the growth of regional markets for producer services all are part of a restructured economic base that is driving physical change in the city. The concentration and accumulation of capital in Buenos Aires is leading to new investment in the built environment. As financial activities increase, a need for expanded office and administrative facilities is being generated. Moreover, changes in capital flows help to create capital surpluses, which are invested in property, the consumption of luxury goods, and in other areas. For example, rehabilitation of the city's public service infrastructure requires a huge capital investment. This investment, in turn, helps to create a demand for labor, construction materials, support services, and administrators.

Historical inertia in the development and circulation of capital in Buenos Aires has retarded the ability of globalization policies to reshape the urban landscape. Just as in the late nineteenth century, when *porteños* shied away from investing in what were perceived as speculative technologies (railroads, tramways, and ports), domestic capital in the 1990s is not flowing into projects that could have important forward and backward linkages in the local economy. The construction of luxury boutiques, glitzy shopping malls, sports facilities, and high-rise apartments, coupled with land speculation and the consumption of luxury imported goods, has done little to broaden the economic base of Buenos Aires or to encourage the investment of capital in public infrastructure. Moreover, a failure to open up participation in the privatization of state-owned businesses to individual investors has hindered the restructuring process. Perhaps the most significant barrier to the reconfiguring of Buenos Aires' circuits of capital, however, is concern about the long-term stability of Argentina's currency and consumer prices.

Changes in the value of Argentina's currency and the annual inflation rate reflect the stability of the local economy. Economic restructuring

Table 5.12 Annual rate of inflation, Consumer Price Index change, and currency exchange rates in the Greater Buenos Aires Region, 1980–1995

Year	Annual rate of inflation (percent)	Consumer Price Index[a] (base 1988 = 100)	Exchange rate For the US$ (selling rate)[b]	
1980	87.6	0.0039453	Australes	0.000184
1981	131.3	0.008067		0.000574
1982	209.7	0.021360		0.002594
1983	433.7	0.09480		0.010540
1984	688.0	0.6889		0.068422
1985	385.4	5.320		0.6011
1986	81.9	10.112		0.9442
1987	174.8	23.39		2.31
1988	387.7	103.62		10.85
1989	4923.6	3294.60		407.10
1990	1343.9	79 530.50		4876.81
1991	70.3	216 061.90		9541.48
1992	10.1	269 861.20	Pesos[c]	0.9915
1993	7.4	287 669.84		0.9945
1994[d]	3.5	290 000.00		0.9975
1995[e]	4.0	295 000.00		0.9800

Source: República Argentina (1993a).

[a] The Consumer Price Index measures price changes in the Greater Buenos Aires Metropolitan Area for a specific group of goods and services represented by the consumption of the population for the period July 1985 to June 1986.

[b] Annual average exchange rate to buy US$1. Exchange rate 1980–1985 has been converted to Australes for comparison.

[c] Changes in Argentina's monetary unit relative to the 1994 Peso:

Until December 31, 1969	M$N	10 000 000 000 000 = 1 Peso
Until May 31, 1983	$Ley	100 000 000 000 = 1 Peso
Until June 14, 1985	$a	10 000 000 = 1 Peso
Until December 31, 1991	$A	10 000 = 1 Peso
Since January 1, 1992	$1	= 1 Peso

[d] Preliminary figures.

[e] Projected figures.

policies have stabilized both currency and consumer prices since 1990 (Table 5.12). Inflation is down to single digits for the first time in over 13 years, consumer prices have leveled off, and the peso has been fixed to the US dollar on a one-for-one basis. Stability in the Buenos Aires financial market is crucial if the city is to attract the global capital needed to fund major infrastructural improvements. During periods of high inflation and weak currency rates, both local and international capital tend to seek more profitable investment arenas. For example, in 1989 alone an estimated US$4.3 billion in private capital left Argentina for more stable areas. Official estimates put the total amount of Argentina's private capital circulating offshore at over US$60 billion in

Figure 5.2 The Hyatt Hotel near Retiro Station

1989. A lack of entrepreneurial and investment capital in Buenos Aires has had extremely negative effects on the city's ability to develop infrastructural projects and to maintain a stable economy.

Liberalization of the capital markets since 1990 has encouraged a net inflow of private funds into Buenos Aires, reversing the negative trends of the 1980s. In 1991, US$2.3 billion in private capital returned to Argentina, nearly US$8 billion was repatriated in 1992, and over US$5 billion returned in 1993. Much of this capital has been invested in real estate development projects. In partnership with multinational companies, local capital is helping to fund the construction of international hotels such as the Hyatt complex near Retiro station (Figure 5.2), major shopping malls like the Bullrich Center (see Figure 3.24), and urban rehabilitation projects such as Puerto Madero. Stability in both currency and inflation rates also has driven the expansion of Buenos Aires' stock market. In 1986, barely US$300 million in shares traded on the stock exchange. By 1992, this figure had exploded to US$32 billion, an indication of a renewed level of confidence in the domestic economy. Transactions in government securities grew from US$13.6 billion in 1989 to over US$94 billion in 1992, with market capitalization exceeding 12 percent. Privatization policies and more efficient tax collection methods also have stimulated an increase in government revenues, enabling vital capital to be redirected from inefficient, loss-making activities to more productive social programs.

In 1993, over 50 major banks and bank representatives maintained offices in Buenos Aires, an indication of the city's growing role as a major financial center in the Southern Cone (Table 5.13). The majority of these

Table 5.13 Major international banks and bank representatives in Buenos Aires, 1993

Bank	Main branch	Location
Banca Commerciale Italiana	Reconquista	City Center
Banca del Gottardo	San Martín	"
Banca della Svizzera Italiana	Reconquista	"
Banca Nazionale del Lavoro	Florida	"
Banco Basel	25 de Mayo	"
Banco Comercial Israelita	Maipú	"
Banco Comercial Uruguay	J. D. Perón	"
Banco de Boston	Florida	"
Banco de Canada	Florida	"
Banco de Galicia	J. D. Perón	"
Banco de Intercambio Regional	R. S. Peña	"
Banco de Italia	Reconquista	"
Banco de Londres	Florida	"
Banco de Napoles	B. Mitre	"
Banco de Paris	25 de Mayo	"
Banco de Uruguay	Esmeralda	"
Banco del Iberia	Esmeralda	"
Banco di Napoli	B. Mitre	"
Banco do Brasil	Sarmiento	"
Banco do Estado de São Paulo	J. D. Perón	"
Banco Español de Río de la Plata	J. D. Perón	"
Banco Europeo para América Latina	J. D. Perón	"
Banco Exterior de España	B. Mitre	"
Banco Florencia	Reconquista	"
Banco Francés del Río de la Plata	Reconquista	"
Banco Hispano Corfín	C. Pelligrini	"
Banco Holandes Unido	Florida	"
Banco Interamericano de Desarrollo	Esmeralda	"
Banco Interfinanzas	Sarmiento	"
Banco Italiano	Corrientes	"
Banco Mediterraneo	R. S. Peña	"
Banco Mundial	B. Mitre	"
Banco Roberts	25 de Mayo	"
Banco Santander	B. Mitre	"
Banco Shaw	Sarmiento	"
Banco Subameris	J. D. Perón	"
Banco Supervielle Société Générale	Reconquista	"
Bank of America	J. D. Perón	"
Bank of Tokyo	Reconquista	"
Banque Nationale de Paris	25 de Mayo	"
Chase Manhattan Bank	25 de Mayo	"
Citibank	B. Mitre	"
Deutsche Bank	B. Mitre	"
Groupe Crédit Lyonnais	B. Mitre	"
Israel Discount Bank	Sarmiento	"
Lloyds Bank	Reconquista	"
Manufacturers Hanover Trust	L. N. Alem	"

Table 5.13   (*continued*)

Bank	Main branch	Location
Midland Bank	25 de Mayo	City Center
Morgan Guaranty Trust of New York	25 de Mayo	"
National Bank of Chicago	Maipú	"
Republic National Bank of New York	B. Mitre	"
Royal Bank of Canada	Florida	"
Swiss Bank Corporation	25 de Mayo	"

Source: Guía Telefónica Buenos Aires 1993/1994.

banks are clustered in the downtown core within a few blocks of the Plaza de Mayo. Buenos Aires' role as a financial node, however, means that changes in other nodes on the global network can have a direct and immediate impact on the city's capital markets. After the January 1995 collapse of Mexico's currency, the Buenos Aires stock market and banking system sustained heavy losses. Despite the successes of globalization in Buenos Aires, the city's banking system teeters on the edge of disaster. Banks in Buenos Aires only insure the first US$1500 of deposits and, at the slightest hint of trouble, local capital frequently flees to offshore locations for protection. While a guarantee of stability is absent in the local financial markets, the federal government will continue to struggle in its attempts to lure capital investment to Argentina. Weak circuits of capital in Buenos Aires have a direct impact on the reshaping of the urban landscape by restricting the availability of funds for urban development projects. A major infusion of investment capital is desperately needed to rehabilitate the city's collapsing public infrastructure and to cope with the demands of participation in the global economy.

For example, increasing levels of specialization in the service and information sectors of Buenos Aires' economy have created a demand for better-educated employees. Yet the city's education system has failed to restructure its curriculum or to adapt to the changing demands of the global marketplace. Although the Federal District of Buenos Aires hosts 19 major public and private universities, as well as several smaller, specialized schools, the education system is poorly managed and maintained. Much of the physical infrastructure is in bad repair and modern equipment is in short supply. As a fundamental component of the capital development process, the education system in Buenos Aires must be able to supply the type of intellectual capital needed to compete in an increasingly sophisticated, integrated, and technologically driven global society. Unfortunately, federal, municipal, and local governments have shown little interest in recent decades in investing in Buenos Aires' rundown education system.

In this new global economic environment, Buenos Aires and its citizens face new challenges. One of these challenges is to balance the realities of global capitalism with the realities of human health, welfare, and development in the city. Restructuring labor markets and circuits of capital in Buenos Aires without comcomitant investments in education, transport, and communication infrastructure, for example, could prove to be a Pyrrhic economic victory for the government. Transport and communication particularly are crucial to the articulation of both city and nation along the local–global continuum of social, political, and economic relationships. The following chapter examines the interactive city and focuses on the role of transport and communication in re-shaping local, regional, and global linkages.

6

The interactive city: transport and communication

All urban areas face difficulties with accommodating the growth of intricate patterns of interaction along the local–global continuum. A concentration of industrial, commercial, and cultural activities in world cities frequently produces demands upon urban transport infrastructure that invariably are greater than available capacity. Moreover, transport modes exist in a competitive environment, which often creates tension between the public and private sectors. Therefore, as Brian Turton (1992, p. 67) observed recently, analyses of contemporary urban transport issues generally have taken "a problem-oriented approach with a particular concern to identify the spatial aspects of transport-planning programmes." At the interurban level, transport analyses have been influenced by the development of world city and world economy hypotheses. World cities are connected by hierarchies of transport networks, services, and infrastructure that provide both horizontal and vertical linkages along the local–global continuum (Keeling 1995).

Transport and communication services and infrastructure facilitate and condition interaction between people, institutions, labor, capital, and the built environment. As suggested in the framework for analysis outlined in Chapter 1, transport functions as the foundation upon which urbanization processes rest. If an efficient, affordable, and multimodal transport system is absent, cities like Buenos Aires suffer from inequities and inefficiencies in connectivity and mobility at several different levels along the local–global continuum. The quality of transport and communication among and within these different levels has a profound influence on the impact of globalization and world city processes on urban environments.

Connectivity and mobility are crucial components of the daily rhythm of life in Buenos Aires, which long has functioned as the dominant transport node of Argentina. Most international airline flights, cargo ships, road and railroad traffic, telephone calls, and computer information originate or terminate in the federal capital. The nation's domestic road, rail, air, shipping, and telephone networks are dendritic in form, converging on Buenos Aires. Within the Greater Buenos Aires Metropolitan Area (GBAMA), urban and suburban development historically have occurred primarily along the four major transport corridors that extend northwest, west, southwest, and south from the city center. Transverse links within the city are rare, and congestion along the urban area's major arterials has reached crisis point. A lack of adequate transport planning, infrastructure, and services in the GBAMA has had a detrimental effect on the shape and structure of the modern city. Since the 1970s, public policy concerning mobility in the city has favored the automobile-based middle class. Urban space has been reshaped to address the needs of the automobile user, not the needs of the majority of the urban population who rely on public transport. Transport inadequacies in Buenos Aires present the contemporary city with one of its most serious challenges for the future. In this chapter, connectivity and mobility patterns within and between Buenos Aires' four distinct transport environments – global, regional, national, and local – are analyzed and their implications for the city's participation in the world city system and in the global economy are discussed.

Global connectivity

One of the major definitional characteristics of a world city is the provision of physical infrastructure to facilitate global interaction (Shachar 1994). The global reach of a world city is sustained by telecommunications networks, international airports, ultramodern port facilities, and high-speed rail systems. Major pathways of communication link the dominant world cities together into a global network (see Figure 1.1). Globalization benefits, in turn, theoretically are diffused throughout a city and its immediate hinterland via an integrated, multimodal urban and interurban transport network. An important symbol of global accessibility in recent years has been the development of a wide network of international airline flights to and from a world city, coupled with high flight frequencies on the network. Airline linkages offer the best illustration of transport's role in the world city system for five reasons: (i) international airline flows are one of the few indices available of transactional activities and interurban connectivity; (ii) airline networks and their associated infrastructure are the most visible manifestation of world city interaction; (iii) great demand still exists for face-to-face relationships, despite the global telecommunications revolution; (iv) air transport is the preferred mode of interurban mobility for the transnational capitalist class, multinational corporate employees, migrants, tourists, and high-value, low-bulk goods; and (v) airline links are a vital component of a city's aspirations to world city status (Keeling 1995). Global connectivity maximizes the potential for personal contacts within the international arena and is a crucial locational factor in the development of global financial, management, and cultural centers.

Intercontinental airline links

For many cities attempting to achieve world city status and enhance their involvement in the global economy, the term "direct flight to London" (or Tokyo or New York) has become a metaphor for success (Abbott 1993). Non-stop air service to major world cities represents both the globalization of society and trade and the emergence of an information- and producer services-based economy. Enhanced levels of global connectivity are perceived to endow certain competitive advantages upon urban areas. Planners and policy makers in Argentina recognize the importance of international trunk routes for the country's articulation with the world economy, and the federal government has pursued an aggressive airline privatization and deregulation program in recent years to stimulate route development and to enhance customer service.

An analysis of Buenos Aires' position on, and accessibility to, the international airline network illustrates how poorly connected the city is at the global level. Although several important factors such as government regulation, airline hubbing practices, supply and demand, and historical inertia exert a strong influence over airline service provision, by any measure Buenos Aires has yet to extend its global reach beyond a few key cities (for example, Miami and Madrid). Within the global airline system, 20 cities function as major hubs on the network and also dominate their respective regional and national hinterlands (Figure 6.1). In 1992, Buenos Aires occupied the penultimate position in this functional hierarchy, with 52 non-stop intercontinental flights per week and direct connections to only 21 cities at the global level (Table 6.1). Moreover, the spatial dynamics of Buenos Aires' global connectivity have changed little since the early 1970s (Table 6.2). Over a period of 22

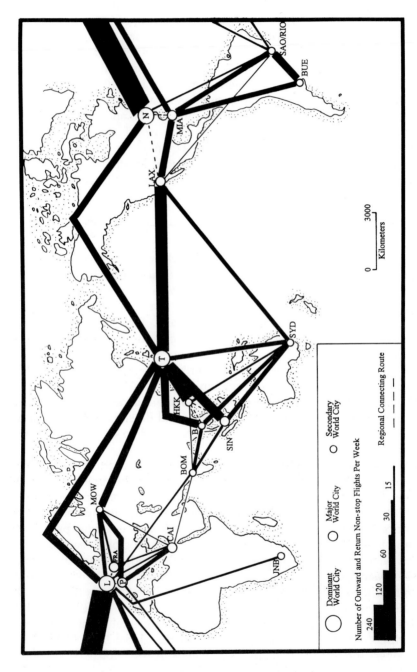

Figure 6.1 Buenos Aires' position on the global airline network, 1992. Source: Official Airline Guide (1992)

Table 6.1 A comparison of Buenos Aires' connectivity on the global airline network, 1992

| Global hub | Non-stop flights[a] | | | Cities served[b] | | |
	Global	Regional	Domestic	Global	Regional	Domestic
London	775	3239	1063	126	116	17
New York	644	634	8837	86	45	126
Paris	565	2264	1436	140	93	53
Tokyo	538	401	1814	62	18	38
Frankfurt	482	1376	771	114	76	19
Miami	311	1389	2146	43	58	61
Cairo	277	34	114	62	16	9
Los Angeles	245	419	7150	47	33	103
Bangkok	231	483	307	57	24	17
Amsterdam	229	1593	0	94	86	0
Singapore	221	831	0	57	39	0
Hong Kong	154	713	0	33	36	0
Zurich	147	1258	155	61	80	2
Sydney	144	89	1541	35	14	53
Rio de Janeiro	93	44	933	28	12	41
Moscow	87	400	1430	64	51	108
Bombay	64	111	313	30	20	31
São Paulo	64	97	1418	27	13	63
Buenos Aires	52	336	414	21	19	41
Johannesburg	40	108	450	18	23	25

Source: *Official Airline Guide* (1992).

[a] Total number of flights per week to the hub city with no intermediate stops between city pairs. Regional flights are those originating and terminating within a hub city's geographical region (i.e. Europe for London, South America for Buenos Aires).
[b] The number of cities served includes all cities with either non-stop or direct flights (one or more intermediate stops between city pairs) to/from the major global hubs.

years, the volume of non-stop flights from Buenos Aires has risen from 21 to 65 per week, with ten cities served in 1994 compared with five in 1972. The volume of weekly direct flights actually has declined by 40 percent since 1972, with six fewer cities served in 1994. The introduction of long-range, wide-bodied jets after 1972 meant that some cities functioning primarily as fuel and service points between major city pairs were dropped from the network (for example, Dakar and Las Palmas). Moreover, economy of scale resulting from the increased use of wide-bodied jets has altered service frequencies to some major hubs.

Changes in the global airline network stemming from privatization, deregulation, and route rationalization policies also have affected Buenos Aires. In the 1990s, Miami has become the dominant gateway city between North and South America, and Buenos Aires has over four non-stop flights each day to this important hub. Argentina's traditional

Table 6.2 A comparison of intercontinental airline connections to and from Buenos Aires, 1972, 1982, and 1994

Region/city	Non-stop 1972	Non-stop 1982	Non-stop 1994	Direct[a] 1972	Direct[a] 1982	Direct[a] 1994
North America						
Baltimore	–	–	–	–	–	2
Chicago	–	–	–	–	–	7
Curacao	–	1	–	–	–	–
Dallas–Fort Worth	–	–	–	–	–	7
Havana	–	–	1	–	–	–
Los Angeles	–	–	–	7	8	4
México City	–	–	–	5	5	3
Miami	–	4	33	15	16	9
Montréal	–	–	–	1	1	1
New York City	5	–	7	22	17	16
Panamá City	2	–	–	7	3	2
San Francisco	–	–	–	3	6	7
Toronto	–	–	–	1	1	1
Vancouver	–	–	–	1	1	–
Washington DC	–	–	–	2	1	–
Europe						
Amsterdam	–	–	–	2	2	3
Brussels	–	–	–	2	–	–
Copenhagen	–	–	–	1	2	–
Frankfurt	–	–	3	8	6	2
Geneva	–	–	–	2	2	–
Lisbon	–	–	–	6	4	–
London	–	–	2	4	4	2
Madrid	4	5	10	10	5	4
Moscow	–	–	–	–	–	1
Nice	–	–	–	1	–	–
Paris	–	1	3	8	6	4
Rome	–	2	3	6	4	3
Stockholm	–	–	–	1	–	–
Zurich	–	–	–	7	5	4
Africa						
Cape Town	–	2	–	–	–	2
Casablanca	–	–	–	2	–	–
Dakar	9	2	–	3	2	–
Freetown	1	–	–	–	–	–
Gran Canary	–	–	1	–	–	–
Johannesburg	–	–	–	–	–	2
Las Palmas	–	1	–	2	–	–
Sal, Cape Verde	–	–	–	–	–	1
Asia/Pacific						
Auckland	–	–	2	–	–	–

Table 6.2   (*continued*)

Region/city	Number of weekly flights					
	Non-stop			Direct[a]		
	1972	1982	1994	1972	1982	1994
Kuala Lumpur	–	–	–	–	–	1
Sydney	–	–	–	–	–	2
Total	21	18	65	130	101	90

Source: *Official Airline Guide* (1972, 1982, 1994).
[a] Flights that use the same plane but stop in an intermediate city before reaching the final destination.

European relationships continue to exert a tremendous influence over connectivity patterns. Buenos Aires has 10 non-stop flights each week to Madrid, as well as less frequent direct service to London, Rome, Paris, and Amsterdam. The Madrid connection not only reflects historic colonial ties but also the relationship with Iberia Airlines of Spain, which now owns a substantial interest in Argentina's national airline (Aerolíneas Argentinas). In early 1994, Buenos Aires had only one direct connection to the African continent and, surprisingly, had yet to develop direct connections to the dynamic economic centers of Southeast Asia such as Hong Kong, Singapore, Taipei, or Tokyo. However, Malaysian Airlines recently introduced a new twice-weekly service between Kuala Lumpur and Buenos Aires via Cape Town and Johannesburg in Africa. Two flights per week to Auckland and Sydney reflect growing socio-economic ties between Argentina and the Oceania region. Many Argentines migrated to Australia during the military rule of the late 1970s.

The importance of connectivity to the global airline network for Buenos Aires is reflected in the rapid increase in traffic volume recorded during the past decade (Table 6.3). Not only have passenger volumes grown to over 4 million annually, but freight tonnage transported by air more than doubled during the 10-year period. Increases in the volume of low-bulk, high-value goods shipped by air are a major indicator of a world city's changing economic dynamism. Economies of scale in air freight movement have encouraged flexible production and just-in-time inventory practices in many high-technology industries, which, in turn, have altered the dynamics of urban economies. Specialized products such as electronics, health supplies, scientific instruments, and telecommunications equipment moving in and out of Buenos Aires not only signify a shift away from traditional industrial activities but also suggest a change in domestic consumption habits. In 1992, for example, electrical

Table 6.3   International airline traffic, Argentina, 1983–1992[a]

Year	Total number of passengers transported	Freight transported (tons)	Mail transported (tons)	Total tons transported
1983	1 672 000	38 583	2141	41 276
1984	1 998 000	43 963	2428	46 895
1985	1 952 000	41 703	1992	44 318
1986	2 546 000	51 838	2165	54 921
1987	2 500 000	52 219	2396	55 438
1988	2 628 000	50 773	2178	53 125
1989	2 887 000	50 578	2127	52 907
1990	3 280 000	54 871	2431	57 302
1991	3 535 000	64 744	2604	67 348
1992	4 054 000	85 258	2985	88 243

Source: Repúblic Argentina (1993a).

[a] Data refer to domestic and foreign companies providing regular services to Argentina. Although the data refer to Argentina, almost all international traffic flows through Buenos Aires.

equipment and precision instruments accounted for 18 percent of Argentina's total imports, up from 13 percent in 1980 (República Argentina 1993a). These high-value products often are shipped by air.

A serious problem with articulating Buenos Aires' global linkages to the national hinterland is the separation of the domestic and international airports. Constructed in 1945, 35 kilometers from the city center, Ezeiza International Airport occupies 6700 hectares of land in the *partido* of Esteban Echeverría. Airport facilities are rudimentary compared to other major international airports. All of Argentina's domestic flights and several flights to neighboring countries (Uruguay and Paraguay) depart from the Jorge Newbery airport near the city center. Newbery was constructed in 1947 along the shores of the Río de la Plata just a few kilometers from the Plaza de Mayo. Transfers from international to domestic flights, or vice versa, can take three hours or longer, as unlike many major international airports (for example, Amsterdam, London, New York, Tokyo, or Paris) Ezeiza has no rail connection to either the city or the domestic airport. Passengers must choose between a private automobile, minibus service (US$14 one-way in 1994), or taxi (over US$35) for the journey between the international terminal and the city center. A multilane freeway connects Ezeiza airport to the downtown area. However, connections by public transport to areas other than the downtown core are difficult and expensive. It often is quicker and easier to travel to the city center and then take the appropriate transport mode to the final destination outside the Federal District.

Other global links

An equally important yet less visible aspect of global connectivity is the provision of telecommunications services in world cities. The development of fiber-optic cable, satellite transmissions, dedicated computer lines, and facsimile capabilities over the last decade has changed the space–time relationships of urban centers. New telecommunications technology theoretically allows almost any individual or institution in Buenos Aires to connect into the global information highway and to interact with other individuals and institutions located in cities around the world. Interurban space has been compressed to such a degree by telecommunications that cities 8000 kilometers apart today are literally seconds apart in information space. For example, access to the Internet computer system allows a college professor in Kentucky to send documents and other data almost instantaneously to a colleague at the University of Buenos Aires.

Telecommunications facilities in Buenos Aires continue to improve daily, primarily through privatization strategies. Until 1989, the ENTEL company, an inefficient, overbureaucratized state monopoly, controlled Argentina's telecommunications sector. Stories of telephone usage problems in Buenos Aires had reached legendary proportions, and commercial growth was being seriously retarded by inadequate telecommunications facilities. Between December 1991 and March 1992, the federal government split ENTEL into four companies and sold them to private consortia. Telefónica de Argentina now provides basic telephone services in southwestern and southern Buenos Aires, Telecom Argentina services the northern and western areas of the city, Telintar provides international services, and Startel operates telex, data transmission, and shore-to-ship services. A curious aspect of the territorial division of telecommunication services is that no allowance has been made for competition among the different operators. A state monopoly over the city's telephone systems effectively has been replaced with two private monopolies, with one company controlling the south and southwest and the other dominating the north and west.

Modernization of the urban telephone network has facilitated an increase in the use of facsimile machines, telexes, and computers for international communication. However, access to the evolving global information highway still is restricted to a select segment of society: certain government departments, universities, and multinational corporate offices. Over 65 percent of all installed computer and telecommunications equipment in Argentina is located in the GBAMA, primarily within the Federal District (Carlevari and Carlevari 1994). Most of this equipment is found in the industrial, commercial, and service sectors.

For many residents of the metropolitan area, making an international phone call usually requires a visit to one of the several telecommunications offices scattered around the city. Calls to North America, western Europe, and the contiguous South American countries (Uruguay, Brazil, Paraguay, Bolivia, and Chile) dominate international telecommunications traffic to and from Buenos Aires (República Argentina 1993a).

The final component in Buenos Aires' network of global connectivity is the international shipping sector. Maritime transport continues to play an important role in Buenos Aires' articulation with the world economy, especially the movement of container traffic and high-bulk, low-value products. During the early 1970s, Buenos Aires ranked as one of the world's major seaports, second only to New York in volume handled in the western hemisphere. Although the port's global ranking has dropped since the 1970s, Buenos Aires still handles about 35 percent of Argentina's total export traffic, which is primarily agricultural in nature, and approximately 85 percent of import traffic. Overall, the port of Buenos Aires handles about 40 percent of Argentina's total international freight tonnage. A variety of international shipping companies maintain offices in Buenos Aires and provide service to most of the world's important ports. The city has biweekly container and general cargo service to South and West Asia, and more frequent connections to North America and Europe. Port facilities are located primarily east and north of the city center. The four enclosed docks of Puerto Madero run parallel to Avenidas Huergo and Eduardo Madero, with access provided via an inner harbor (*Darsena Norte*). Most of Puerto Madero's facilities have been decommissioned and work is underway to rehabilitate the area with offices, condominiums, and restaurants. Container, bulk, and tanker traffic now is handled primarily by a series of six docks (*Darsena A to F*) located adjacent to the *barrio* of Retiro, although Dock Sud in the *partido* of Avellaneda also handles some traffic.

The port of Buenos Aires continues to suffer from serious infrastructural and management problems (Roccatagliata 1993). A lack of adequate long-term policies, intermittent planning, continued infrastructural disinvestment, bureaucratization of port management, jurisdictional conflicts, and labor disputes all have contributed to massive inefficiencies in the port system. To move 1 ton of cargo through the port of Buenos Aires costs approximately 12–14 dollars, compared with under 6 dollars a ton at Brazilian ports (Roccatagliata 1993). Moreover, Buenos Aires is not a deep-water port and cannot accommodate large ocean-going vessels. A port facility at least 15 meters (45 feet) deep is necessary if Buenos Aires is to take advantage of the economies of scale provided by bulk carriers and giant container ships. At present, port capacity is limited to ships with less than 10 meters (32 feet) of draught and no more than 170 000 displacement tons. Rapid worldwide growth in container traffic also presents problems for Buenos Aires. The port only has two operational cranes for container transhipment and it lacks sufficient storage and loading space near the docks for efficient container management. Thus, a major issue for the future is the city's continuing inability to participate fully and competitively in the global maritime network. Some planners envisage Buenos Aires as a major Atlantic gateway for a future South American landbridge between the Atlantic and Pacific economies. However, absent adequate port infrastructure and massive harbor improvements, Buenos Aires is likely to lose its position as a major cargo transhipment center.

Government officials, academics, business people, planners, and policy makers in Buenos Aires clearly appreciate the importance of connectivity to the world city system and the global economy. One of the principal objectives of Argentina's economic and social restructuring program is an "intensification of trade, financial and technological integration of the Argentine economy in world markets" (República Argentina 1993b, p. 63). The efficient, rapid, and inexpensive movement of people, goods, and information is central to the achievement of a more dynamic role for Buenos Aires in the new world order. In particular, increased levels of global connectivity are fundamental to Buenos Aires' role as gateway to the Southern Cone and are vital to the city's ability to diffuse the benefits of globalization to the regional and national hinterlands. Yet despite the rhetoric of change and ambitious privatization strategies, contemporary Buenos Aires remains firmly ensconced in the global semiperiphery and on the fringe of mainstream global interaction.

Regional connectivity

Relationships between Buenos Aires and its regional urban neighbors historically have been superficial at best. Inertia in the city's traditional connections with Europe and, more recently, North America, coupled with an absence of regional economic and social complementarity, kept Buenos Aires relatively isolated from other regional urban centers well into the twentieth century. A national trade and transport network more concerned with bringing export products to port than with fostering connections to other countries further exacerbated poor regional connectivity (Keeling 1994). However, recent progress in the organization of regional trade alliances, particularly the Common Market of the Southern Cone (MERCOSUR), has quickened the pace of interaction between Buenos Aires and its urban neighbors. Since 1991, Buenos Aires

Table 6.4 A comparison of regional airline connections to Buenos Aires, 1972, 1982, and 1994

| | Number of weekly flights | | | | | |
| Buenos Aires | Non-stop | | | Direct[a] | | |
to/from	1972	1982	1994	1972	1982	1994
Antofagasta	–	–	–	2	–	–
Arica	–	–	–	1	–	–
Asunción	9	6	9	8	5	9
Bogotá	–	–	4	6	4	2
Cali	–	–	–	1	–	–
Caracas	2	2	4	–	2	1
Cochabamba	–	–	–	1	–	–
Colonia	–	–	13	–	–	–
Curitiba	–	–	–	–	–	7
Florianopolis	–	–	3	–	–	9
Guayaquil	–	1	–	3	4	5
Iguassu, Brazil	–	8	3	–	–	–
La Paz	2	1	–	4	4	4
Lima	5	3	7	19	8	2
Montevideo	148	115	83	–	–	5
Porto Alegre	10	3	11	–	7	13
Punta Arenas	–	–	–	2	–	–
Punta del Este	12	51	7	–	–	–
Quito	–	–	–	3	3	3
Recife	–	–	–	–	1	–
Rio de Janeiro	18	18	15	32	42	45
Salvador	–	–	–	–	–	7
Santa Cruz	2	4	5	–	2	1
Santiago	29	36	70	6	5	6
São Paulo	21	23	49	11	23	25
Total	258	271	283	99	110	144

Source: Official Airline Guide (1972, 1982, 1994).

[a] Flights that use the same plane but stop in an intermediate city before reaching the final destination.

has enjoyed increased levels of trade and communication with Curitiba, Porto Alegre, Rio de Janeiro, and São Paulo, Brazil's major southern urban centers.

An analysis of regional airline connections between 1972 and 1994 highlights the recent growth in connections to Brazilian cities (Table 6.4). Buenos Aires enjoyed direct airline service to only three Brazilian cities in 1972, compared with seven cities in 1994. Moreover, flight frequencies between São Paulo and Buenos Aires have doubled, although frequencies between Rio de Janeiro and Buenos Aires have remained about the same. The MERCOSUR regional trade agreement also has stimulated increased airline service to and from Asunción, Paraguay, and Santa Cruz, Bolivia. A reduction in the number of weekly flights between Buenos Aires and Montevideo is a result of increased aircraft capacity (wide-bodied jets) and more competitive hydrofoil and ferry services in the Plata estuary. Punta del Este on Uruguay's Atlantic coast is a favorite destination for many Argentine vacationers during the summer months, and it continues to stimulate high levels of connectivity with Buenos Aires. Increased tourist activity in the Río de la Plata region also has encouraged new airline service across the estuary to Colonia in Uruguay. Although Chile has yet to participate in the development of a regional trade bloc, interaction between Santiago and Buenos Aires is increasing. However, the volume of airline flights between the two cities in 1994 stemmed more from the routing practices of foreign airlines (Iberia, Lufthansa, KLM, etc.) than from real growth in intercity trade and communication.

Regional surface links

Inadequate surface links between Buenos Aires and the major cities of neighboring countries long have been a source of exasperation to regional development strategists (Basco et al. 1988, Padula 1993). Poor infrastructure and a lack of political will to develop cross-border routes have reinforced the economic, political, and social control Buenos Aires exerts over Argentina, thus contributing to megacephalous urban growth in recent decades. Interior provinces, cities, and towns have been unable to develop strong economic and social ties to neighboring countries and have been forced to rely on Buenos Aires as the primary source of economic dynamism. Moreover, poor regional surface connectivity has hindered the city's ability to diffuse the benefits of world city and world economy involvement to the national and regional hinterlands.

Suprastate regional railroad links now are almost nonexistent, despite efforts to improve connectivity and mobility across national boundaries to take advantage of increased trade stimulated by MERCOSUR. There are no through passenger trains from Buenos Aires, or any Argentine city for that matter, to a neighboring country, and through freight trains are rare. Twenty years ago, one could travel from Buenos Aires to Santiago and Valparaíso, Chile, by train across the Andes mountains. A journey from Buenos Aires to Antofagasta, Chile, via Salta was possible, as well as journeys from Buenos Aires to La Paz and Santa Cruz in Bolivia and to Asunción, Paraguay (Thomas Cook 1974). Part of the problem stems from incompatible railroad gauges. A mixture of broad, standard, and narrow track gauges complicates integrated operations

Table 6.5   International bus connections to Buenos Aires, 1994

City	Distance (km)	Frequency (buses per week)	Journey time (hours)	Index of connectivity[a]
Asunción	1375	44	21	0.92
Ciudad del Este	1255	5	18	0.86
Curitiba	2392	15	34.5	0.86
Florianopolis	2122	15	26	0.74
La Paz	2770	4	55	1.19
Montevideo	715	28	8.5	0.71
Porto Alegre	1692	8	22.5	0.80
Potosí	2196	2	50	1.37
Rio de Janeiro	2870	15	42	0.88
Santa Cruz	2463	3	47	1.14
Santiago	1540	14	24	0.94
São Paulo	2757	15	36	0.78
Uruguaiana	1001	8	16	0.96
Valparaíso	1550	3	24	0.93

Source: Thomas Cook (1994); Various company timetables.

[a] The index of connectivity is calculated by dividing journey time by total kilometers. A connectivity index of 0.60 represents an average speed of 100 kilometers per hour.

both in Buenos Aires and throughout Argentina. The railroad line from Buenos Aires to the northeastern provinces and the Brazilian border is standard gauge (1.435 meters), whereas the Brazilian line from Argentina's northeastern border to Porto Alegre is narrow gauge (1 meter). Piecemeal privatization of Argentina's railroads has split the national railroad system between several different operators, none of whom have yet to find any economic incentive to coordinate their systems or to develop through passenger and freight services to neighboring countries.

Almost all surface passenger and freight traffic between Buenos Aires and urban centers in Bolivia, Brazil, Chile, Paraguay, and Uruguay moves by road. Yet highway links from Buenos Aires to neighboring countries are inadequate, poorly maintained, and unsuitable for efficient regional interaction. Despite poor roads, however, international bus connections to Buenos Aires maintain journey times on a par with long-distance bus service in the United States. For example, daily bus service from São Paulo covers the 2757-kilometer journey in 36 hours at an average speed of 77 kilometers per hour (Table 6.5). The slowest international connection is between Buenos Aires and Potosí, Bolivia. Difficult operating conditions and unpaved roads in the Northwest restrict overall running time on this route to an average of less than 45 kilometers per hour. Regional freight haulage by road has grown rapidly since 1990, reflecting the increase in trade with Brazil and Chile. Overall freight rates per ton between Buenos Aires and São Paulo, for example, declined by 32 percent between 1990 and 1992. The elimination of many cross-border restrictions and improved operating efficiency have lowered the average rate per ton of general cargo from US$125 to US$85. Refrigerated cargo such as fruit from Buenos Aires to São Paulo now costs about US$2.70 per box compared with US$4.10 per box in 1990. Improved delivery speeds and lower costs are crucial to many manufacturers and retailers in Buenos Aires who operate the just-in-time inventory system in order to reduce operating costs and remain competitive.

Plans are on the drawing board for a major infrastructural project designed to improve Buenos Aires' regional connectivity by linking Rio de Janeiro, São Paulo, Montevideo, Buenos Aires, and Santiago together along an Atlantic–Pacific superhighway. A combination road and rail bridge across the Río de la Plata, estimated to cost upwards of 1000 million dollars, would connect Brazil and Uruguay more directly to Argentina. Planners are evaluating four possible routes across the Plata estuary from Colonia de Sacramento to Buenos Aires, the favored interchange location being the area around Retiro railroad station and Catalinas Norte in the downtown core. In keeping with the Argentine government's privatization ideology, and drawing on the experiences of the Channel Tunnel venture linking Britain and France, the Río de la Plata Bridge Project would be funded by the private sector and operated under a long-term concession.

Telecommunications and maritime traffic between Buenos Aires and its regional neighbors follow similar patterns found at the global level. Most regional telephone and telex traffic flows between Buenos Aires, Santiago, Montevideo, Rio de Janeiro, and São Paulo. Buenos Aires has a well developed hydrofoil, ferry, and catamaran service across the Plata estuary to Uruguay. Colonia is reached in an hour from Buenos Aires, with bus connections on to Montevideo, and the Buquebus company covers the 300 kilometers between Buenos Aires and Montevideo several times daily in just under 3 hours. Although many business people utilize the ferry services, most travelers between Buenos Aires and Uruguay are day-trippers or tourists. The port of Buenos Aires also provides regularly scheduled container, bulk, and general cargo service to and from Uruguay, Brazil, and other South American countries. High on the list of regional transport improvement projects is the development of the Plata River Basin, which covers some 3.2 million square kilometers of territory in Argentina, Bolivia, Brazil, Paraguay, and Uruguay. The multinational Permanent Commission for Transport in the Plata Basin has been put together to take advantage of regional integration opportunities based on expanding usage of this important fluvial corridor.

Regional connectivity long has been the weakest aspect of Buenos Aires' local–global relationships. An economy geared historically to the North Atlantic countries, poor cross-border transport facilities, and long-established feelings of enmity toward Brazil and Chile have inhibited the development of strong relationships between Buenos Aires and other regional urban centers. However, the seeds of regional economic integration, planted in the early 1950s, seem to be flowering with the early successes of MERCOSUR. Growth in intraregional trade has stimulated increased levels of communication between Buenos Aires and its regional counterparts and has encouraged government officials, planners, and others to consider seriously transport infrastructure improvements between the urban centers. Articulating the economic and social dynamism of world city processes at work in Buenos Aires, São Paulo, and Rio de Janeiro with the regional hinterland could have a positive effect on the overall long-term development of both urban and rural environments in the Southern Cone.

National connectivity

A great deal has been written about the dominance of Buenos Aires over the national transport and communication system. Most researchers seeking answers to the paradox that has been Argentine development since the nineteenth century have acknowledged either implicitly or explicitly the importance of transport development in shaping Buenos Aires' national hegemony (see, for example, Scobie 1971, Rock 1987). Without the development impetus of cross-country transport infrastructure and the stimulation of socioeconomic demand for transport services between interior cities and towns Buenos Aires naturally became the focal point for traffic. Moreover, with approximately 40 percent of the nation's population now concentrated in the GBAMA, demand has continued to grow for interaction with the capital city. Since 1991, the federal government's Project for Territorial Reorganization has recognized that the benefits of globalization and world city status cannot be diffused adequately to the national hinterland without an integrated, multimodal transport and communication system (República Argentina 1994). Unfortunately, Argentina's airline routes, major highways, telecommunication links, and railroads still focus almost exclusively on Buenos Aires. Argentina continues to function as a bifurcated state, split between the dynamic, wealthy (in relative terms) world city and an impoverished, maldeveloped, poorly connected interior.

For the few who can afford it, the airline system is the preferred mode of internal transport to and from Buenos Aires. In 1993, 27 interior cities

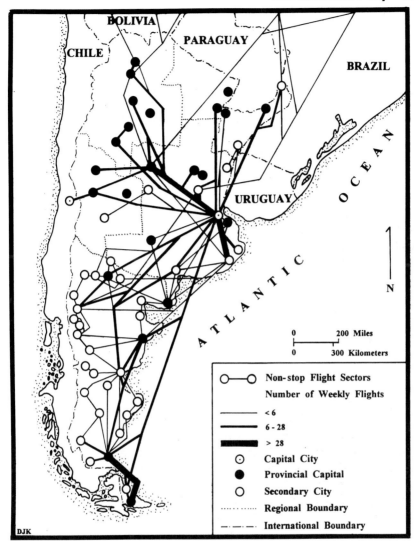

Figure 6.2 Argentina's domestic airline network, 1993. *Source*: Official Airline Guide (1992)

and towns had non-stop flights to the capital, with an additional 26 towns connected to Buenos Aires via an intermediate city (Figure 6.2). Buenos Aires accounted for 26 percent of all daily flight departures in Argentina, up from 19 percent in 1972 (Official Airline Guide 1972, 1993). However, traffic on the domestic airline network continues to be lost to road-based transport. Between 1983 and 1992, the total number of kilometers covered by the domestic airline system declined from 54 million to under 40 million. The total amount of freight transported by air also registered declines, falling from 43 000 tons in 1983 to 27 000 tons in 1992 (República Argentina 1993a). Passenger traffic has remained stagnant at the national level, although Buenos Aires has experienced steady increases in the total number of passengers arriving and departing on domestic flights. Indications are that contemporary Buenos Aires exerts more dominance over Argentina's airline network than at any period in recent history. For example, the federal government passed a law in 1983 requiring all international air cargo destined for the interior provinces to be unloaded in Buenos Aires and carried on Argentina's national airlines. Few foreign carriers are permitted to serve cities in Argentina other than Buenos Aires. Moreover, inequities in levels of regional connectivity continue to characterize the airline system. Coastal and pampas cities have far more accessibility to Buenos Aires than do the cities of northwest or northeast Argentina. All of these processes at work within the ambit of Argentina's national transport environment continue to reinforce Buenos Aires' position as the dominant node in the national urban network.

Surface links to the national hinterland

Until the mid-1980s, air transport completely dominated external and internal accessibility to most world cities. Over the past 5 years, the development of high-speed rail systems in Europe and Japan has provided an alternative mode of transport for interactions over short to medium distances (150–650 kilometers). Studies of the impact of France's high-speed rail system (TGV) on urban connectivity suggest that new surface links accentuate and strengthen the dominant nodes of national and supraregional transport systems (Benoit et al. 1993). These nodes usually are the urban centers at the upper end of the hierarchy of world cities.

High-speed surface transport also is playing an instrumental role in spreading the development impetus of world city and world economy involvement to national and regional hinterlands. Heightened levels of interurban, intraregional, and interregional connectivity can stimulate socioeconomic interaction and can provide a new dimension to stagnant local economies. A comparison of interurban railroad links in 1994 highlights the important role high-speed surface transport plays in national and supraregional connectivity (Table 6.6). World cities such as London, Tokyo, New York, Paris, Madrid, and Melbourne now enjoy high levels of interurban railroad connectivity. Unfortunately, in recent years Buenos Aires has suffered serious declines in railroad accessibility

Table 6.6 A comparison of interurban railroad connectivity from selected world cities, 1994

Origin	Destination	Distance (kms)	Journey (time)	Index of connectivity[a]
0–499 Kilometers				
Tokyo	Sendai	351	1 hour 46 minutes	0.30
Paris	Nantes	396	1 hour 58 minutes	0.30
London	Manchester	304	2 hours 25 minutes	0.48
New York	Washington	362	2 hours 55 minutes	0.48
New York	Boston	373	4 hours 10 minutes	0.67
Buenos Aires	Mar Del Plata	400	5 hours 10 minutes	0.77
Buenos Aires	Rojas	220	4 hours 14 minutes	1.16
São Paulo	Qurinhos	450	9 hours 12 minutes	1.23
500–999 Kilometers				
Paris	Lyon	512	2 hours	0.23
Tokyo	Osaka	553	2 hours 30 minutes	0.27
Madrid	Seville	574	2 hours 45 minutes	0.29
London	Edinburgh	632	4 hours	0.38
Melbourne	Sydney	961	10 hours 23 minutes	0.65
Istanbul	Ankara	578	7 hours 20 minutes	0.76
Santiago	Concepción	577	8 hours 40 minutes	0.90
Buenos Aires	Bahía Blanca	680	11 hours 15 minutes	0.99
México City	Guadalajara	613	11 hours 25 minutes	1.12
Buenos Aires	Santa Rosa	606	11 hours 45 minutes	1.16
Buenos Aires	Necochea	503	9 hours 55 minutes	1.18
Buenos Aires	General Pico	524	11 hours 25 minutes	1.31
1000+ Kilometers				
Paris	Madrid	1489	12 hours 32 minutes	0.51
México City	Monterrey	1022	14 hours 10 minutes	0.83
Los Angeles	Seattle	2233	34 hours 15 minutes	0.92
Johannesburg	Cape Town	1530	25 hours 25 minutes	1.00
Buenos Aires	Tucumán	1170	20 hours 30 minutes	1.05
Santiago	Puerto Montt	1088	20 hours 20 minutes	1.12
Buenos Aires	Bariloche	1741	36 hours	1.24

Source: Thomas Cook (1994).

[a] The index of connectivity is calculated by dividing journey time by total kilometers. A connectivity index of 0.30 represents an average speed of 200 kilometers per hour.

to other urban centers. Privatization of the railroad sector in Argentina has decimated interurban passenger services and left Buenos Aires with railroad links to only a handful of cities. For example, a 400-kilometer journey from Paris to Nantes takes just under 2 hours, whereas the journey from Buenos Aires to Mar del Plata, a similar distance, takes over 5 hours. It takes 4 hours to cover the 632 kilometers between London and Edinburgh, giving the two cities a 0.38 connectivity index.

Contrast the 680-kilometer journey between Buenos Aires and Bahía Blanca, which takes over 11 hours and has a connectivity index near 1.0. The index of connectivity is an excellent indicator of comparative levels of development in high-speed surface transport and it illustrates how some world cities have become much closer in time–space to important secondary and tertiary urban centers.

Although privatization of Argentina's national railroad system continues apace, the importance of passenger railroad service as a social obligation requiring some form of federal subsidy continues to be debated. The long-term fate of intercity passenger services between Buenos Aires and the major provincial capitals has yet to be determined. The provincial government of Tucumán has stepped in to subsidize and operate a twice-weekly service between the city of Tucumán and Buenos Aires, but service was guaranteed only until April 1995 and could be withdrawn at a moment's notice. Other provincial governments have retained the rights to run passenger service or have abandoned service completely. The only viable franchise for intercity passenger service is along the 400-kilometer Buenos Aires–Mar del Plata corridor. Nearly 2 million passengers annually are carried along this corridor despite its unattractive journey time and poor ride quality (Richter 1993).

In the 1990s, road-based traffic dominates Buenos Aires' connectivity to the interior provinces. Most of the country's major highways parallel the railroads and fan out from Buenos Aires in all directions. Interurban access to and from the capital is provided by a series of two-lane paved highways plus a few multilane freeways. Roads have reinforced the dendritic nature of Argentina's surface transport network, with Buenos Aires serving as the focal point for the major national arterials. Although plans remain on the drawing board for a series of interurban freeways connecting Buenos Aires to the major pampas cities, a lack of funds and political will have stymied the projects. The Menem government sees privatization of the national road network as the only viable means of infrastructural improvement. A network of privately operated toll roads has been planned to support the proposed Southern Cone superhighway and to feed traffic more efficiently into and around the GBAMA.

Most people and goods access Buenos Aires from the provinces by bus, private automobile, or truck. Regular bus service to and from Buenos Aires is provided in almost every city and town of the interior. For example, from Buenos Aires each day seven buses serve Mendoza, 20 buses run to Bahía Blanca, 40 buses go to Córdoba, and Rosario enjoys at least half-hourly service from the capital. Over 65 percent of all passenger buses registered in Argentina are located in the GBAMA, as are nearly 50 percent of all registered trucks. In addition, nearly 60 percent of all private automobiles in use in Argentina in 1991 were registered in the Buenos Aires area (Carlevari and Carlevari 1994).

Domestic river transport is operated largely on the 3000-kilometer navigable inland water network consisting of the Río de la Plata estuary and its tributaries, the Río Uruguay, Río Paraná, Río Paraguay, and Río Alto Paraná. The absence of navigable rivers in the interior gives Buenos Aires a natural geographic advantage, as nearly all domestic fluvial traffic is concentrated on the Plata system. In 1976, the Emilio Mitre Canal was completed between Buenos Aires and the Paraná river to facilitate access and egress to Argentina's river ports. Over 50 kilometers long, about 130 meters wide, and 10 meters deep, the canal cost 90 million dollars to construct. Although the canal has improved internal connectivity, the problem of deep-water facilities still remains.

Telecommunication patterns follow the same pathways as the other modes of transport. The dominant linkages are between Buenos Aires and the provincial capitals. Although a national network of fiber-optic cable and other telecommunications hardware is under construction, the primary links will be between Buenos Aires and the major urban centers of the interior. Improvement of the national telecommunications network is vitally important to Argentina's incorporation into the contemporary world economy, yet reinforcing dendritic patterns of communication could serve to strengthen Buenos Aires' economic and social dominance over the nation.

Metropolitan connectivity and mobility

In this final section of the chapter, the transport environment of the municipalities outside the Federal District is examined, followed by a discussion of mobility patterns within the 200-square kilometer Federal District. Buenos Aires long has been endowed with one of the best urban transport networks in Latin America, despite the system's chronic inefficiencies and poor infrastructure. Suburban railroads developed in the late nineteenth century encouraged the type of urban sprawl experienced in the industrialized countries of the North Atlantic and helped the development of a property-owning, mobile urban middle class (Sargent 1974). Electric trams in the Federal District enabled high levels of inner-city mobility during the early decades of the twentieth century and encouraged population densification in many of the district's *barrios*. The construction of subways and the growth of an urban bus network further improved the interaction of people, goods, and information within the GBAMA. After 1950, however, investment in the public transport system declined rapidly. Service inefficiencies, chronic labor problems, bureaucratic ineptitude, rampant fare evasion, and increasing levels of private automobile ownership contributed to steady declines in ridership. Thus, although the physical spatial distribution of the metropolitan public transport network has changed little since the early 1900s, modal shifts in traffic and changing patterns of urban development have altered the dynamics of connectivity and mobility in Buenos Aires.

The metropolitan transport system ties Buenos Aires together in a way that is important for understanding the contemporary city. *Colectivos* (private buses), for example, allow suburbanites to participate in the daily life of the city and to take advantage of the phenomenon known as *el microcentro* (the central city district). Almost unique among world cities, Buenos Aires has a powerful sense of a center or downtown core that is available for every resident of the metropolitan area and that is heavily used day and night. The downtown core, stretching from Retiro railroad station to the docks of La Boca, contains the majority of the city's entertainment facilities, bars and nightclubs, tourist districts, and glitzy new shopping centers. Moreover, *el microcentro* contains the financial and administrative heart of the city, providing service sector jobs for hundreds of thousands of *porteños*. Every day millions of people flood into the center for work, recreation, or shopping, creating a very distinct pattern of urban movement.

Three-quarters of all passenger traffic in the GBAMA in 1982 moved by road, with suburban railroads handling 16 percent and subways 8 percent of the remaining traffic. By 1992, the percentage of traffic handled by suburban railroads had fallen to 8 percent, whereas traffic on the road network had increased to 84 percent of the metropolitan total. Despite the considerable change in modal split during the 1980s, approximately the same number of passengers, 2.6 billion, were transported within the GBAMA in 1992 compared with 1980 (República Argentina 1993a). Although many people have switched from rail to bus, the most staggering growth in urban traffic has been in the number of private automobiles used for daily commuting. There are no concrete figures for the total number of daily trips generated by private automobiles in Buenos Aires, but reports in local newspapers suggest that over one million cars a day move in and out of the downtown area (*La Nación, Buenos Aires Herald* May 1994). In addition, approximately one million buses, trucks, and taxis each day vie for precious space on the Federal District's roads.

Other modes of transport within the metropolitan area include ferries, taxis, horses and carts, skateboards, rollerskates, bicycles, and walking. Apart from the Tigre delta and the routes to Uruguay, ferry travel in Buenos Aires is minimal. Although a hydrofoil service along the north shore of the city has been proposed in the past, water-based transportation does not seem likely to become an important component of the urban transport network in the near future. In the suburban areas of the city many people move about the neighborhood on bicycles or they walk. Walking accounted for 9.2 percent of all journeys taken in the GBAMA in 1991 compared with 8.1 percent of all trips in 1970 (Câmara and Banister 1993). In the suburbs, the number rose to 11.5 percent, an indication of rising levels of poverty and declining levels of public service provision outside the Federal District. Rollerskating and skateboarding are becoming increasingly more common among the younger generation for getting to school or for just moving about the neighborhood. The horse and cart remains an important mode of transport in the more peripheral and rural suburbs, although it is not uncommon to see a horse and cart on the busy streets of major satellite cities such as Luján or Cañuelas.

Buses are the most important means of mobility within the metropolitan area, with Buenos Aires served by a three-tiered urban network. A system of private buses or *colectivos* operates on a regular schedule within the Federal District along fixed routes. Intraurban buses provide scheduled links between the Federal District and the suburban areas and also within and between suburbs. Interurban buses, many of which depart from the Retiro national bus terminal, serve the satellite communities that sit along the main roads leading to urban centers beyond the metropolitan area. A recent phenomenon in Buenos Aires is the growth of charter buses, special services that have predetermined routes to distinct zones in the suburban periphery. Charter services offer superior speed and ride quality compared with other forms of public transport and are attracting riders away from regular buses and trains.

Despite increased congestion on the urban road network that continues to slow average journey times, urban bus use has grown steadily since 1989, exceeding 2 billion riders in 1992 (Table 6.7). However, ridership shows tremendous variation from area to area within the metropolitan region. The southern and northwestern bus routes in the inner suburbs are the most heavily traveled because many of the city's major industrial centers and *villas de emergencia* are located here. Low-income families especially depend on the *colectivos* as their only means of transportation. In contrast, bus journeys to and from the outer suburbs have shown little increase in recent years, despite substantial population growth in the middle and outer suburban rings. Price and journey time deter many people from riding the bus from outlying areas. For example, the express bus from Luján to Once railroad station in the Federal District cost US$5 in 1994, with a journey time of between 75 and 120 minutes (Table 6.8). A train journey along the same route cost only US$1.10, although the service was less frequent, involved a

Table 6.7 Passengers carried by the urban bus network of Buenos Aires, 1989–1992

Territorial division	(millions)			
	1989	1990	1991	1992
Federal District	513	517	522	527
Inner Suburban Ring[a]	1414	1412	1426	1440
Outer Suburban Ring[b]	39	37	37	38
Metropolitan Region	1966	1966	1985	2005

Source: República Argentina (1993b).

[a] The 19 *partidos* of the Inner Ring.
[b] The remaining *partidos* served by the metropolitan bus system.

Table 6.8 Suburban bus service, Greater Buenos Aires, 1994

Buenos Aires to/from	Distance (kms)	Frequency (buses per day)	Journey time (hours)	Index of connectivity[a]
Chascomús	115	6	3	1.56
Coronel Brandsen	65	1	2.25	2.08
La Plata	50	39	1	1.20
Luján	66	14	1.75	1.59
Mercedes	100	9	2.25	1.35
Paname	115	4	2.75	1.43
Zárate	100	54	2	1.20

Source: Thomas Cook (1994) and posted company timetables.

[a] The index of connectivity is calculated by dividing journey time by total kilometers. A connectivity index of 1.20 represents an average speed of 50 kilometers per hour.

change of train at Moreno, and took nearly 2 hours. For many who live in the outer suburbs and need to commute to the Federal District, the private automobile is the preferred mode of transport, although railroads remain important.

The suburban railroad network

For over 100 years, suburban railroads have played a crucial role in shaping the spatial dynamics of growth and change in Buenos Aires. During the 1850s and 1860s, the first four urban railroad lines began to radiate out northwest, west, southwest, and south of downtown Buenos Aires. By the mid-1870s, the railroads had helped to determine the basic physical framework of the GBAMA (Sargent 1974). Several small agricultural and speculative settlements were strung out along the four principal railroad corridors leading from the rapidly expanding city center. For the next 50 years, the railroads alone determined the spatial dynamics of suburban growth. Yet suburban settlements did not become fully functional components of the Buenos Aires urban system until the 1900s, when train facilities, speeds, frequencies, and costs improved sufficiently to encourage daily commuting. Moreover, suburban expansion beyond the railroad catchment area did not take place until after the introduction of automobiles and buses in the 1930s.

The suburban railroad network reached its operational zenith during the 1930s. Several of the suburban lines had been electrified between 1916 and 1931, which resulted in an outward shift of the effective commuting realm. Suburbs such as Tigre, Moreno, Merlo, and Morón became more accessible from the city center and began to expand areally away from the railroad station. Railroads also encouraged new linear population nuclei, ever more distant from Buenos Aires, and spurred nuclear growth increasingly farther afield from the railroad lines. When automobiles and buses were introduced to the transportation environment during the early 1930s, non-urbanized land between the various railroad corridors became a primary target for urban expansion. Indeed, Luis Sommi (1940) credits the first *colectivos*, essentially oversized taxicabs mounted on truck chassis, with creating a new suburban Buenos Aires by providing rapid transportation to areas of the city that previously had been isolated. The flexibility of *colectivos* offered stiff competition to the railroads and, within a few years, passenger loadings on the major suburban lines began to drop sharply in favor of road-based transport.

At the same time, the suburban railroads started to suffer the effects of a lack of infrastructural investment. British companies who owned the railroads had spent little money on service improvements since the end of World War I in 1918. When President Juan Perón nationalized the railroads in 1948, hopes for a new era in suburban railroad travel were high. However, railroad nationalization proved to be a transportation disaster for Buenos Aires. For 45 years, poor management by the state, a lack of investment, deteriorating physical infrastructure, and abysmal service drove the Buenos Aires railroad network into the ground. In 1980, the federal government created the Metropolitan Railroad Authority, under the auspices of Ferrocarriles Argentinas, the national railroad company, with the task of recapturing a substantial share of urban and suburban traffic in Buenos Aires. Parts of the Roca line were electrified and upgraded in 1985 with an overhead catenary system, but little could be done to stem the financial hemorrhaging and loss of ridership. Overall, little progress was made during the decade and the railroad network fell further into disrepair.

With a new federal government in 1989 came a reappraisal of state involvement in the urban transportation arena. As part of the Menem government's privatization policies, a new state corporation known as Ferrocarriles Metropolitanos (FEMESA) was created in 1992 as an intermediate step between state management and full privatization. FEMESA has authority over approximately 800 kilometers of suburban railroad lines. The government also is considering the creation of an independent Metropolitan Transit Authority with the aim of integrating passenger traffic flows within the GBAMA. Portions of the suburban railroad system were fully privatized in 1993. A consortium including Burlington Northern and Morrison Knudsen from the United States, the Argentine construction company of Benito Roggio & Sons, and Consorcio Metropolitano de Transporte (Cometrans), an association of bus operators in Buenos Aires, bid successfully for the Mitre, Sarmiento, and Urquiza commuter lines as well as for the five lines of the Buenos Aires subway system. The federal government retains ownership of the rights-of-way, equipment, stations, and facilities. Any property not required for railroad operations will be franchised to real estate developers. On the top of the development list are the four major railroad terminals in the Federal District – Retiro, Once, Lacroze, and Constitución.

Commuter railroad service is crucial to connectivity and mobility in the GBAMA. In 1993, an estimated 15 million daily trips were taken in Buenos Aires, over 90 percent of which were on public transport. Although commuter railroads now have a relatively small share of this daily market, they still carry in excess of one million riders each day. The actual level of ridership is impossible to estimate because fare evasion on the system is tremendous. Everyday hundreds of thousands of riders evade payment because the railroads do not have a functional system in place to control access and ticket sales. One of the first tasks of the new private ownership consortia is to improve revenue collection and to crack down on fare evasion. The second important task is to improve service and facilities because infrastructural deterioration and unreliable service have discouraged ridership in recent years.

In 1980, over 380 million passengers were carried on the urban and suburban railroad system. By 1992 this figure had declined by 45 percent to just over 209 million passengers. Moreover, the total passenger kilometers covered by the urban and suburban railroads dropped precipitously from 8.5 billion in 1980 to under 4.5 billion in 1992, a 47 percent decline (República Argentina 1993a). For many, riding the Buenos Aires suburban railroads can be an uncomfortable experience. Carriages often have broken windows, torn and damaged seats, and ineffective doors. Overcrowded trains and irregular running times are the norm, especially along the western and southwestern corridors.

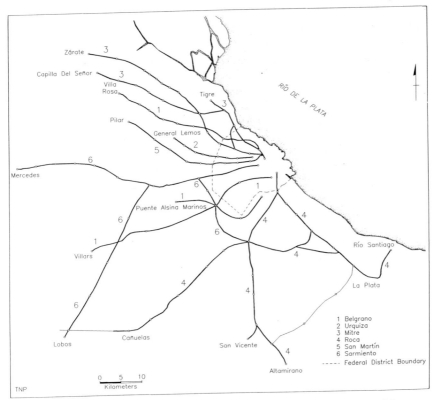

Figure 6.3 The suburban railroad network in Buenos Aires, 1994. *Source:* After Stoetzel (1993)

Station facilities are generally poor, with graffiti and trash everywhere. The railroad rights of way are used as open garbage dumps in many parts of the city. Railroad service rarely is integrated with other forms of transport; intermodality is a term frequently used in transport planning circles but it has yet to be achieved in Buenos Aires. One of the barriers to integrated operations is the existence of three different track gauges in the suburban railroad system. Moreover, an absence of transverse links between the major corridors or around the suburban rings of Buenos Aires reinforces the flow of traffic to and from the downtown terminals. For example, a person who lives in the northern suburb of San Fernando and works in the Mercedes Benz factory in western La Matanza has little choice but to journey to the city center, change trains, and then journey out to their place of employment.

Six major commuter railroad lines handle passenger traffic in the GBAMA (Figure 6.3). The 214-kilometer, broad-gauge Mitre line serves 54 stations along the northwestern corridor. Fifty-seven kilometers of the

Mitre system are electrified with an 800-volt, third-rail system, linking Retiro terminal to the suburbs of Tigre, Suarez, and Bartólome Mitre. The Bartolomé Mitre–Tigre Delta branch paralleling the Río Luján and the Plata coast, and closed to passenger traffic since 1961, is being revived as a light-rail line. Tren de la Costa SA, a wholly owned subsidiary of Comercial del Plata, bid successfully in 1993 for the 30-year concession to operate the project (Garibotto 1994). In keeping with the government's policy of disengagement from public transport provision, the light-rail project will be entirely self-financing and will not require a government subsidy. Originally part of the Mitre broad-gauge network, the new system will operate on standard-gauge track (1435 mm) with rolling stock constructed in Spain. Compatibility with Mitre's existing broad-gauge network was not considered important. Rehabilitation of the line includes the refurbishing of the station buildings, with each location to have its own architectural "personality," and a new shopping complex at the Maipu terminal. At Maipu, shops will be located on an air-conditioned bridge designed to link the light-rail system with the suburban network at Bartolomé Mitre. The *barrios* of Borges, Anchorena, Barrancas, San Isidro, Punta Chica, Marina Nueva, San Fernando, Canal San Fernando, and Tigre Delta all will benefit from the refurbished rail infrastructure and from enhanced public transport services. The Tren de la Costa project will be the first serious upgrading of Buenos Aires' suburban railroad system in over a decade. On the remaining 157 kilometers of the active Mitre system, diesel trains provide service to the suburban terminals of Capilla del Señor and Zárate in the Outer Ring. In 1992, the Mitre line carried approximately 45 million passengers.

The narrow-gauge Belgrano line is split into three sections totaling 102 kilometers. The northwestern branch serves 19 stations from Retiro with diesel trains and terminates at Villa Rosa in the *partido* of Pilar. Along the western corridor, one branch of the Belgrano system connects Estación Buenos Aires in the Federal District to Villars in the municipality of Marcos Paz, serving 16 intermediate suburbs. A second branch connects 16 stations between Alsina in the *partido* of Lanús and Marinos del Crucero General Belgrano in Merlo. Approximately 15 million riders annually are carried on the Belgrano network. Of all the suburban railroad lines, the Belgrano has the most infrastructural problems and is the most prone to service disruptions and breakdowns.

The shortest suburban network in Buenos Aires is the standard-gauge General Urquiza railroad which operates from Federico Lacroze terminal in the *barrio* of Chacarita. Urquiza is a 25-kilometer, 550-volt, third-rail system that serves 23 stations between Lacroze and General Lemos in the *partido* of Sarmiento along the northwestern corridor. In 1992, Urquiza carried approximately 15 million passengers. Another relatively short line is the 55-kilometer, broad-gauge San Martín railroad running from Retiro station to Pilar in the northwest corridor. Diesel trains provide access to 17 intermediate suburbs, and they carried approximately 10 million riders in 1992.

Traditionally the busiest of Buenos Aires' suburban railroads, the 192-kilometer, broad-gauge Sarmiento line operates from Once de Septiembre terminal in the *barrio* of Balvanera. In 1992, the Sarmiento network carried in excess of 70 million passengers over four distinct sectors. Service to the 15 stations between Once and Moreno is provided by an 800-volt, third-rail system. The latest traffic projections by the private consortium that has taken over operation of the system are that more than 80 million passengers annually now are carried along the electrified sector. To highlight the importance of this line to the Buenos Aires transport network, more passengers are carried along this 36-kilometer stretch than on the entire Long Island Railroad, North America's largest commuter railroad system (Stoetzel 1993). Diesel railcars operate over the remaining 156 kilometers along three stretches of line: between Moreno, Luján and Mercedes to the northwest, between Merlo and Lobos to the west, and between Haedo and Temperley to the south.

The Haedo to Temperley route is unusual in the Buenos Aires railroad network because it is the only intercorridor passenger line in the system. It also functions as an important interchange link between the Sarmiento and Roca systems for cargo trains. In the early 1980s, the Centro de Investigaciones Ferroviarias y del Transporte (1985) carried out an extensive study on the feasibility of a Buenos Aires ring railroad. Cognizant of the absence of transverse connections in the passenger railroad network, the study proposed a semicircular route from Retiro terminal to La Plata via Caseros, Haedo, and Temperley. The route would connect the San Martín and Sarmiento lines between Caseros and Haedo, the Belgrano and Sarmiento lines between Haedo and Elia/Tapiales, and the Belgrano and Roca lines between Elia/Tapiales and Temperley. More importantly, several major industrial areas such as Química Argentina and the Haedo manufacturing zone, as well as the Palomar military college and airfield, the Buenos Aires Central Market, and the Faculty of Agronomy could be served by the ring railroad. Although the study presented a convincing argument, supported by solid financial projections, the ring railroad idea did not receive government support. In 1994, only the section of line between Haedo and Temperley carried passengers, and there are no other intercorridor connections in the metropolitan area.

Buenos Aires' sixth and most widespread network is the broad-gauge General Roca railroad covering over 250 kilometers along the western, southwestern, and southern corridors. The network has three main branches and a city terminus at Plaza Constitución. The Cañuelas branch is electrified as far as Ezeiza, where diesel service takes over toward Cañuelas and Lobos along the western corridor. On the Altamirano branch along the southwestern corridor, electrified service extends as far as Glew in the *partido* of Almirante Brown, with diesel railcars running on to Altamirano and San Vicente. La Plata is served by hourly diesel service from Constitución, although plans to electrify the line via Florencio Varela and Villa Elisa have been on the drawing board for several years. Some overhead catenary infrastructure extends to Villa Elisa, but electric trains have yet to be seen on the branch. The Roca line serves only one station (Yrigoyen) inside the Federal District, but connects 16 stations between Temperley and Lobos and over 30 stations along the southwestern and southern corridors toward Altamirano and La Plata, respectively. Fifty-five million passengers were carried in 1992, the only line to show an increase in passenger loadings during the previous decade.

Mobility in the Federal District

Until the 1900s, the Federal District remained mononuclear in form. A lack of transport away from the urban core where most people worked inhibited residential expansion and limited commuting to the suburban railroad corridors. With the development and growth of the electric trolley after 1900, residential expansion in the Federal District became linear and distant from the city center as well as nuclear, with concentric accretions to the core *barrios* (Sargent 1974). Trolleys reached out to the *barrios* of Flores, Belgrano, and Chacarita, and to the slaughterhouses and factories of Villa Lugano. By 1914, much of the downtown core and the more important surrounding *barrios* were interconnected by the electric trolley network. However, as in many cities of the United States, electric trolleys in Buenos Aires eventually succumbed to competition from buses, automobiles, and subways. By the 1950s, only a few exposed trolley tracks along some minor streets remained as evidence of the once extensive network.

Buenos Aires' first subway, and the first to be built in Latin America, came into service in December 1913. Subway construction had been proposed by the private railroad companies as a means to connect the outlying railroad termini with the central business district. Even though the Retiro and Constitución railroad terminals sat just on the fringe of the downtown core, passenger interchange and transfer to the financial district was time-consuming and relatively inefficient. By the late 1920s, Line A carried traffic equal to 10 percent of the entire trolley system, even though its length totaled only 1.5 percent of the trolley network

Figure 6.4   Light-rail system along the southwest corridor of the Federal District

(Pastori 1929). Subway Line A runs 6.8 kilometers between the *barrio* of Caballito and the Plaza de Mayo and serves a total of 14 stations. Between the Once railroad terminal and the Plaza de Mayo, stations are spaced about three city blocks apart, and west of Once they are spaced about five blocks apart.

A second subway, Line B, opened in 1931 linking the Federico Lacroze railroad terminal to the financial district around Avenida Leandro N. Alem near the central post office. This 8.7-kilometer line runs its entire length under Avenida Corrientes and has 13 stations spaced about five blocks apart. Three other subway lines also opened during the 1930s, completing the contemporary network. Line C, the city's only transverse route, links the Retiro and Constitución railroad terminals. Line D runs northwest from the Plaza de Mayo to the *barrio* of Palermo, and Line E runs west from the Plaza de Mayo to the Plaza de los Virreyes in southwestern Flores. Lines A and B operate unique equipment, whereas lines C, D, and E are compatible. In 1986, the government authorized the construction of a short light-rail system (Premetro) to connect the Savio municipal housing complex in Villa Lugano with subway line E at Plaza de los Virreyes (Figure 6.4). The light-rail system runs through the Almirante Brown recreation area serving the City Amusement Park and a large *villa de emergencia* along Avenida Mariano Acosta.

Buenos Aires' five subway lines and short light-rail system cover 46 kilometers in the Federal District. Between 1960 and 1980 ridership declined from 300 to 200 million passengers annually. By 1982, annual ridership had dipped to 182 million. A lack of investment in new infrastructure and competition from automobiles and buses seriously affected subway ridership during the 1970s and 1980s. The subways traditionally carried many passengers who commuted into the Federal District on the suburban railroads. As the railroads deteriorated and lost traffic to *colectivos* and automobiles, the subways began to suffer accordingly. However, since the mid-1980s ridership has improved steadily and the total number of passengers transported in 1992 reached 198 million (República Argentina 1993a).

As part of the federal government's globalization strategies, the Buenos Aires subway system was privatized in 1994 (International Railway Journal 1993). Consortium operators Metrovías and Trainmet have a concession to operate the five subway lines in the Federal District for 20 years. At the same time, the municipal government in the Federal District is considering plans for several extensions to the subway system as well as for three new lines (Figure 6.5). An extension of Line D from Palermo to Ministro Carranza has been in operation for several years, and work continues to take the line forward along Avenida Cabildo toward Plaza Balcarce near the Federal District boundary. Several north–south lines are planned, including an extension of Line C south along Avenida Montes de Oca from Plaza Constitución to the Pueyyredón bridge. Many of the southwestern and southern *barrios* of the Federal District are poorly served by public transport, and the two planned southern extensions would improve mobility in these traditional working-class areas immeasurably. Even if the planned extensions go forward, expanding the subway network to 74 kilometers, the system still would compare unfavorably to other world cities. Paris, for example, has a 200-kilometer subway network, Madrid has 100 kilometers, México's system covers 158 kilometers, and the New York subway extends over 400 kilometers.

Buenos Aires' five principal suburban railroad terminals – Retiro, Federico Lacroze, Once, Constitución, and Buenos Aires – function as the city's most important transport nodes. The proximity of the national bus terminal to the Retiro railroad complex makes this area one of the busiest in the Federal District. Other important transport nodes include the Jorge Newbery airport, Plaza de Mayo, the international ferry terminal, and the Avenida 9 de Julio freeway interchange. Within the city center, people, goods, and information circulate using various transport modes. Taxis, private messenger services, delivery trucks, local area computer networks, and telephones all facilitate accessibility, mobility, and communication in the commercial zone. Bicycles are not encouraged in the downtown core because traffic conditions make their use extremely dangerous. In the city center, Avenida Florida between Plaza San Martín and Plaza de Mayo functions as a *peatonal* or

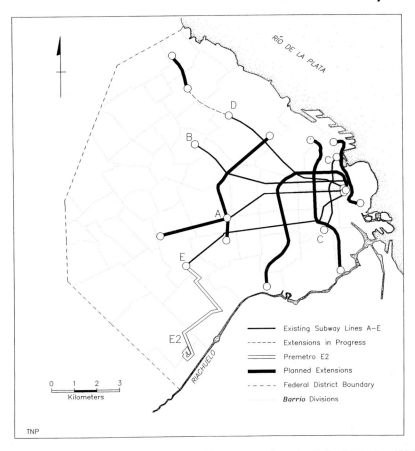

Figure 6.5 The present and proposed subway network in the Federal District, 1994.
Source: La Nación **(1994)**

pedestrian walkway. Vehicular traffic is forbidden on Avenida Florida, and the *peatonal* has become the premier shopping street in Buenos Aires (Figure 6.6). Crossing Avenida Florida from east to west between Avenidas San Martín and 9 de Julio is another *peatonal*, Avenida Lavalle. Home to Buenos Aires' 24-hour entertainment zone, Lavalle is thronged day and night by thousands of *porteños* who visit the many restaurants, cafés, and cinemas that line the street or who simply mingle with the crowds.

Colectivos are the most popular form of public transport in the Federal District. Approximately 146 routes crisscross the inner-city *barrios*, linking the major transport nodes and commercial areas to the neighborhoods and recreational areas of the city. The vast majority of the Federal District's 3 million residents are no more than two or three blocks away

Figure 6.6 Avenida Florida, Buenos Aires' premier shopping street in the city center

from a *colectivo* route. Few world cities have an urban bus network with coverage as comprehensive as the *colectivos* of Buenos Aires. Many of these bus lines follow two or more routes through the city depending on the time of day and *barrios* served. Despite overcrowding, surly drivers, snarled and chaotic traffic, and overly zealous inspectors, the *colectivo* system is surprisingly efficient and functions as a crucial component of the urban transportation network.

Freeways, major arterials, and neighborhood streets in the Federal District facilitate the circulation not only of taxis, *colectivos*, and trucks, but also of private automobiles. In recent years, private automobile use in the Federal District for commuting and routine mobility has increased exponentially, as has the volume of suburban traffic moving in and out of the inner city. The road system in the Federal District has surpassed saturation point and now is routinely jammed with traffic most of the day and well into the evening hours. Noise levels, air pollution, accidents, road damage, and clogged streets caused by vehicular traffic have pushed the city to the very brink of transportation anarchy. Every day, 42 000 taxis, 11 000 buses, and nearly 2 million private automobiles circulate through the streets of the Federal District. To paraphrase a title from Spanish film director Almovar, Buenos Aires seems like a city on the edge of a nervous breakdown!

Five major arterials collect and distribute traffic between Avenida General Paz, the boundary between the Federal District and the suburbs, and the downtown core (Figure 6.7). Avenida Libertador runs north from Plaza San Martín parallel to the Retiro railroad yards toward

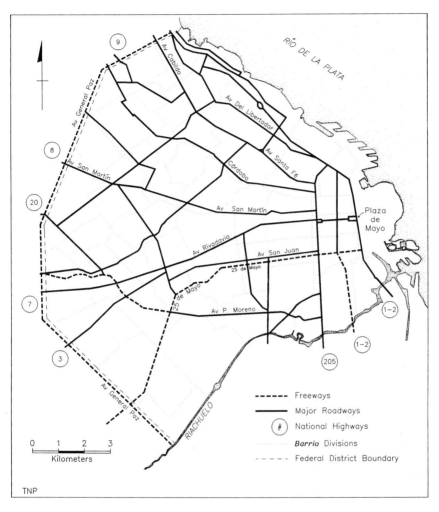

Figure 6.7 Major arterials in the Federal District, 1994. *Source:* After Wheaton (1990)

Vicente López. From the west corner of Plaza San Martín, Avenida Santa Fé runs northwest through the *barrios* of Palermo and Belgrano and becomes Avenida Cabildo before merging with Avenida General Paz. Avenida San Martín is the major arterial that runs through Caballito, Paternal, and Villa Devoto toward the suburban *partido* of General San Martín. Buenos Aires' longest continual street, Avenida Rivadavia, functions as the Federal District's major western arterial and runs through Almagro, Balvanera, Caballito, and Flores on its way to Liniers and the western suburbs. The fifth major arterial is the east–west freeway from Puerto Madero to Avenida General Paz. Several other important roads carry traffic across the city along a north–south axis and serve as tributaries to the major arterials.

Urban freeways were introduced to the Federal District in 1978 during the military *Proceso*. Transport planners envisioned a 75-kilometer freeway network crisscrossing the Federal District that would speed traffic from the suburban arterials to the heart of the city and out again. Five major freeways were planned: the east–west Autopista 25 de Mayo, the Central, Transversal, Nueve de Julio, and the Occidental. Private companies would operate the toll freeways, with the federal government guaranteeing the financial credits sought by the concessionaires. Autopista 25 de Mayo was the only one completed during the military period. It runs from the boundary between Puerto Madero and San Telmo in the city center to Parque Avellaneda where it bifurcates. One branch, the elevated Perito Moreno freeway, runs northwest to Avenida General Paz, and the other section becomes the international airport freeway running southwest through Villa Lugano. In 1981, the government started work on extending Avenida 9 de Julio at both its southern and northern ends. From the interchange with the east–west freeway near Plaza Constitución, the southern extension of 9 de Julio runs to the Riachuelo river. At the northern end, the Avenida 9 de Julio was to be extended out over the Retiro railroad yards to link up with the future coastal freeway. In 1994, work had been suspended on the extension for lack of funds. Critics of the urban freeways suggest that construction is a complete waste of money because the time saved by driving the freeway is more than lost in the traffic jams at the freeway exits.

Plans are underway to extend the La Plata to Buenos Aires freeway, now under construction in the *partidos* of Avellaneda and Quilmes, through the downtown core via Puerto Madero. Several possible routes have been suggested by the city's public works department (*La Nación* May 28, 1994). The most favorable route would use the land currently occupied by the railroad tracks that used to service Puerto Madero. This route has received vociferous objections from the companies who are financing the "City Port" project in Puerto Madero. They argue that the freeway would separate City Port practically and perceptually from the city center and make it extremely difficult to market the project as a residential and commercial center. A second route has been proposed that would take the freeway out over reclaimed land along the Río de la Plata and bypass Puerto Madero to the east. Environmentalists and ecologists strongly oppose this route because of possible damage to the flora and fauna of the river bank. Other opposition comes from groups who claim the project is just too expensive and that a better solution would be investment in public transport.

Contemporary traffic problems in Buenos Aires have been compounded by poor urban planning and development, and by the deterioration in the city's public transport system. In addition, many of the narrow colonial-era streets in the Federal District are not suited for modern urban traffic. Pedestrian sidewalks along these streets are extremely narrow and crowded.

A scathing editorial in the *Buenos Aires Herald* on May 13, 1994, blamed the traffic congestion on city engineers who have been:

> allowed to carry out all sorts of preposterous plans which have gouged out the living cores of many parts of the city, draining off the population into the suburbs so as to give way to the tyranny of the car. Whole chunks of the city have been demolished to build interchanges, flyovers, parking-lots and far from improving inner city traffic, such a policy has simply aggravated the matter further by pouring more vehicles into an ever-congested area.

Responding to the growing congestion, in May 1994, the government passed the Traffic Emergency Law to ban cars from the Federal District 1 day per week. In effect for a trial period of 180 days, the law bans cars based on the last number of their licence plate. For example, cars with plates ending in 0 or 1 must remain off the streets on Mondays, plates ending in 2 or 3 are banned on Tuesdays, and so on. Government officials argue that the law will keep approximately 500 000 vehicles each day off the city's streets. Unfortunately, no long-term traffic management plans have been forthcoming to address the other 1.5 million vehicles that still will clog the Federal District daily. Restrictions on automobile circulation in the Federal District were tried between March 1974 and May 1976 in response to the global oil crisis, but they had little long-term effect on calming traffic growth in the city.

In many of the industrial world's biggest cities, traffic planners have come to the realization that increasing demands for road space created by growing private automobile traffic can never be met adequately. One of the automobile's greatest advantages, spatial flexibility, also creates a monumental problem for transport planners. Roads and freeways tend to spread mobility, and thus transport demand, over a wide area, whereas public transport helps to concentrate movement along a specific corridor. Moreover, the enormous environmental and economic cost of freeways to the urban environment has stimulated a reappraisal of the role of both freeways and public transport. For example, the extension of the Avenida 9 de Julio freeway across Avenida Libertador and the Retiro railroad tracks is estimated to cost at least 10 million dollars per kilometer. Freeway opponents hope that new investment in light rail, traditional rail, buses, and bikeways in world cities such as Buenos Aires will revitalize urban centers and redress the imbalance between public transport supply and demand. The current traffic crisis in Buenos Aires has reinforced the fact that monomodal solutions to transport problems are doomed to failure. World cities like Buenos Aires can only progress in an environmentally sustainable manner along the local–global continuum by employing multimodal solutions to urban transport problems. With transport-related environmental issues in mind, the following chapter examines environmental management in Buenos Aires and looks at the general health and welfare of the city's residents.

7

The living city: managing the urban environment

Situated on the southern bank of the Río de la Plata estuary at an average 25 meters above mean sea level, the Greater Buenos Aires Metropolitan Area (GBAMA) has a distinct physical environment (Figure 7.1). To the north, the temperate waters of the Río Paraná and its many tributaries form a great delta at the head of the Plata estuary. The waters of the large estuary to the east of Buenos Aires have a tremendous influence over the urban climate, with the heat and humidity modifying winter temperatures. Buenos Aires enjoys a humid subtropical climate, with mean annual temperatures that fluctuate at about 17°C. Monthly temperature means during winter (June–August) average about 11°C and summer (December–February) monthly means average approximately 25°C. The annual mean precipitation in Buenos Aires is 1000 mm, with monthly extremes of 60 mm in July and over 120 mm in March. Away from the coast, the flat, urbanized landscape stretches out in clearly discernible corridors, with a number of streams and small rivers cutting eastward toward the estuary. Flooding and standing water are perennial problems in the city, especially along the banks of the arroyos and rivers and in low-lying areas where poorer families have established shantytowns and temporary dwellings.

Management of Buenos Aires' physical environment has been piecemeal for most of the twentieth century, with responsibilities divided among a number of government institutions and agencies. Environmental management difficulties are exacerbated in Buenos Aires because no "environmental problem" has ever been defined. Moreover, there is institutional confusion about how to manage environmental issues and

Figure 7.1   Satellite view of Buenos Aires and the Río de la Plata estuary, reproduced with permission from Juan A. Roccatagliata

policies and about who has responsibility for particular problems. As a result, in the GBAMA, the various components of environmental management are split among multiple institutions and between multiple jurisdictions, with almost no coordination between them (Pace 1992).

Throughout the twentieth century, urban growth has occurred in Buenos Aires with little concern for environmental implications. Laws frequently have been passed to address garbage disposal, human waste, industrial effluents, air pollution, and other by-products of urbanization, but enforcement has been negligible and sporadic. Constant political and economic turmoil between the 1930s and the 1980s pushed environmental concerns to the very bottom of the government's urban management agenda. In the contemporary climate of privatization, deregulation, and globalization of the urban economy, environmental concerns are being subordinated to the overwhelming desire of individuals, institutions, and bureaucrats to incorporate Buenos Aires and Argentina rapidly into the world economy. Economic growth in an expanding free-market global environment is paramount, with governments and planners merely paying lip-service to environmental issues. Indeed, multinational industrial companies are attracted to Buenos Aires in part because lax environmental laws allow greater production flexibility and help to lower costs. More serious, however, has been the reluctance of public, private, and foreign enterprises to invest in pollution awareness and reduction campaigns. As a result, problems with illegal toxic waste dumping, industrial effluent discharge into the urban waterways, exhaust emissions into the local atmosphere, and perhaps irreversible damage to the city's flora and fauna have contributed to the increasing environmental degradation of Buenos Aires.

In 1991, the Menem government responded to concerns about the city's deteriorating environment by creating the National Secretariat on Natural Resources and the Human Environment. However, little evidence of the Secretariat articulating a comprehensive environmental strategy has emerged. At the non-governmental level, the environmental or ecological movement has grown since the return to democratic government in 1983. Yet the lack of previous experience and the absence of coordinated social organizations have limited the political role of the environmental movement in Buenos Aires. About 100 environmental non-governmental organizations (NGOs) are active on a continuous basis, with activities ranging from broader development issues to more focused habitat and ecological issues (Pace 1992). Despite the serious environmental problems confronting Buenos Aires, however, environmental NGOs have yet to propose a workable social or political plan to address the issues.

Compounding the problem for NGOs and governments alike is that environmental issues rarely have been at the forefront of *porteño* concerns about the city. A 1993 survey of 600 city residents by Mansilla, Delich, and Associates found that the economy, political corruption, and rising unemployment were the most pressing urban concerns, with environmental issues barely rating a mention (*Buenos Aires Herald* May 6, 1993, p. 11). Since the introduction of Perón's social state in the 1940s, the residents of Buenos Aires have become accustomed to government employees cleaning up after them. Many *porteños* have lost their sense of civic pride and they litter the streets and pollute the environment with impunity and with little consideration for the community. Trains, buses, urban streets, open lots, city parks and plazas, sidewalks, and gutters are used indiscriminately as garbage receptacles. Wealthier areas of the city are cleaner than poorer areas, not because residents are more environmentally aware but because they can afford to pay for cleanup crews. Overcoming general apathy toward the state of the urban environment remains a major challenge to the city's environmental advocates and urban planners.

Three major aspects of environmental management in Buenos Aires are examined in this chapter. First, we analyze the city's metropolitan green belt and its impact on the urban environment and explore the distribution and function of green spaces throughout Buenos Aires. Second, urban pollution is examined, with a specific focus on the contamination of the air and water in the city. Finally, we comment briefly on the health and welfare of Buenos Aires' citizens, the provision of water and sewer services in the city, and the relationship between urban quality of life and environmental deterioration.

Green belts and public spaces

As Buenos Aires industrialized during the first half of the twentieth century, factory smokestacks, industrial machines, and motor vehicles came to represent progress and modernity. Economic and demographic growth expanded the city areally and reshaped the physical environment. A lack of integrated urban management strategies in Buenos Aires encouraged unrestrained growth with little concern for environmental conditions in the city. Trees were uprooted, green spaces became manufacturing plants and housing estates, and permeable surfaces disappeared under a sea of concrete and asphalt. Municipal governments struggled to cope with industrial and human wastes, and motorized transport increasingly clogged the urban highways and byways. Surface runoff became a serious problem, especially along the rivers and arroyos that snake across the urban landscape. Buenos Aires' overstressed drainage system constantly backed up, which caused massive street flooding and frequent inundation of low-income *barrios*.

Industrialized urban life also created a growing problem with solid waste disposal. Up until the late 1980s, recycling did not exist in Buenos Aires and garbage filled up every available spot on the landscape. A haphazard system of incinerators and garbage-burning on open dumps evolved around the outskirts of the Federal District and in peripheral areas of the suburban Inner Ring. During the 1970s, soot and ash fallout over the city reached an astonishing 80 tons per day (Carty 1981). Railroad tracks, arroyos, vacant lots, and street gutters across the city functioned as unofficial garbage dumps. Even in well-organized *barrios*, garbage could be found piled up on street corners, a practice that still continues to this day (see Figure 3.18). Almirante Brown Park in the southwestern corner of the Federal District, for example, had become essentially a huge open garbage pit by the 1970s. Images of thousands of people scraping a living by picking rubbish from garbage dumps had always been associated with other Latin American cities, not Europeanized, civilized Buenos Aires. Yet direct evidence could be found throughout the city of a trend toward this unsavory aspect of urban life. In 1994, both human and animal scavengers still could be observed on several of the open garbage dumps in Greater Buenos Aires (GBA).

In 1970, lawyer and urban planner Guillermo Domingo Laura began to develop the idea of creating parks and open spaces from sanitary landfills that could be used to reclaim low-lying land around the city. He envisioned a green belt some 150 kilometers long and covering 300 square kilometers that would cope with Buenos Aires' garbage problem for at least the next 30 years (Carty 1981). After setting out the appropriate administrative, financial, and engineering steps needed to bring the green belt plan to fruition, Laura submitted the idea to the government, which quickly adopted the plan. The green belt idea fit nicely into the urban planning strategies of the military government that were designed to reshape and reinvigorate Buenos Aires. In 1977, an agreement between the Municipality of the City of Buenos Aires and various provincial authorities created the Cinturón Ecológico del Area Metropolitana or CEAMSE (the Metropolitan Area Ecologial Belt). CEAMSE proved to be one of the few instances of interjurisdictional agreement in the GBAMA that had any practical application. Prior to the creation of CEAMSE, garbage services had been run by over 20 administrative jurisdictions across the metropolitan area with little or no coordination and integration of policies.

In June 1980, the open dumps and incinerators across the city were closed, new laws on land use, pollutant emissions, and population densities were drafted, and CEAMSE plunged into the garbage business. Private companies are contracted to bring what amounts to over 10 000 tons of garbage daily to the several modern transfer stations scattered around the city. The trash is compacted by a giant press and sent to the landfill sites for burial. Dump trucks compact the garbage into trenches and cover it with a 2-foot layer of compressed earth. Long-term plans call for a system of recreational parks and for the recovery and forestation of floodland using millions of tons of waste as fill. Setting aside over 40 000 hectares of land for the green belt also will aid in the recovery of damaged river banks. Supporters of the project argue that the landfill terrain can be shaped for golf courses, soccer fields, parks, or roadbeds.

The green belt follows the course of the Río Reconquista from the Paraná delta due west for approximately 30 kilometers toward the *partido* of Merlo (Figure 7.2). It then winds southward for about 40 kilometers following several of the small arroyos that cut across Merlo, La Matanza, and Esteban Echeverría. South of the Ezeiza International Airport, the green belt turns east toward the Arroyo de las Piedras before ending near Highway 53 in the *partido* of Florencio Varela. A projected green belt scenic highway has yet to materialize, but a number of parks, tree-planting projects, and recreation areas have proved successful. For example, Reconquista Park near Bancalari railroad station in San Fernando served originally as a demonstration park for the green belt project and was equipped with tennis courts, soccer fields, and children's playgrounds.

Many cities and international agencies have watched the development of CEAMSE very closely, noting that the green belt idea could be a realistic solution to urban environmental problems in other countries. Initial enthusiasm for the project in Buenos Aires, however, has turned into long-term frustration. Inadequate funding and problems with land

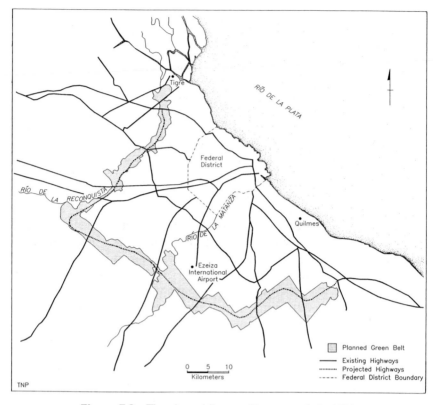

Figure 7.2 The planned Buenos Aires green belt, 1994

acquisition have stymied the full implementation of the original plan. Many municipalities in GBA are financially bankrupt and cannot afford the fee to deposit garbage at the CEAMSE landfill. As a result, CEAMSE has had financial problems in recent years (Bartone et al. 1991). Moreover, at least 100 open garbage dumps have sprung up around the city since the late 1980s. Another serious problem for the green belt's future is the lack of control over the type of garbage that enters the landfill. Since 1990, vociferous complaints about possible toxic chemical dumping and other hazardous materials, particularly along the northwestern corridor, have cast doubt on the viability of the project and on the suitability of the reclaimed land for activities such as children's playgrounds and golf courses.

A further complication is the federal government's determination to disengage itself from all public service provision. Private sector participation in municipal solid waste collection and disposal has increased dramatically since 1989. Less than 25 percent of collection services in the

Federal District now are handled by the municipal government. In the 19 *partidos* of the suburban Inner Ring, only two municipalities directly participate in solid waste collection. Residents are discouraged from using landfills because of the costs involved, especially now that many public landfills have been privatized. For example, the large Villa Dominico landfill in Avellaneda is operated by SYUSA, a private company, and a local subsidiary (ASEO) of a major US company operates the Gonzales Catán landfill in La Matanza. A major issue for the future of solid waste management in Buenos Aires under a privatized system is the monitoring and supervision of private contractors by local governments to ensure adequate environmental protection. Moreover, costs must be controlled to prevent illegal dumping on open land and along green belts, especially in the suburbs.

Green belts, wooded recreational areas, tree-lined avenues, and riparian zones long have been considered the lungs of the city, nature's method of removing pollutants harmful to humans and oxygenating the air. For example, despite the high volume of automobile traffic flowing along the Avenida General Paz ring road compared with many city center streets, air quality is vastly superior along General Paz because its many trees help to break down the emissions. With the exception of the Plaza de Mayo and several other important plazas, few trees are found in the central city area. Historically, in Buenos Aires the "uncontrolled alienation of public and private lands through land speculation" has severely restricted the development of open spaces and recreational areas (Sargent 1974, p. 88). There are many parks and plazas in Buenos Aires, but the areas within the metropolis set aside for green spaces are considerably less than in comparable world cities. In 1933, the Federal District only had 960 hectares or about 5 percent of the urban area in open space. This compared unfavorably to Vienna, London, and Berlin, which had in excess of 20 percent of their urban areas devoted to open space. Paris had 12 percent of its urban area in open space without including the huge Bois de Boulogne Park. In 1994, only 1078 hectares in the Federal District were open and unpaved. This equates to approximately 3 square meters per resident, far less than the 10 square meters of green space per capita recommended internationally (Brailovsky and Foguelman 1992).

Within the Federal District, four major zones of green space exist, complemented by several minor areas. Palermo Park along the northwestern corridor is the most developed green space in the metropolitan area. Palermo comprises several sections, including the Botanic, Zoological, and Japanese Gardens, a lake, and several plazas. Second is the coastal ecological zone, which stretches east from Puerto Madero to the Río de la Plata shoreline. The third major green space is

Presidente Sarmiento Park, which occupies a substantial portion of Villa Devoto near the Avenida General Paz ring road. Finally, the most undeveloped area of open land and green space is found in the southwestern corner of the Federal District alongside the channelized Riachuelo river. Once the site of an immense open garbage dump, much of the land in Villa Soldati and Villa Riachuelo has been rehabilitated. Parks, lakes, soccer fields, and an autodrome, golf course, and amusement park now comprise the complex known as Parque Almirante Brown.

Overall, the Federal District is not well endowed with trees, and those that do exist are found primarily along the northwestern and western corridors. In 1970, approximately 300 000 trees provided shade and oxygen in the downtown area. Since 1977, more than 250 000 new trees have been planted, with 100 000 trees planted in 1980 alone. Unfortunately, many of the trees in the central city area still are too young to have any significant foliage, and the overall number of trees remains insufficient to ameliorate poor air quality in Buenos Aires. The municipal government has remodeled and cleaned up about 50 of the city's plazas, with plans to remodel others when funds become available. Throughout the metropolitan area, 70 hectares of green belt have been added recently, with 639 additional hectares in the process of conversion to green belt status.

Many environmentalists and planners in Buenos Aires have been critical recently of the lack of attention given to the actual and potential green spaces in the city (Randle 1991a). Patricio Randle (1991b) argued that contemporary urban society is destroying the community in Buenos Aires by focusing on economic growth and ignoring spatial considerations. The wide Avenida 9 de Julio, for example, has become an inhospitable and antiurban open space. It slices through the heart of the downtown core, separating the western and eastern sections of the financial district and creating a perceptual and physical barrier that pedestrians find particularly difficult to negotiate. Increasing traffic congestion, noise, and air pollution along Avenida 9 de Julio have devalued the area practically and perceptually.

The human scale of the city also is changing, as 20- and 30-story apartment towers spring up on every piece of vacant land. Children are denied access to the urban environment because few safe playgrounds exist for them. Freeways carve up and divide *barrios*, creating new and hostile edges and often absorbing what little open space is available in a neighborhood. Parks, plazas, and open spaces bear the brunt of the frequent financial difficulties of municipal governments and become neglected landscapes, left to deteriorate and stagnate. Those open spaces that are heavily used by Buenos Aires' citizens, such as the Tigre Delta area and the Palermo complex, are being loved to death. Overcrowding, pollution, and a lack of management have eroded the aesthetic and practical value of many of the city's popular recreational and congregational open spaces. Moreover, rising levels of air, water, and ground pollution throughout Buenos Aires are changing the way *porteños* interact with the urban environment and are eroding the city's quality of life.

Urban pollution

There is little disagreement among environmentalists, bureaucrats, planners, and the general public in Buenos Aires that urban pollution has reached intolerable levels. However, debate continues over the cause and effect relationships between economic growth and environmental deterioration and over the role government should play in urban environmental management. The dominant view among critics of globalization is that Buenos Aires' involvement in the world economy is generating environmental costs that are beyond the fiscal and management capacity of both government and society. The government believes that sound environmental management is best achieved through privatization policies, and it long has subscribed to the "polluter should pay" principle (Brailovsky and Foguelman 1992). For example, a 1978 law required companies that contaminated groundwater through a lack of proper environmental controls to pay an annual fee to the Obras Sanitarias de la Nación (OSN) or National Sanitary Company. Fees were to be used for the construction of water treatment plants in Buenos Aires, but lax enforcement of the law and inadequate management controls resulted in few fees and no new plants. By 1994, air and water pollution in Buenos Aires had reached critical levels, especially in the city center, along the northwest corridor, and along the Matanza–Riachuelo river system.

Air pollution

Buenos Aires lacks any control over industrial and vehicle emissions, the main source of air pollution in the city. Part of the problem stems from a lack of technological equipment and resources to diagnose and treat emissions. Moreover, the city is hampered in its efforts to restrict pollution by inconsistent environmental policies. With globalization and free-market ideologies driving the government's economic restructuring efforts, little consideration is given to the social costs of pollution.

Everyday millions of *porteños* breathe the thick, choking, polluted air of Buenos Aires, yet fatalistically accept the problem as part of city life. Catalytic converters and unleaded gasoline for vehicles are unknown in Buenos Aires. Thousands of vehicles clogging the streets of the downtown core spew out carbon monoxide and thick, black diesel fumes. The pollution is bad especially along the narrow, one-way streets of the city center, where pedestrians walk barely a meter away from vehicle exhaust pipes. Levels of air pollution in the Federal District frequently exceed the maximum tolerable smog level of 9 parts per million set by the World Health Organization (WHO). For example, during a 1-week stretch between May 20 and 27, 1994, air pollution levels reached as high as 11.8 parts per million on consecutive days (*La Nación* 1994). Fortunately, Buenos Aires' position at the edge of the flat pampas next to a large body of water, coupled with prevailing atmospheric conditions, allows for the fairly rapid dispersion of air pollution throughout much of the year. However, the city's air can be shockingly poor and stagnant at times.

The principal contaminants in the Buenos Aires air are dust, solid particles, carbon dioxide from industrial and residential heating, carbon monoxide from vehicles, sulfur dioxide from industry, and nitrogen oxides from incinerators, vehicles, and industrial plants. Precipitation sampling in the Federal District between 1983 and 1988 revealed little evidence of acid rain pollution (Canziana et al. 1989). However, since 1989 increased levels of sulfuric acid have been detected in two specific areas of Buenos Aires: Berisso, which is adjacent to the industrial and port complex of La Plata, and Beccar, which is close to several major industrial plants. Estimated annual emissions of pollutants within the Federal District exceed 35 000 tonnes of sulfur dioxide, 240 000 tonnes of carbon monoxide, 30 000 tonnes of nitrogen oxides, and 4000 tonnes of suspended particulate matter (Earthwatch 1992). Despite some short-term declines in pollution levels, overall pollution counts have increased steadily since the 1970s, reflecting in part the greater number of vehicles transiting the Federal District and the lax environmental controls over industrial emissions.

Air pollution from electricity generating plants in Buenos Aires has been reduced since the 1970s. In 1970, over 90 percent of Argentina's electricity came from thermal power stations that burned primarily oil and coal. By the early 1990s, nuclear and hydro generation accounted for over 40 percent of electricity production, which reduced the overall emission of sulfur and carbon pollutants (Carnevali and Suárez 1993). A greater percentage of Buenos Aires' industrial and residential electricity and natural gas now comes from generating plants in the interior, resulting in less pollution from urban power generation. Nonetheless, the three thermal power stations in Buenos Aires produced nearly 90 000 tonnes of sulfur dioxide emissions in 1988 (Earthwatch 1992).

Water pollution

One of the more worrying environmental problems in Buenos Aires is the pollution of surface water and groundwater sources. Industrial activity in Buenos Aires and the uncontrolled discharge of untreated household sewage continues to pollute seriously the Río de la Plata and its tributaries. A large percentage of people in Buenos Aires consume drinking water totally or partially drawn from polluted water courses or underground wells. Moreover, pesticides from the expanding agricultural frontier in Brazil are becoming increasingly evident in the Plata estuary. Swimming along the Buenos Aires shoreline has been prohibited for several years because of heavy pollution, and the consumption of contaminated fish caught in the estuary continues to pose serious problems for the city's health officials. Isolated cases of cholera also have been reported recently in the city.

Buenos Aires' various governments lack adequate funding for environmental control of industrial wastes. Each day, tremendous volumes of toxic wastes and other hazardous materials find their way into the arroyos, streams, and rivers of the metropolitan area. Particularly at risk are poor people who live in shantytowns along the banks of these heavily polluted waterways. Estimates for toxic waste production in Buenos Aires are not easily obtained. However, evidence of serious water pollution caused by industrial effluent suggests that significant volumes of toxic and hazardous waste are not receiving adequate treatment or disposal (Pace 1992). Environmental groups estimate that at least 1.2 million tonnes of hazardous solids, toxic mud, and diluted solvents are dispersed annually (legally and illegally) into the waterways and soils of the GBAMA. For example, the area around Dock Sud in the *partido* of Avellaneda is at particular risk. Dock Sud is the center of operations for numerous petroleum, chemical, alcohol, and grain companies. Over 700 storage tanks contain nearly 1.5 million cubic meters of toxic substances and potentially explosive materials. A fire on June 28, 1984, at the Perito Moreno petroleum plant nearly led to a major disaster in the area. Only a fortunate change in wind direction saved dozens of tanks containing toxic and highly flammable materials from exploding (Brailovsky and Foguelman 1992).

The density of surface water in Buenos Aires has reached unheard of levels because of industrial and domestic wastes. The Río Matanza-Riachuelo watershed provides an excellent example of a small urban ecosystem and its pollution problems. The watershed is approximately 2300 square kilometers and contains 3.5 million people, 30 percent of whom live in the Federal District, 20 percent in the *partido* of La Matanza, 10 percent in Lanús and Lomas de Zamora, with the remaining 40 percent shared among the *partidos* of Almirante Brown, Avellaneda, Cañuelas, Esteban Echeverría, Las Heras, Merlo, Marcos Paz, and San Vicente. In the suburban *partidos* included in the river basin, only 17 percent of the population have sewer service, and only 55 percent have piped potable water. Inside the Federal District, over 90 percent of the *barrios* included in the Riachuelo basin are connected to the sewer system and over 95 percent have piped water. The *barrios* of La Boca and Barracas account for almost all of the Federal District homes inside the basin without sewer or water service. A 1980 study commissioned by the Cinturón Ecológico company (CEAMSE) and conducted by London's Thames Water Consultancy Service showed evidence of both legal and illegal untreated domestic and industrial wastes being discharged into the river system. Estimates put the number of factories discharging waste water into the Matanza–Riachuelo system somewhere between 20 000 and 40 000, with over half of the factories located inside the Federal District. In the neighborhood of Aldo Bonzi in La Matanza, for example, the study recorded a daily discharge into the Río Matanza of 17 000 cubic meters of water in a complete state of putrefaction (Brailovsky and Foguelman 1992).

An analysis of dissolved oxygen in the Matanza-Riachuelo river further highlights the serious problem of water pollution in Buenos Aires. A ratio of 5 mg of oxygen to 1 liter of water is required for fish to survive in rivers. Fifty kilometers inland, where National Highway 3 crosses the Río Matanza, levels of 8.4 mg/2 l have been recorded (Berón 1981). Near the Ricchieri freeway in the suburban Inner Ring, the ratio drops precipitously to 2.6 mg/2 l. Inside the Federal District, measurements revealed a 0.1 mg/2 l ratio, and at the Nicolás Avellaneda bridge near Dock Sud the river was essentially dead with a ratio of 0.0 mg/2 l. Moreover, since 1981 pollution of the Matanza–Riachuelo river system has worsened!

Management of Buenos Aires' water supply has evolved through three specific stages since 1945. At the end of the 1940s, the government created a state agency (Obras Sanitarias de la Nación – OSN) to provide potable water and sewer service in Buenos Aires and to control atmospheric and water pollution. Territorial conflicts between the federal, provincial, and local governments over management policies occurred frequently and contributed to the inefficient operation of OSN. The second stage in water management ran from the end of the 1970s until 1992. During this period, attempts were made to decentralize OSN's functions. Management responsibility for water supply and pollution control passed to the provincial governments and to local municipalities. At the same time, an interjurisdictional body was created to coordinate water and sewer service between the Federal District and the suburban municipalities. During this second stage, however, little progress occurred in the provision of new infrastructure. The third stage in urban water management began in 1992 with the transfer of control over water contamination issues from OSN to the Secretary of Natural Resources and the Human Environment as a first step toward privatization. It is premature to evaluate the spatial consequences of privatization, but to date little has changed in the management of the urban water and sewer system. Interjurisdictional conflicts continue to pose serious barriers to water management. For example, the catchment area of the Matanza–Riachuelo river is administered by 22 authorities, with another 19 organizations exercising some type of authority over the 64-kilometer length of the river (the Subsecretary of Maritime and Fluvial Transport, the National Director of Navigable Waterways, the Port Administration, and the Provincial Director of Hydrology are just a few). Thirteen *partidos* along with various national and provincial authorities have an interest in the management of the Reconquista river basin. Because flooding is a serious and ongoing problem in suburban Buenos Aires, local governments are demanding more control over the waterways that pass through their jurisdictions.

The impact of flooding on Buenos Aires is considerable. Three factors combine to exacerbate the flooding problem. First, Buenos Aires suffers from an obsolete storm and surface water drainage system (Pace 1992). In some parts of the city there is no provision at all for surface runoff, so water just collects and floods the surrounding area. Second, a lack of funds and adequate legal building sites has encouraged uncontrolled settlement by poor communities along river banks, floodplains, and other lowlands, particularly in the Inner Ring suburbs. Flooding thus affects tremendous numbers of people and exerts a significant social cost. Third, the creation of the Cinturón Ecológico around Buenos Aires has eliminated many natural drainage pathways, thus contributing to the flooding problem. The combination of periodic flooding, inadequate water and sewer provision, industrial pollution, and lax environmental regulations in Buenos Aires is taking a serious toll on the health and welfare of the city's citizens.

Health and welfare in Buenos Aires

Health and welfare in Buenos Aires is being affected negatively by the failure of government, institutions, and individuals to address the city's environmental problems. Many of these problems are the direct result of a failure to coordinate management of the urban environment and of a lack of short- and long-term environmental planning. The various municipal governments of Buenos Aires have primary responsibility for environmental health within their boundaries, although the federal government also has jurisdiction over the entire metropolitan region. However, there remains a clear spatial imbalance between the provision of basic services in the Federal District and in the suburbs. For example, nearly 95 percent of the houses inside the Federal District have running water and direct sewer connections (Table 7.1). In contrast, barely 25 percent of the population residing in the 19 *partidos* of the suburban Inner Ring have direct access to both running water and a sewer. A staggering 3.5 million people in the Inner Ring alone are without sewer service or running water. The lack of access to basic services such as potable water and sewers is most acute in the shantytowns that lie along the banks of the city's streams and rivers.

Infant mortality rates in the suburban areas are 50 percent higher than in the Federal District, in part because of poor access to prenatal services and other necessary health care. In 1992, approximately 70 percent of all health-care services furnished to children under the age of 14 was provided in the Federal District by private facilities (República Argentina 1993a). In GBA, 60 percent of such services was provided by welfare fund facilities and by public hospitals. Approximately 12 percent of health-care services provided to adults in the Federal District came from public hospitals; this figure jumps to 25 percent in GBA. Residents of the Federal District also fare better in comparisons of affiliations with health-care systems (Table 7.2). An estimated 2.85 million people in GBA were without primary health care in 1992, a number that has been increasing steadily since the early 1980s. Out-patient consultations in public-care facilities within the Federal District rose from 5.3 million in 1984 to over 6.6 million in 1991, despite little change in the size of the population. The Federal District has 66 hospitals to cater for 3 million permanent residents, with more beds available per capita than in the suburban *partidos*. Thus, as a result of better medical facilities inside the Federal District, many suburban residents frequently travel to the inner city for their primary health care. In addition, hospitals in the Federal District are better equipped to cope with major health problems such as cholera epidemics and the AIDS virus. There are few reliable statistics on the spatial distribution of AIDS in Buenos Aires, but anecdotal evidence suggests that the suburban areas of the city have a disproportionately larger number of cases than the Federal District. A particular problem in the poorer suburbs is the use of infected needles by drug addicts.

Table 7.1 Availability of services in the home in Buenos Aires, 1991

Political division	Total	Running water and sewer	Only running water		Sewer only	No running water or sewer	Unknown
			with toilet	without toilet			
Federal District							
Houses	978 330	936 251	5183	15 306	635	156	20 799
Households	1 023 464	970 969	5748	18 981	659	182	26 925
Population	2 871 519	2 714 532	20 224	64 725	1734	555	69 749
Percentage	100	94.54	0.70	2.25	0.06	0.02	2.43
19 partidos of GBA							
Houses	2 083 676	588 178	484 723	40 863	41 366	824 189	104 357
Households	2 172 716	606 928	506 606	42 511	42 819	858 065	115 787
Population	7 924 424	1 975 000	1 821 574	172 433	155 648	3 397 037	402 732
Percentage	100	24.92	22.99	2.18	1.96	42.87	5.08

Source: República Argentina (1993a).

Table 7.2 Percentage of the urban population affiliated to health-care systems, 1989 and 1992

Age groups	Federal Capital		Greater Buenos Aires	
	1989	1992	1989	1992
0–4	78.74	72.60	54.50	55.83
5–9	73.40	79.94	58.34	56.62
10–14	78.14	81.63	59.64	61.75
15–19	76.93	81.30	57.91	56.49
20–29	74.84	76.58	58.53	55.31
30–39	77.61	80.81	63.78	64.66
40–49	79.32	84.95	62.60	65.99
50–59	82.27	84.33	72.05	71.28
60+	93.52	94.88	86.03	87.85
Total	81.16	83.79	64.20	64.27

Estimated population without primary health-care coverage, 1992

Federal Capital = 480 000 residents
Greater Buenos Aires = 2 850 000 residents

Source: República Argentina (1993a).

The future of urban environmental management in Buenos Aires

It certainly is a major understatement to say that Buenos Aires faces some serious environmental problems. Although the city has a vibrant and rapidly growing environmental movement, with many people dedicated to improving the overall health of Buenos Aires, no clear environmental management strategy exists. Globalization of the urban economy has pushed much of the responsibility for environmental management into the hands of private individuals and companies. The federal government is trying to liberalize economic conditions, which has meant a relaxation of environmental standards. Exacerbating the environmental problem is the absence in Buenos Aires of the infrastructure necessary to handle industrial, commercial, and residential wastes. The pollution risk is particularly high in the areas along streams and rivers that are home to many of the city's low-income households. Moreover, municipal governments in Buenos Aires have neither the funds nor the expertise (or, some will argue, the political will) to enforce existing environmental laws. For example, state inspections of waste disposal practices have been severely curtailed in recent years. Companies can pollute with impunity because corporate managers know that discovery is unlikely given the government's weak financial position, its ideological stance toward uninhibited economic growth, and its desire to participate more fully in the global economy.

Perhaps the most visible and oft-debated environmental problem in Buenos Aires is the future use of private automobiles in the city center. The relationship between urban environmental management, transport, accessibility, and mobility in Buenos Aires is crucial, but it has received scant attention in recent years. Massive traffic congestion in the Federal District, coupled with horrendous levels of air pollution and public outcry over the intolerable road situation, have pressured the government to construct more freeways to speed accessibility to the downtown core. However, little consideration has been given to the spatial composition of the city center. Narrow colonial-era streets, a lack of parking facilities, and increased commercial–bureaucratic activities combine to create an environment unsuited to the automobile. As more and more people demand automobile access to the city center, urban planners become trapped in a vicious cycle of urban freeway construction. Neighborhoods are disrupted and people are forced out of the Federal District to accommodate new roads. Freeways attract more traffic because the suburbs continue to grow and people need access to the city center. More traffic leads to more congestion, more pollution, and more debate over accessibility. Planners are pressured to address the demand for more freeways to cope with the growing traffic, and the vicious cycle begins once again.

Part of the problem, of course, is the way that automobiles are mythologized and packaged for urban consumption. Private automobile ownership is seen as the pinnacle of middle-class achievement in Buenos Aires and is the dream of every poor immigrant. Automobile ownership functions as a metaphor for success in Buenos Aires. The government proudly proclaims the latest increases in automobile production at the Ford, Mercedes, or Volkswagen plants and strongly supports the industry through a bewildering variety of subsidies, tax incentives, and public infrastructure. At the same time, public transport is starved of capital and left to fend for itself. Privatization of the suburban railroads and subways essentially relieves the government from having to face the transport issue. At stake for future Buenos Aires from a transport–environment perspective is the very essence of *porteño* life. Will the city center become like Caracas, dissected by urban freeways and no longer with a definable historic urban core? Is Buenos Aires on the road to becoming the Southern Cone's equivalent of México City, choked daily with traffic and pollution? Unfortunately, these scenarios appear inevitable while a clear strategy for urban traffic calming and the revitalization of public transport facilities is absent.

Buenos Aires faces myriad environmental challenges in the future. However, conversations with planners, environmentalists, geographers, bureaucrats, and others in the city suggest that there are six components of the urban environment puzzle that need immediate attention. First, Buenos Aires must address the unequal role of the automobile in the transport arena. Priority ought to be given to improving suburban rail services, the subway network, and alternative transport modes such as walking, cycling, and ferry boats. Automobiles are a fact of life in world cities, but they should be part of an integrated, balanced transportation strategy and not the only alternative. Second, strict enforcement of environmental laws is necessary, especially in the industrial suburbs of the northwestern and southern corridors. New laws are required to protect against random garbage dumping, toxic waste pollution of waterways, and air pollution. Third, the city desperately needs more green spaces and trees. Green spaces need to be strategically placed around the urban area, not concentrated in exclusive neighborhoods. Fourth, a massive clean-up of the Paraná delta and the Río de la Plata shoreline is needed. Restoring the health of the waterways is vital to overall quality of life in Buenos Aires and to the city's image as a dynamic, progressive world city.

Fifth, a massive public and private works program is needed to address the shortage of sewer and water facilities in the suburban *partidos*. Increased levels of groundwater contamination from inadequate waste facilities are beginning to have a serious long-term effect on health and welfare in the city, particularly in the outer suburbs. The Federal District's aging and crumbling water and sewer system also needs immediate maintenance, especially in the low-income *barrios* along the Riachuelo and in the southwestern corner. Finally, a campaign to raise the level of environmental awareness in Buenos Aires is desperately needed. Environmental concerns have not been high on the agenda of most *porteños* in recent years. Globalization of the Buenos Aires economy and the pursuit of world city status brings with it many environmental implications that need to be addressed in both the public and private arenas.

8

The cultural city: developing a sense of place

The role of world cities as concentration points for global capital, corporate headquarters, financial centers, and advanced producer services creates a demand for a rich assortment of social and cultural infrastructure. With the professionalization of the service sector in many world cities, local middle- to high-income groups are expanding as a percentage of the total urban population. These groups have demands and aspirations related to quality of life and to access to social and cultural infrastructure. Transnational corporate élites, international financiers, tourists, and the global "jet-set" (*los elegantes*) also create a demand for this infrastructure. The provision of formal and informal meeting places, highly reputable schools, and universities is necessary to stimulate intellectual growth and to maintain, nourish, and expand the urban social networks so vital for continued development and change. Moreover, opera houses, theaters, art galleries, museums, historical buildings, restaurants, night clubs, and open green spaces play crucial roles in the attempts by world cities to attract and retain those groups of people necessary to expand a city's global reach. The development of a city's social and cultural infrastructure, therefore, is crucial to the growth and change of urban identity and sense of place.

Buenos Aires' physical and cultural landscapes have been shaped by the hands and minds of four centuries of *porteños*. In turn, the city's physical and cultural landscapes have shaped the way *porteños* think about themselves and the world around them. How individuals perceive themselves as actors within a family, community, *barrio*, or city plays a powerful role in shaping their sense of place. However, sense of place is possibly the most elusive world city characteristic. It is an extremely slippery concept, often better understood by more subjective analysis than by quantification and modeling. In many instances, sense of place has a very intangible quality. It deals with how individuals and communities feel about a particular space, icon, historical figure, public landmark, or building and how that feeling becomes a part of the mythologies humans create for and about a place. These mythologies are essential components of culture. They help people to define who and what they are. Like sense of place, though, culture is a very untidy concept. It often is defined as the "learned collective human behavior" that forms a way of life held in common by a group of people. As Yi-Fu Tuan (1974) puts it, culture is the local, customary way of doing things.

In this chapter, the focus is on three elements critical to the development of Buenos Aires' distinctive urban identity and sense of place. First, an overview of some of the basic characteristics of *porteños* and their culture helps us to understand urban identity in Buenos Aires more clearly. Second, we examine the landscapes of pleasure that serve as mini-stages and backdrops for the drama of daily life played out in Buenos Aires. Landscapes of pleasure are fundamental components of urban society and economy. They can provide valuable evidence of how different groups within a city interact and how cultural influences diffuse through an urban environment. Third, the tourist landscapes of Buenos Aires are explored. Many components of the city's history, mythology, and urban space are commodified and marketed to residents and visitors alike for a variety of economic, social, and political reasons. Moreover, these components frequently function as cultural metaphors for *porteño* society and way of life (see Gannon 1994). Finally, we delve briefly into the consequences of latinamericanizing and globalizing the cultural space of Buenos Aires. What influences are these processes having on the way *porteños* view themselves, their urban environment, and the world around them? Is Buenos Aires experiencing the end of the European myth that has dominated the city for so long?

Urban identity and sense of place

Buenos Aires society can be divided into two very different socio-economic spheres. The upper middle class and élite inhabit Barrio Norte and the northern suburbs, where status, family, and personal wealth are the defining characteristics of *porteño* society. Their lives revolve around the chic cafés and boutiques of Calle Florida and Avenida Santa Fé, the galas and glittering performances at the Teatro Colón, luxury country clubs, and substantial country estates (*quintas*). As the city's oligarchy, they generally have university degrees, maintain overseas bank accounts, and send their children to study in North America or Europe. Many have vacation homes in the resorts of Bariloche, Mar del Plata, or Punta del Este and travel frequently to Miami, New York, or Paris for both pleasure and business. Buenos Aires' bankers are linked to the world's important financial centers, the industrialists depend on foreign franchises and distributorships, and the agriculturalists rely on export markets for their products. Although their relationships, ideologies, and sense of place often are international in scope and context, economic attitudes often are conservative and very resistant to change.

The "people" of Buenos Aires, by contrast, include the factory workers, shopkeepers, clerks, bureaucrats, day laborers, schoolteachers, domestics, office workers, and taxi drivers who inhabit the middle-class neighborhoods, often run-down *barrios*, and shantytowns of the city. The people's relationships, ideologies, and sense of place generally are more locally focused, grounded in family, community, and *barrio*. Many fear the process of economic globalization, with its free market, free trade, and free competition ideology. Economic modernization and labor-saving technologies threaten their role as wage earners and small producers. For the people of Buenos Aires, state control over industry and services represented job stability and a guaranteed share of the modest local market. A lack of trust or sense of common goals between the people and the oligarchy has resulted in what Paul Lewis (1990, p. 502) has called "perpetual standoff." The living standards of the masses cannot be raised and the oligarchy remains unwilling to invest its wealth in what are seen frequently as high-risk, speculative long-term infrastructural improvements. Thus, a differentially scaled sense of place contributes to a clear spatial and ideological separation in Buenos Aires between the two groups. Little wonder, then, that sociocultural relationships in Buenos Aires between the people, the oligarchy, and the government are fragile, ambiguous, and occasionally volatile.

The Menem government's enthusiastic embrace of globalization policies has renewed nationalist sentiments in Buenos Aires. Since independence from Spain at the beginning of the nineteenth century, nationalism has played an important role in the development of a distinct urban identity. In the past, Nationalists upheld "authoritarian rule and the concept of the organic society; they opposed liberalism, democracy, and communism" (Rock 1993, p. xx). They conducted campaigns against immigration, and xenophobia often broke out into overt and ugly racism. The Jewish families in Buenos Aires who owned grain-exporting houses and beer factories often were the target of nationalistic vitriolic attacks. Even the British, whom Raúl Scalabrini Ortiz (1968, p. 198) described as "an enemy whose techniques of world domination have the following features: astuteness, cunning, indirect maneuvers, ill-faith, constant lies, [and] the subtle manipulation of its local agents," were the targets of nationalistic attacks. Such sentiments have survived into the 1990s. Buenos Aires is experiencing a resurgence of antiforeign feelings as most of the country's public services are sold off to overseas investors and operators. Critics of urban restructuring in Buenos Aires argue that dependency on the federal government has been replaced by a far more insidious evil: dependency on multinational corporations and foreign governments. Increased property ownership, business control, and corporate involvement in the day-to-day activities of *porteños* by foreign interests are changing not only the built landscape but also individual urban identities and sense of place. Many *porteños* argue that globalization is leading to the homogenization of urban life and the loss of many of the characteristics that make Buenos Aires such a unique world city.

Nationalistic feelings also have exacerbated tensions between Buenos Aires, the interior, and neighboring countries. The growth and dominance of Buenos Aires over Argentina between 1880 and 1940 encouraged increased contact with the capital, which Bruno Jacovella (1953, p. 5) bemoaned ended the "corporate spirit and the organic community" of Argentina and resulted in the genesis of "the extremes of individualism and 'massification'." Buenos Aires was viewed from the outside as a hotbed of corruption, prostitution, and bureacratic ineptitude, and in the 1930s the Nationalists renewed demands for immigration controls to reduce "the parasitical hordes of the metropolis" (Ibarguren 1969, p. 26). Nationalist rhetoric in the 1990s, which frequently takes on racist overtones, is directed against residents from Bolivia, Peru, and Paraguay, derogatorily called *cabecitas negritas* (greasers or little black heads), who have flocked to Buenos Aires in recent decades. In 1994, the government was considering immigration law reforms that would fine companies employing illegal immigrants and that would make migration a more "selective" process. One of the government's primary goals with immigration reform is to stem the flow of migrants to Buenos Aires in an attempt to preserve the city's European identity.

Surveys carried out recently on racist attitudes in Buenos Aires suggest that racism and discrimination could be linked closely to the lack of a strong Argentine identity. Civilized, sophisticated Buenos Aires, for example, often is portrayed as the essence of Argentina. The identity of Buenos Aires *is* the national identity. Interior regions, cities, and towns, along with the people who come from these places, are viewed as parochial, underdeveloped, unsophisticated, and even barbaric. For example, a late 1992 survey conducted by Edgardo Catterberg revealed serious discrimination against migrants from interior provinces as well as negative attitudes toward Paraguayan migrants, considered the "most despised" group in Argentina (*Latin American Weekly Report*, September 9, 1993, p. 417). The survey also highlighted anti-Semitism as a serious problem. Moreover, there remains a deep-seated distrust in Buenos Aires of anything not of an understandable European origin. Racism also stems in part from Buenos Aires' lack of community or culture beyond the environments of family and *barrio*. Buenos Aires society is broken down into small social groups which are wary of each other in business, sport, and individual human contact.

The people of Buenos Aires

A popular joke in Buenos Aires is that *porteños* think of themselves as Spaniards who dress like the French, talk like the Italians, act like the North Americans, and think they are British. Another *bon mot* has *porteño* babies refusing to leave the womb until being assured they are in a European city. Eduardo Crawley (1984, pp. 5–6) noted that Buenos Aires "playacts at being a city that really belongs in the northern hemisphere, and although it somehow drifted to the South Atlantic, it is still attached to the parental body [Europe] by an imaginary umbilical cord." Indeed, more blondes adorn the billboards of Buenos Aires than in Sweden (*Economist* November 26, 1994). Such ambiguities about cultural origins and identities are not unique to Buenos Aires and its residents. Most societies have expressed desires to imitate, adapt, or adopt some aspects of other culture groups. However, despite attempts to recreate a European image, Buenos Aires and its residents have evolved a unique Latin American urban identity, one characterized by sophistication, style, self-importance, introspection, and a deep desire for respectability.

Buenos Aires is home to over 13 million unique individuals, each with his or her own cultural backgrounds and biases. Yet despite the myriad influences of Italians, English, Spanish, Turks, Jews, Slavs, indigenous Argentines, and Creoles on Buenos Aires, the city has achieved a fairly homogeneous character. Although individual native cultural expressions are being preserved in Buenos Aires, there are certain characteristics that are present in most typical *porteños*. Attempts to generalize the character of *porteños* certainly run the danger of cultural stereotyping and gross generalization, and I caution that my interpretation of these characteristics is based purely upon personal observations and interaction, and is colored by my own cultural biases. *Porteños* are hard-working, friendly, polite, and extremely conscious of their public image. The achievement of public respectability is the Holy Grail of *porteño* life;

respectability anoints a person as a full member of the urban middle class and it epitomizes urban civilization and progress. *Porteños* are passionately proud of their city and its heritage. Few world cities exhibit such an intensely personal relationship between people and place as that experienced by *porteños* with Buenos Aires. Jorge Luis Borges (1974, p. 17) expressed it beautifully:

> The streets of Buenos Aires
> Are the roots of my soul.

As Baldomero Fernández Moreno (1956, cited in Arocena 1982) observed, city and personal life are inextricably intertwined:

> Buenos Aires encapsulates the universe
> and in its clay, its asphalt, or its stone
> my renewed verse is nurtured;
> and I remain as faithful as ivy,
> with a song on my back, convinced
> that it thrives on your blood and mine.

Porteños are vibrant, animated, passionate, and excitable about *futbol* (soccer), *la guita* (money), and the opposite sex. They are very attuned to international politics, fads, and fashions, and have a particular fondness for North American popular culture. North American-style fast-food restaurants, English-language rock music, fast cars, recreational drugs, and Hollywood-inspired street slang all are *de rigueur* for the young and the restless in Buenos Aires and these influences have become as much a part of the local culture as they have in Tokyo, London, Paris, or Sydney.

Fast-food outlets such as Pumpernic vie with established multi-nationals like McDonald's, Burger King, and Kentucky Fried Chicken in the downtown core for control of the market. Coca Cola and Pepsi have become an omnipresent part of the urban landscape, from giant floodlit billboards and electronic signs to sweatshirt logos and crumpled cans littering the highways and byways of the city. Grunge fashion has flooded the boutiques dotted along Avenida Santa Fé and Calle Florida. Songs by Guns N'Roses, Madonna, Billy Joel, and countless other English-language rock stars blare out from radios and compact disc players at every turn. The teenage crowds that gather around the Buenos Aires Sheraton or Hyatt hotels to scream adulation at whichever rock star heroes happen to be in town perhaps are no different from teenagers in other world cities. It's just that there seems to be more emotion, a greater sense of urgency, and far more frenzy in Buenos Aires than elsewhere. Many Buenos Aires residents even have acquired a taste for handguns and crack cocaine, long considered by many to be symptomatic of North American not Argentine urban decline.

Another defining *porteño* characteristic is a tendency toward melancholy and introspection. No other world city has a populace so fascinated with life's daily complications, dark sides, and vagaries. In Buenos Aires there are three times more psychiatrists and psychologists per capita than in New York (Hollander 1990, Wheaton 1990). Certainly six decades of economic and political instability took their toll on the *porteño* psyche, as did the period of the "Dirty War" in the late 1970s when thousands of people disappeared and the military controlled the city through repression and terror (Andersen 1993). *Porteños* also seem to have developed a chronic sense of malaise about their city and country, perhaps fueled by the belief that little would or could change despite one's best efforts. Although the 1990s have brought some measure of political and economic stability to Buenos Aires, a certain level of fatalism continues to exist among the populace. Such questions as "How long will order and stability last?" and "When will the next social upheaval arrive?" are grist for the conversation mill in the city's cafés, bars, and restaurants.

A *porteño's* sense of place and urban identity is related intimately to his or her *barrio*. A peculiar characteristic of Buenos Aires, one that distinguishes it from other world cities in the western hemisphere, is the quality and diverse nature of neighborhood life. The *barrio* grew up as a small parish centered around the neighborhood church and Spanish-style plaza. Urban growth during the nineteenth and twentieth centuries melded the various neighborhoods together into a huge urban expanse, one part seemingly indistinguishable from another. However, the *barrios* and their edges and boundaries remain, celebrated in poetry and tango, and reinforced by fierce rivalries between neighborhood sports teams, political affiliations, ethnic divisions, and traditional attitudes. Indeed, the essence of the *barrio* has remained relatively unchanged for over 100 years.

A sense of belonging or neighborhood familiarity is reinforced by the local *boliche* (snack bar), pharmacy, market, bread store, and butcher. Although supermarket chains have sprung up across the metropolitan area, along with megamalls and jumbo outlets, people still utilize the services of the *barrio*. Many believe that the unique characteristics of the *barrio* are disappearing as urban mass society encourages a depersonalized, rootless, homogeneous environment. Yet, on the other hand, as Buenos Aires increasingly becomes inaccessible for daily life experiences, the physical and social immediacy of the *barrio* takes on a greater importance in both the spiritual and physical geography of the city. Although it has lost its preeminence in recent decades, the *barrio* continues to play a central role in defining community and individual sense of place. Describing oneself as from San Telmo, Palermo, or Flores still conveys a host of powerful social, cultural, and emotional messages.

Ethnicity, religion, and language further define the *porteño* character and help to shape the *porteño's* sense of place. At the end of the 1970s, approximately half of the city's population claimed Italian descent. Twenty percent had Spanish roots, 20 percent claimed a Creole heritage, and the remaining 10 percent were divided among Slavic, Oriental, Jewish, and Arabic ethnic groups (Etchepareborda 1982). In the 1990s, the ethnic composition of Buenos Aires is changing, with important consequences for *porteño* culture. The city has absorbed substantial numbers of *mestizos*, indigenous peoples, and Asians in recent years and the built environment is beginning to show signs of their cultural influence. Most visible are the speciality shops of the Koreans and Chinese, as well as the street-level workshops of migrants from the interior. Although clear spatial patterns of ethnic concentrations are difficult to discern in Buenos Aires, some neighborhoods are known for certain ethnic groups. Italians are found in La Boca and Avellaneda, Germans in San Isidro and Martínez, Jews in Villa Crespo, the English in Hurlingham, and Koreans in Flores and Once.

Nearly 85 percent of the Buenos Aires population professes Catholicism, although a smaller percentage practice the religion on a regular basis. The Catholic Church long has functioned as a pillar of Buenos Aires society, a crucial component of the power triad that controls both city and nation: church, oligarchy, and government (often the military). Buenos Aires hosts over 200 Catholic churches, more than 150 churches serve other Christian denominations, and about 80 synagogues serve the city's Jewish community, which numbers over one-quarter of a million. In addition, Buenos Aires functions as a regional headquarters for the Armenian, Orthodox, and Ukrainian Catholic churches, and has several mosques for the city's small Muslim population. Koreans, Japanese, Chinese, and other Asian migrants to the city have begun to leave evidence of the Buddhist, Hindu, Shinto, and Confucian religions on the urban landscape.

Porteño attitudes toward sexuality in Buenos Aires are influenced strongly by church, family, and *barrio* and always have been relatively conservative, at least on the surface. However, since the return of democracy in 1983, sex has begun to play a major commercial role in the daily lives of *porteños*. Sexuality is used to sell products on television, on billboards, and in magazines, and sexually explicit films, videos, and magazines find an eager market in the city. Critics of globalization and privatization policies argue that free trade is exposing the local market-place to "undesirable" influences such as pornography. Moral decay among urban youth is an oft-discussed topic in newspaper editorials, over dinner tables, and in cafés. Most *porteños* are sexually active before finishing high school, and discreet affairs often take place in the *telos* or officially regulated trysting establishments scattered across the city (Wheaton 1990).

Lifestyles that were the target of political repression during the military *Proceso*, such as homosexuality, lesbianism, and transvestism, are becoming more evident, although tolerance levels still are highly debated. The neighborhoods of San Telmo and La Boca, with their Italianate and French buildings and narrow cobblestoned streets, have become important centers of gay life in Buenos Aires. However, the heart of the city's gay community is found along the middle-class shopping boulevard of Avenida Santa Fé (Miller 1992). Many bars, restaurants, and discotheques in this area of Buenos Aires cater to the gay community and still are targets for periodic raids by *La Moralidad* or vice squad. Even President Menem has attacked the gay community verbally. In a speech to an audience of medical students in his home province of La Rioja, Menem criticized homosexuality as against nature, thus incurring the wrath of the Buenos Aires liberal press (Goñi 1994).

Porteños also have a fascination with transvestism, particularly male-to-female crossdressing. As in many other cultures (North American, English, Australian), crossdressing is a prominent theme in Buenos Aires' television soap operas, comedies, and commercials. The most visible display of transvestite and transsexual lifestyles is closely associated with Buenos Aires' gay community, where transvestites can be found on any given night in the gay bars of Barrio Norte and along Avenida Santa Fé. Many transvestites perform in drag shows along Santa Fé and are known for their flamboyant and often outrageous behavior. The highest percentage of Buenos Aires' crossdressers, however, is found among the heterosexual community. As in northern hemisphere cities, there are no evident patterns to the spatial distribution of crossdressers in Buenos Aires. Crossdressing, almost exclusively male-to-female, is a phenomenon that transcends socioeconomic lines and cultural barriers. Unlike the gay community in Buenos Aires, however, heterosexual crossdressers have no city-wide organization or group to cater to their needs or to lobby for social recognition. Crossdressers usually meet discreetly in small groups at a neighborhood hotel or at a private house. "Gabriela," a heterosexual crossdresser and friend of a group of university students that I met in a café in the Recoleta neighborhood, said that most of the crossdressers she knew lived in the wealthier *barrios* along the city's north shore. Perhaps this makes sense when the cost of maintaining both a male and female wardrobe is considered. Few *porteños* in the current economic climate of Buenos Aires can afford such an expense.

Nonetheless, estimates suggest that today there are over 50 000 hetero-sexual crossdressers in the Buenos Aires metropolitan area.

A major inhibiting factor in *porteño* society for accepting the gay and transvestite communities is the very macho and aggressive parade of masculinity that characterizes the male environment in Buenos Aires. Expressions of manliness and virility among *porteños*, argued James Scobie (1974, p. 228), stem from Argentina's gaucho heritage, where "sentiments or attachments represented unacceptable weaknesses or softness in a virile world." Moreover, the Catholic church exerts a tremendous moral influence over *porteños* and it continues to brand "alternative" lifestyles as sinful and deviant behavior.

Language is another important defining characteristic of the cultural city. *Porteños* speak a rich Buenos Aires slang called *lunfardo*, which originated in the southern, working-class, immigrant *barrios*. *Lunfardo* vocabulary has been enriched over the past 100 years by the mixture of ethnic groups, languages, and cultural identities in Buenos Aires and by the autochthonous indigenous idioms. Most *porteños* use this slang language in everyday speech, and *lunfardo* has been incorporated into tango lyrics, poetry, and literature. A classic example of the poetic use of slang is found in Carlos de la Púa's (1954) poem called "The Everyday Thrashing:"

La durmió de un cochete,	He knocked her out a slap,
gargajeó de un colmiyo	spat aside,
se arregló la melena	Fixed his hair
y pitándose un faso	and smoking a cigarette
salió de la atorranta	Left the shabby room
pieza del conventiyo	of the tenement house
y silbando bajito	And whistling low
rumbió pal escalso	he headed for the gambling den

In addition to *lunfardo*, many English words have become incorporated into the daily vocabulary of the *porteños*. Now that we have fleshed out the basic characteristics of *porteño* culture, let us journey into Buenos Aires' landscapes of pleasure and examine how and where *porteños* spend their leisure time.

Landscapes of pleasure

Certain areas of any city, as well as certain functions, are dedicated to the pursuit of pleasure. Entertainment and recreational landscapes are fundamental components of urban life and often they become defining characteristics of a city. Tokyo's Ginza District, Greenwich Village in

New York, Soho in London, Sydney's Kings Cross, and the Reeperbahn in Hamburg are just a few of the areas in world cities that are synonymous with entertainment and recreational activities. Globalization forces in the urban economy have a direct impact on landscapes of pleasure. Local and national governments strive to enhance the attractiveness of these landscapes in order to entice international tourists and the transnational élite. Moreover, local entrepreneurs in Buenos Aires have reacted to increased involvement in the global economy by investing capital in entertainment and recreational infrastructure. Plans are on the drawing board to enter a bid to host the quadrennial Olympic Games and the soccer World Cup tournament at some point in the future. Other projects involve the rehabilitation of industrial landscapes for leisure activities (for example, Puerto Madero). Some landscapes of pleasure have a distinctive physical location, character, and ambiance, while others are more intangible and often subject to the whims, fads, and fashions of the day. What ranks as the hottest nightclub, top restaurant, coziest café, or most tranquil park all are matters of personal taste and subjective judgment. Nonetheless, some level of continuity does exist in the general location of areas designated in any city as landscapes of pleasure. Although the general populace of Buenos Aires entertain themselves in a variety of different ways, landscapes of pleasure in the city can be divided into three general categories: sports and outdoor recreational activities, the arts, and nightlife. Activities in the latter two categories take place primarily in the downtown core of Buenos Aires, whereas outdoor activities are more dispersed across the various neighborhoods and municipalities of the city.

Sports and outdoor life

Buenos Aires has 17 major sports stadiums, dozens of yacht clubs, several racecourses, parks, and a growing number of golf and tennis courses to cater to the sporting needs of *porteños*. In addition, there are over 180 neighborhood athletic clubs and several North American-style health and fitness clubs scattered across the metropolitan region. However, of all the sports and outdoors activities enjoyed in Buenos Aires, none is as important to urban identity and sense of place as the game of soccer. Passion for soccer runs deep in Buenos Aires, pervading family, community, and *barrio* life. Unlike North American football, basketball, hockey, or baseball, where team loyalties usually are at the city level, support for soccer in Buenos Aires is rooted in the *barrio*. The *barrio* where a person is born or raised more often than not decides which team to support.

Although the national team represents Argentina and domestic soccer leagues draw teams from around the country, soccer is primarily a Buenos Aires affair. The major professional leagues are dominated by Buenos Aires clubs, and the national squad mostly comprises players from the big city teams such as Boca Juniors, River Plate, or Velez Sarsfield. Of the 20 teams that make up Division A soccer in Argentina, eight teams are located in the Federal District and six are found in the Greater Buenos Aires (GBA) suburbs. The city also has eight clubs playing in the second division. Buenos Aires' soccer stadiums dominate both skyline and *barrio* and function as important neighborhood landmarks. In La Boca, the stadium known affectionately as *La Bombonera* (the chocolate box) towers over the warehouses and two-story wooden buildings of the surrounding area. Covering two city blocks and reaching 60 meters into the air, *La Bombonera* becomes the focal point for interneighborhood passions and rivalries on game days. Unfortunately, in recent years gangs of rival La Boca and River Plate supporters have started to direct their energies toward antisocial behavior outside the arena.

Passion for Argentine soccer at the international level frequently brings together Argentinos of disparate political and economic persuasions. In the middle of a brutal and repressive period of military rule in the late 1970s, Buenos Aires hosted the 1978 soccer World Cup finals. Argentina won the championship, played at River Plate's Monumental Stadium along the north shore of the Río de la Plata. Success united both city and nation in an outpouring of emotional nationalism. Forgotten for a few joyous weeks were such mundane problems as the military's campaign of terror against political dissidents, divisive relationships between labor and management, and ideological clashes between right and left wing students.

A major figure in the cultural mythology of both city and nation is the soccer player, Diego Maradona. Since 1982, Maradona has become a cultural icon, a sports hero, and a personality of extraordinary talent who has made the headlines more often for his activities off the soccer field than on. Like thousands of aspiring soccer players, Maradona grew up in a poor working-class *barrio*, learning his craft on vacant lots in Villa Fiorita just beyond the Federal District. After playing for Boca Juniors in the immigrant neighborhood of La Boca, Maradona went off to Europe to make his fortune scoring goals for the Italian club, Napoli. Even though Maradona had not played on the Argentine national team for some time, having been suspended for cocaine abuse, overwhelming public support pressured the coach of the national team to place Maradona back on the squad in 1994. Buenos Aires had gone into shock during the 1994 World Cup qualifying games, when Colombia came into Monumental Stadium and thrashed Argentina's national team by five goals to zero. According to public sentiment, only Maradona could help the country survive a do-or-die playoff series against Australia and thus qualify for the final games in the United States. It would be a tragic blow to the national pysche if Argentina did not participate in the greatest sporting event in the world: the World Cup Finals. Argentina's President Menem even flew to the United States to watch the national team play their first match of the 1994 tournament against Greece in Boston's Foxboro Stadium. Maradona's suspension from the 1994 World Cup for substance abuse and the national team's unceremonial departure from the tournament caused tremendous anguish in Buenos Aires. Soccer afficionados may mourn for a few months and then rebound to cheer on a new campaign and new heroes, but Maradona will live in the hearts and minds of many *porteños* as perhaps the greatest soccer player of all time. In many ways, Maradona has become a metaphor for Argentine socioeconomic restructuring, raising the question of whether Argentina can be a modern country that plays by the rules of international society. Many *porteños* see Maradona as a victim, not as a gifted cheat from the *barrios* who thought he could play by his own rules. In Buenos Aires, *viveza criolla* or street-smartness still is a valued commodity, with quick fixes, rule-bending, and corruption frequently the preferred *modus operandi* in daily life.

On most days of the week, crowds of people can be found at the *hipódromos* or horse racing tracks that dot the landscape of Buenos Aires (Figure 8.1). Horse racing retains a huge following in Buenos Aires with regular meetings at the famous San Isidro stadium or in downtown Palermo. The five grandstands of Palermo's Hipódromo Argentino have changed little over the past century. They are divided into four distinct categories originally intended to separate high society from the commoners. A coat and tie dress code is still enforced for the center grandstand at Palermo. Horse racing of a different kind occurs on the polo fields. Buenos Aires is the home of Argentine polo, a game essentially for the rich which is played at the fashionable Hurlingham Club in Morón as well as in the Federal District at the Campo Argentino de Polo in Palermo. Popularized in Britain by Prince Charles and certainly overexposed in the Buenos Aires media at every opportunity, polo belongs almost exclusively to the landed gentry. Yet the sport has become a part of Argentina's national identity, known by most people but experienced by few.

One of the most popular outdoor activities for *porteños* is a weekend visit to the Paraná delta area in the suburbs of Tigre and San Fernando. The streams, canals, and backwaters of the Paraná delta have been a popular weekend refuge for urbanites since the late 1890s. Near Tigre's

Figure 8.1 San Isidro Racecourse along the north shore of the Río de la Plata, reproduced with permission from Juan A. Roccatagliata

railroad terminal, dozens of small wooden ferries jockey for position with larger cruise boats and eager rowers. These vessels crisscross the delta's waterways bringing residents and visitors alike to the restaurants, stone mansions, English-style cottages, and humble shacks scattered across the myriad islands of the delta. Rowing clubs with ostentatious clubhouses and huge grounds strategically positioned near the junction of the Luján and Tigre rivers primarily cater to the wealthier *porteños*, although membership is open to most urbanites. On most weekends, the boat ramps near these clubs spew determined rowers out on to the murky brown waters at a constant rate.

Porteños also flock to the city's major park complex in Palermo in huge numbers. With a zoo, botanic gardens, velodrome, tennis courts, planet- arium, horse riding trails, and paddle boats, the park is alive with people almost every day and night throughout the year. Smaller neigh- borhood parks and plazas also draw substantial numbers of people, particularly on Buenos Aires' warm spring and fall evenings. *Porteños* love to congregate in parks and plazas, especially for political rallies or protests. Plazas especially play a crucial role in the identity of Buenos Aires' residents. For example, every Thursday a group known around the world as the Mothers of the Plaza de Mayo gather in front of the Casa Rosada (presidential palace) in the heart of downtown Buenos Aires. The Mothers have been protesting in the Plaza de Mayo for over 16 years against the disappearance of thousands of young people, including their own children, during the brutal military *Proceso* of the late 1970s (Bouvard 1994). For the Mothers, the Plaza de Mayo has become their world stage, a symbolic location from which to pursue their search for justice, as well as a symbol of political power.

Arts and entertainment

Buenos Aires always has prided itself on being a cultured, civilized, European city and *porteños* are avid supporters of the arts and popular entertainment. According to many *porteños*, the physical remoteness of Buenos Aires from Europe is simply a question of geography, not one of culture, sophistication, or style. *Porteños* are extremely proud of, and vocal about, their city's cultural life. Everyone seems to have an intimate and personal relationship with each *confitería* (café), theater, plaza, discotheque, and museum in Buenos Aires. Indeed, cultural and intellectual life in Buenos Aires remains unrivaled in Latin America and is matched by few of the major world cities.

In a study of pre-World War II Buenos Aires, Richard Walter (1993) observed of the city's social classes that development since 1910 was marked as much by continuity as by change. The same observation can be made about the development of the cultural city since the 1940s. The *gente bién* or upper classes still concentrate in the northern *barrios* and orient much of their daily lives around *el microcentro* (the downtown core). Newspapers and magazines in Buenos Aires continue to report on the parties, celebrations, travels, scandals, marriages, and divorces of the social aristocracy. Performances at the famous Colón Theater on Plaza Lavalle still attract the doyens of Buenos Aires society, with tuxedoed men and suntanned women in fur coats alighting from limousines and taxis, setting the standards of urban fashion, taste, and elegance.

Over 70 museums, 130 art galleries, and nearly 50 functioning theaters are found in Buenos Aires, offering everything from opera to drama and comedy. Thousands of public lectures are presented annually in the city on topics as diverse as Greek archaeology and the presence of alien life on earth. High levels of literacy and education among both the élites and the ordinary *porteños* in Buenos Aires spur an almost insatiable demand for the printed word. The city has a strong and internationally renowned literary tradition. Jorge Luis Borges, Ernesto Sábato, María Elena Walsh, Carlos Guido Spano, Raúl Scalabrini Ortiz, and Rubén Dário are just a few of the literary notables who have celebrated their love for, and frustrations with, Buenos Aires in novels, poems, and short stories.

Kiosks located strategically around the downtown core sell magazines, newspapers, and journals from around the world, although the US$17 price tag for a Sunday New York Times in April 1993 probably was beyond the financial means of most *porteños* and visitors! The

Figure 8.2 Avenida Lavalle, the entertainment center of Buenos Aires

concentration of bookstores and kiosks along the pedestrianized Avenida Florída, the most popular street in Buenos Aires, is unmatched elsewhere in Latin America. Major city newspapers include *La Prensa, La Nación, Clarín,* and the English-language *Buenos Aires Herald,* each offering a unique and often biased view of daily events at home and overseas. There are over 750 bookstores in Buenos Aires and 140 public libraries. Dozens of radio stations play music that runs the gamut of styles from tango to classical, heavy metal, and urban rap. Buenos Aires has four major television stations, as well as access to the global information network via cable, satellite, and the now ubiquitous CNN. In addition to dozens of museums, galleries, and concert halls in the Federal District, there is a tremendous concentration of cinemas and theaters in the downtown core. The pedestrians-only Avenida Lavalle between Avenidas 9 de Julio and Florída is home to Buenos Aires cinema with 16 screens (Figure 8.2). Other cinemas are located close to Lavalle on Avenidas Suipacha, Santa Fé, and Corrientes, the latter considered the "Broadway" of Buenos Aires. Cinema attendance in Buenos Aires, however, has declined since the early 1980s, in part because of the rapid growth of the home video market. In 1980, over 24 million people attended a cinema in the Federal District (República Argentina 1993a). By 1992, the total number of spectators had dropped to just over 10 million.

Entertainment choices for *porteños* on any given day are many and varied, and reflect the importance of global culture in daily life. During the last week of April 1993, for example, 54 cinema screens in the downtown core and 13 screens in the surrounding *barrios* were showing both popular English-language as well as European and Latin films. At the Ideal Theater *porteños* could watch *Lorenzo's Oil*, *The Bodyguard* played at the Iguazu, *Last of the Mohicans* screened at the Suipacha, *Unforgiven* at the Monumental, *The Crying Game* at the Ambassador, and *Hoffa* at the Normandie. The titles of North American films often do not translate literally into Spanish and some amusing titles result. For example, *Home Alone* became *My Poor Little Angel*, and *Sister Act* was retitled as *A Change of Habit*. Moreover, there is a tendency to add a spicy, sexual element to film titles whenever possible. *The Sound of Music* ran under the provocative title of *The Rebel Nun*!

At the Colón Theater, *porteños* and visitors could enjoy a performance by the Buenos Aires Philharmonic Orchestra on Monday evening, Berg's opera *Lulú* on Tuesday, Friday, and Sunday, and the Moscow Philharmonic on Wednesday and Thursday. Performances of *Cyrano* and *Species in Danger*, among others, were available at the General San Martín Municipal Theater on Avenida Corrientes. *El Loco de Asis*, Florencio Sánchez's *En Familia*, and *Electra* played at the Cervantes National Theater on Avenida Libertad. At Café Tortini on Avenida de Mayo, patrons could enjoy the jazz and blues music of the Creole Jazz Band, and *Jesus Christ Superstar* played at L'Orange on Avenida Corrientes. Dozens of other musical comedies, dramas, concerts, recitals, and ballets were on offer at myriad clubs, cafés, theaters, and auditoriums in the downtown core of Buenos Aires.

Buenos Aires after dark

Porteños are creatures of the night. An evening out on the town for food and entertainment, known locally as *una salida*, generally starts late and ends at dawn. *Porteños* have over 13 000 restaurants and bars to choose from in the Federal District alone, and can prepare themselves for a night on the town at over 3000 beauty and barber shops. The most popular restaurants along the Costanera, in San Telmo, or in the downtown core begin to fill up with customers after 10 o'clock in the evening and really begin to hop around midnight. Many of the city's nightclubs do not even open their doors to customers until after midnight. The *Transnoche* or weekend late-night shows at the cinemas are extremely popular, and often begin at one-thirty in the morning. As in any city, the names, ownership, and popularity of nightclubs, dance halls, restaurants, and bars change as frequently as fashion and the economy dictate, although location usually remains a constant. Many of Buenos Aires' most popular nightspots have undergone several incarnations since the late 1980s. This process is part of the dynamic, ever-changing urban theater within which the daily drama of life in Buenos Aires is played out. For example, one of the hot places for *porteño* youth to be during 1991 was the Samovar de Rasputín blues bar in the La Boca neighborhood. In the more upscale Recoleta district, a bar called Newport attracted the upwardly mobile crowd in droves. Some bar and nightclub owners still complain bitterly about police corruption and the ubiquitous problem of the "protection" rackets. Periodic police raids often are designed to intimidate owners into paying a monthly "fee" for protection against customer harrassment. However, bars and nightclubs frequented by Buenos Aires' gay community, such as the Bunker club in Barrio Norte, continue to be the targets of discrimination and police persecution.

Buenos Aires does not have a clearly defined zone that could be characterized as a "red light" district. Unlike Times Square in New York, Soho in London, or certain parts of the Ginza in Tokyo, Buenos Aires' "activities of the flesh" remain somewhat decentralized. Escort services and massage parlors are scattered over the downtown area, most operating relatively discreetly from a phone service or in an upstairs apartment along one of the main avenues. The famous brothels of Calle Necochea in La Boca have long since disappeared along with authentic tango music. Now lined with pizzerías and garish cantinas, Necochea attracts mostly middle-class urbanites and tourists and is reminiscent of San Francisco's North Beach or Soho in London.

Crime has become a serious problem in Buenos Aires since 1989 and many critics blame the government's globalization policies for the deterioration in public safety. Growing social polarization has forced increasing numbers of *porteños* closer to the poverty line, many of whom turn to criminal activities in order to survive. Middle-class suburbs especially to the west and north of the downtown area increasingly are becoming targets for petty criminals. As a result of rising crime rates and poor police protection in the suburbs, many wealthier suburbanites are moving back into the Federal District, where crime is perceived to be much lower. The Federal District does have 35 000 police, one for every 85 residents, which is a ratio far superior to that enjoyed in the suburbs. However, contrary to popular perception, public safety in the Federal District has declined since 1980. In 1991, the delinquency rate in the Federal District was 144.5 per 1000 habitants, compared with 81.5 in 1980. Although overall crime rates in the downtown area have declined since peaking in 1988, serious crimes such as burglary, carjacking, armed robbery, and murder are on the increase. Like any major city, residents and visitors alike are prone to such crimes as muggings, purse-snatching, sexual offences, and petty theft.

Moreover, drug use has increased dramatically since 1989, with cocaine the recreational drug of choice among wealthier *porteños* and students. Buenos Aires has become one of South America's most important shipment points to North America and Europe for cocaine. Many *porteños* believe that the Bolivians and Peruvians who have migrated to the city in recent years are responsible for the recent upsurge in drug-related criminal activity, although official statistics do not support their argument. Nonetheless, despite increasing problems with drugs and crime, Buenos Aires remains a relatively safe city compared to other major urban areas of the world. Tourists especially appreciate the ability to roam the streets of Buenos Aires' many *barrios* safely and without fear of personal injury, although certain areas of the city should be avoided after dark.

Tourist landscapes and the commodification of place

Intimately related to the evolution of a world city's social and cultural infrastructure is the development of its tourist potential. Many world cities long have functioned as major tourist destinations in the global system (for example, London, New York, and Paris). Others cities such as Buenos Aires, Sydney, Miami, and Tokyo are beginning to exploit the attention generated by world city processes by commodifying and packaging urban events, mythologies, and infrastructure in an attempt to lure both regional and global tourists. Tourism is one of the fastest growing sectors of the global economy and it can have a profound effect on urban identity and sense of place. Tourist arrivals in Argentina from foreign sources have been increasing at a steady rate since 1982, when 1.3 million visitors came to the country. By 1993, the number of annual foreign visitors had surpassed 3 million (Repúblic Argentina 1993a). Approximately 85 percent of all visitors to Buenos Aires come from the Americas, with Uruguay and Chile alone accounting for nearly 60 percent. About 10 percent of the city's tourists come from Europe and the remaining 5 percent come from the rest of the world. The average length of stay by visitors from contiguous countries is 5 days, whereas visitors from overseas generally stay twice as long. Government officials in Buenos Aires estimated that the tourism industry has an impact of over US$2 billion annually on the domestic economy. Tourism in both Argentina and Buenos Aires is the third largest industry after petrochemicals and automobiles, and accounts for 6 percent of GNP. Since 1989, tourism has been growing at rates of up to 8 percent annually and over 42 000 jobs are being created each year. In 1993, nearly 500 000 people were engaged directly in tourist activities, with many thousands more engaged indirectly (*Buenos Aires Herald* May 12, 1993, p. 12).

If the commodification of urban images, mythologies, and landscapes plays a central role in the tourism industry, what images are being commodified and sold in Buenos Aires? The city does not have the physical attributes of Rio de Janeiro, Sydney, or San Francisco and therefore relies heavily on more culturally based marketing strategies. In particular, Buenos Aires sells its Europeanized image as the "Paris of Latin America" and relies on the city's art, entertainment, and business sectors to attract visitors. Buenos Aires' tourist landscapes can be divided into six major districts: *el microcentro* or the downtown core, the southern "old quarter," the fashionable neighborhood of Recoleta, the recreational area of Palermo, *el macrocentro* or the fringe neighborhoods of the Federal District, and the outer suburbs. Each of these six tourist districts is packaged and commodified in a different manner, depending on the specific cultural iconography, mythology, or landscape deemed of interest to visitors.

El microcentro

The downtown core of Buenos Aires, known locally as *el microcentro* is the heart and soul of the city's tourist landscapes. Most visitors to Buenos Aires headquarter themselves in *el microcentro* as the majority of the city's shops, restaurants, bars, cafés, cinemas, hotels, and transportation nodes are located here. In the central city area, about 30 major landmarks and sites comprise the core of the tourist experience in Buenos Aires (Figure 8.3). Stretching approximately 12 city blocks from north to south and 16 city blocks from east to west, *el microcentro* is anchored by four major sites. Retiro station and the Plaza General San Martín mark the northeastern boundary, and the Plaza de Mayo functions as the southeastern boundary of the downtown core. Avenida de Mayo from the Plaza de Mayo to the Congress complex functions as the southern boundary, Avenida Santa Fé functions as the northern boundary, and Avenida Callao marks the boundary between the downtown core and the inner city suburbs. The most important landmarks and historical sites in Buenos Aires are located within the downtown core, and the majority of the city's visitors circulate through this zone. The built landscape of *el microcentro* is changing as global capital flows into the city. Luxury international hotels, upscale boutiques, postmodern shopping malls, and recreational facilities provide evidence of new circuits of capital in Buenos Aires and suggest a realignment of traditional patterns of tourism.

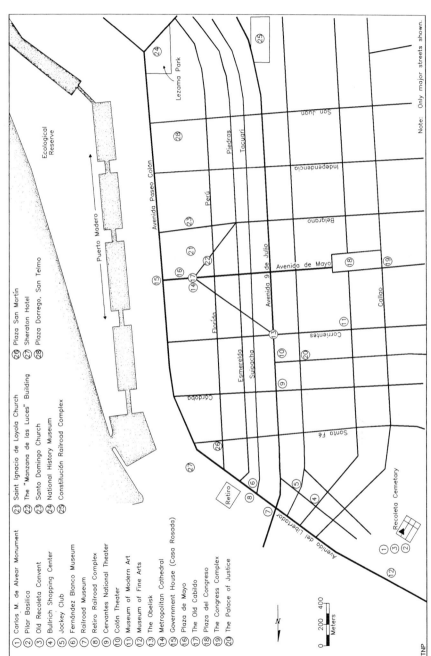

Figure 8.3 Major cultural landmarks and tourist destinations in the downtown core of Buenos Aires, 1994. *Source*: After Wheaton (1990)

① Carlos M. de Alvear Monument
② Pilar Basilica
③ Old Recoleta Convent
④ Bullrich Shopping Center
⑤ Jockey Club
⑥ Fernández Blanco Museum
⑦ Railroad Museum
⑧ Retiro Railroad Complex
⑨ Cervantes National Theater
⑩ Colón Theater
⑪ Museum of Modern Art
⑫ Museum of Fine Arts
⑬ The Obelisk
⑭ Metropolitan Cathedral
⑮ Government House (Casa Rosada)
⑯ Plaza de Mayo
⑰ The Old Cabildo
⑱ Plaza del Congreso
⑲ The Congress Complex
⑳ The Palace of Justice
㉑ Saint Ignacio de Loyola Church
㉒ The "Manzana de las Luces" Building
㉓ Santo Domingo Church
㉔ National History Museum
㉕ Constitución Railroad Complex
㉖ Plaza San Martín
㉗ Sheraton Hotel
㉘ Plaza Dorrego, San Telmo

Note: Only major streets shown.

TNP

A footbridge and several walkways lead from the commercial center to the Costanera Sur, a prolongation of the reclaimed Río de la Plata shoreline. Palm trees, statues, and old stone arches grace the area that accommodates the School of Fine Arts, Naval Observatory, and Boca Juniors sports complex. Ciudad Deportiva is built on a series of landfill islands that pushed back the shoreline of the river. In the mid-1960s, some 70 hectares of private land were donated to the club for development, but like many projects in Buenos Aires funding dried up and the complex remains incomplete. A bird sanctuary occupies open land along the Costanera Sur behind the Boca club. Just off Avenida Belgrano, east of the Puerto Madero docks, sits an old café called Munich that doubles as the Museum of Telecommunications. Built in 1927 by a German architect, the Munich building is an excellent example of *porteño* fascination with European architecture and design. Distinctly out of place among the industrial dock buildings, the Munich café looks as if it belongs in southern Bavaria, with turrets, stained-glass windows, and gnomes carved into the walls. Puerto Madero, the decommissioned port area between the Plaza de Mayo and the Costanera, is undergoing extensive rehabilitation (see Chapter 4). Planners and architects are drawing on the experiences of inner city renovation schemes in cities such as Baltimore, London, and Sydney in an attempt to revitalize this run-down section of Buenos Aires.

Tango and the Old Quarter

San Telmo, La Boca, and Barracas south of the Plaza de Mayo in the city center are packaged as the "Old Quarter." Here tourists can experience the historic colonial ambience and immigrant lifestyles of Buenos Aires, replete with nineteenth century housing, red brick warehouses, tango clubs, and artists of all types. The area's edges are the Riachuelo, Parque Lezama, and Avenida Paseo Colón. Few visitors venture across the Riachuelo river into the industrial neighborhoods of Avellaneda and Quilmes. San Telmo coalesced during the eighteenth and nineteenth centuries around the Plaza Dorrego. Original settlers in the *barrio* included fishermen and dockhands, many of whom were of Genoese, African, Creole, or Irish extraction. Today, the Plaza hosts a weekly Flea market, and is a popular spot for painters, filet designers, musicians, and antique dealers (Figure 8.4). One of the most popular spots in the Old Quarter is a narrow alley known as Caminito, situated between Magallanes and Lamadrid streets in La Boca across from the Rocha harbor (Figure 8.5). The area's modest two-story houses are painted in bright pastels, deep reds, and muddy browns, and the alleyway is lined

Figure 8.4 Plaza Dorrego in San Telmo

Figure 8.5 Caminito, the artists' street in the *barrio* of La Boca

with sculptures and murals by renowned Argentine artists. In 1986, the city decreed that every January the Quinqela Martín Festival of Color be held along Caminito, and throughout the year neighborhood artists gather to show and sell their work. Caminito was named after a tango composed by a La Boca resident, Juan de Dios Filiberto.

As Buenos Aires' most authentic form of popular music, the tango is inseparable from the history of the city and functions as a major component of landscape and cultural mythology. Indeed, the tango functions as an important cultural metaphor for daily life in Buenos Aires. It is one of the city's most commodified items, and tourists flock to the many clubs and restaurants in the Old Quarter in search of the "authentic" tango dance. Tango music came to life during the 1880s in the backstreets of the city's immigrant *barrios* and on the fields and muddy roads of the *arrabales* (urban fringes). The rapid growth of Buenos Aires after its federalization in 1880 attracted a polyglot mixture of *criollos* from the poor interior provinces, discharged soldiers, descendants of African slaves, and Italian, Spanish, Jewish, and East European immigrants. These groups' myriad cultural "voices" merged and blended in the tenements and on the street corners of the expanding *barrios*. Music became an important expression of the changing mood of Buenos Aires' new urbanites, with its focus on such personal concerns as individual experiences, love, female betrayal, and the changing landscapes of *barrio* and community. In the bars and bordellos of La Boca, San Telmo, and the port district, flamenco guitars, Italian flutes, *criollo* milongas, and African candombles fused together the melodies of the early tango. The rapidly changing urban environment featured prominently in early tango lyrics, as the songs summarized the new urban experiences of the first generation of *porteños*. For example, a popular tango laments changes in what would become one of the city's most well-known tourist areas:

Caminito of what you once were
bordered by clover and flowering rushes
a shadow soon you will be
a shadow, just like me.

Other tangos focused on specific areas or streets and anthropomorphized their characteristics. "An Alley of Pompeya" ("Sobre El Pucho"), "A Street in Barracas al Sud" ("Silbando"), and "The Love Nest on Calle Ayacucho" ("El Bulín de la Calle Ayacucho"), for example, all focused on specific locations and were characterized by nostalgia for the past (Walter 1993, p. 101). Streets began to take on unique and personal characteristics and played powerful roles in the *porteños*' emerging sense of place and urban identity. The "'Corrientes' Tango" (1926) both praises and curses the "Broadway" of Buenos Aires:

Corrientes . . . . Street of Vice
One Night You Intoxicated Me With Your Wickedness
And the Venom You Gave Me Was So Strong
    That Nobody Could Resist
    Your Fatal Brilliance

Corrientes . . . . Damned Street,
I Shall Never Exchange You For My Suburban Slum
Even Though There Are Times When I Want To Abandon You
I Cannot Leave You
Street Of My Wickedness

By the turn of the twentieth century, the vulgar dance and music of the tango had become a cultural phenomenon, scorned by the culturally conservative élite as lascivious and extremely common. Manuel Gálvez (1910, p. 129), one of Argentina's leading Nationalist writers, derided the tango as a "product of cosmopolitanism, hybrid and ugly music, . . . a grotesque dance, . . . the embodiment of our national disarray." Part of Gálvez's distaste for tango music stemmed from the reputation of Buenos Aires at that time as the epicenter of white slave traffic in the Southern Cone. From the perspective of both the provincials and the urban élite, much of Buenos Aires was seen as a great market of human flesh, where prostitution, white slavery, and sexual decadence ran rampant (see Guy 1991). Tango music encapsulated all that the élite deemed distasteful about lower-class urban life.

Respectability for the tango came only after its acceptance in the nightclubs of New York, Paris, and Berlin. Success for the tango in Europe allowed it to be embraced by the Buenos Aires urban élite, who were awed by, and enamoured of, European fashions, fads, and ideologies. Among Buenos Aires' urban aristocracy, the tango quickly was adopted as a symbol of national creativity. However, although transformed from neighborhood ballad to international anthem, the tango and its lyrics retained their focus on landscapes, relationships, and personal concerns. Moreover, many élite *porteños* still despised what the music represented: the rise of an urban middle class that challenged the élite's monopoly on power.

Tango became a national commodity after 1917 with the success of a little-known musician called Carlos Gardel. Himself an immigrant from either France or Uruguay (nobody is really sure), Gardel came to epitomize both *porteño* and tango. A career in movies and radio catapulated Gardel to stardom, and between 1929 and 1935 he enjoyed fame throughout the Americas. Gardel's death in a plane crash in 1935 secured his place in Buenos Aires' cultural mythology. Carlos Gardel became an icon, a legendary figure in tango folklore, and the object of much adulation. Even today, if someone has reached the peak of individual achievement, he or she is likely to be called "Gardel." Thus, both Gardel and the tango have become major commodities in the marketing of Buenos Aires' tourist landscapes. Gardel's plaque-covered tomb in Chacarita cemetery near Lacroze railroad station is an important

Figure 8.6 The tomb of Carlos Gardel in Chacarita Cemetery

pilgrimage site for his legions of fans and is one of the most visited attractions in Buenos Aires (Figure 8.6). Although the tango has become a symbol of Buenos Aires and an important cultural export, it has struggled to survive since the 1950s against the onslaught of newer musical forms such as rock-and-roll. The La Boca and San Telmo districts retain the essence of the tango in many nightclubs and bars, yet spontaneous tango is not easy to find. Tango music and dancing have become a respectable, middle-class folk phenomenon, packaged for tourists at US$40 and upwards per show and somewhat lacking the sexuality and emotion of earlier years.

Recoleta and the landscapes of the dead

Recoleta, northwest of the downtown core, remains the most fashionable area in Buenos Aires. The *barrio* takes its name from a Franciscan convent, which dates from the early eighteenth century, and it became a favorite location among upper-class *porteños* during the latter half of the nineteenth century. Visitors to Buenos Aires are drawn to the *barrio* by the famous Recoleta Cemetery, which contains the impressive sepulchers of the city's rich and powerful. Other important landmarks near the cemetery include the eighteenth century Pilar basilica, the recently renovated Recoleta Cultural Center, the Museum of Fine Arts, an old convent, and a variety of plazas (see Figure 8.3). The Buenos Aires School of Law sits across from the Fine Arts museum and the antiquated

Figure 8.7 Recoleta Cemetery and the landscapes of the dead

Ital Amusement Park fronts Avenida Libertador near the boundary with the *barrio* of Retiro.

After decades of dining at Au Bec Fin and drinking coffee and eating rich desserts at the Café de la Paix, the *porteño* élite move ceremoniously into Recoleta Cemetery (Figure 8.7). Recoleta is the "marble heart" of Buenos Aires, where class, family name, or military rank are necessary to assure a coveted place among the ostentatious mausoleums (Wheaton 1990). The city's most revered figures are honored not on the day of their birth but on the day of their death! One of the cemetery's most visited tombs contains the body of Eva Duarte Perón. A plaque above the Duarte family tomb states "Volveré y seré millones" (I will return and be millions), a reference to Evita's popularity among the city's working classes. During her short life (she died in 1952 in her early thirties), Evita Perón became a symbol of hope to the urban masses. She encouraged legislation which gave women the vote, and through the Eva Perón Foundation she built schools, clinics, orphanages, and old age homes for the city's working class. Evita generated a cult following among the Buenos Aires poor with regular distributions of food, money, medicine, and clothes (Lewis 1990). Her humble rural background and extraordinary public presence generated a cult of personality that remains strong to this day. Posters of Evita adorn the city streets, people hang framed pictures of her in their houses, often creating a mini-shrine to their heroine, and her grave remains a popular pilgrimage site. Evita's ghostwritten autobiography, *La Razón de mi vida*, even became required reading in the schools after her death. Evita Perón is both myth and icon, an enduring legacy of attempts to create a social state in Argentina and to better the lives of the urban masses. Whether you love or hate her, agree or disagree with her politics, or find the entire personality worship cult too unusual, there can be no doubt that Eva Perón remains a powerful part of Buenos Aires' urban identity and sense of place.

Palermo parks

Tourists and residents alike converge on the open, verdant spaces of Tres de Febrero Park in the heart of Palermo. As Buenos Aires' major inner-city green space, the park belongs to the urban masses even though it is located in a resolutely upper middle class *barrio*. The Palermo neighborhood contains parks, gardens, embassies, and museums, a zoo, racetrack, and world-class polo field, and the Rural Society show-grounds, pride of the Argentine rural élite. During August, the annual Cattle Show becomes the focal point of the Buenos Aires social calendar, with enough pomp, ceremony, and blue-ribboned champions to last the entire year. Many *porteños* involved in Buenos Aires' "gray" economy ply their trade in the park area. Ice cream vendors, portrait takers, sweet peanuts and popcorn sellers, professional dog walkers, and young artisans vie for attention and space along the many paths and sidestreets that crisscross the park. Palermo is the place to see and be seen in Buenos Aires, especially on a Sunday afternoon.

El macrocentro

The outer suburbs of the Federal District are not packaged or com-modified like the areas and landmarks of the downtown core. Essentially, the landscapes of this area are for those visitors who want to explore the city by themselves and who are confident enough to venture off the beaten track. Those who do usually head for the Parque de Diversiones (Amusement Park) in the southwest corner of the Federal District or to one of the small parks or *barrios* that make up the outer area of the central city. Chacarita Cemetery is a popular destination and perhaps is best known as the location of arguably the world's largest urban cemetery. Occupying nearly half of the *barrio's* territory, Chacarita Cemetery contains the tombs of notables such as President Juan Domingo Perón, tango singer Carlos Gardel, aviator Jorge Newbery, comedian Luis Sandrini, and Madre María Salomé, a disciple of famous healer Pancho Sierra. The cemetery also is the last resting place of most ordinary *porteños*, many of whom are buried in simple plots to the west of the more impressive mausoleums or have their ashes stored in urns displayed in small wall openings along Chacarita's northern edge. Although less elegant and famous than Recoleta Cemetery, Chacarita does receive a significant number of daily visitors. Tourists frequently find their way here to marvel at the impressive tombs or to pay homage at the graves of Gardel or Madre María. In the northwest corner of the complex sit the British and German cemeteries, where headstones and sepulchers provide excellent insights into the importance of both cultures to Buenos Aires society. The names on the graves may not be immediately recognizable, but they are a powerful testimony to the influence that Britain had over the city during the nineteenth century and the Germans have had since the 1920s.

The urban–rural fringe

The final area of importance to the tourist industry in Buenos Aires is the urban–rural fringe. Again, few tourists venture to the periurban zones of Buenos Aires independently unless they are taking a day trip to the Paraná delta zone around Tigre, to the Basilica at Luján, or to the city of La Plata. Although several of the urban satellite cities such as Chascomús, San Antonio de Areco, Lobos, and Mercedes offer sites of interest to visitors, a well-developed and sophisticated tourist information system does not exist in Buenos Aires to market these areas. Many foreign visitors are intimidated by the public transport system in Buenos Aires, by the high rental car prices, and by the city's aggressive drivers. Nonetheless, the more experienced visitors and hardy explorers are rewarded for their efforts to absorb the city's suburban atmosphere by the diversity of the social and cultural landscapes found beyond the Federal District's boundary.

In terms of sense of place and cultural landmarks, the city of Luján perhaps is the most important of GBAs' suburban centers. Located approximately 65 kilometers from the Plaza de Mayo, Luján grew after the seventeenth century as an important stop along the cart road west toward Upper Peru. However, Luján is better known today as the holy city of Argentina, site of a huge neo-Gothic basilica (finished in the 1930s) dedicated to the Virgin Mary. Legend suggests that a cart carrying two small statues of the Virgin from Brazil to Peru in 1630 became stuck crossing the Río Luján. Only after removing one of the statues would the cart finally move, so the driver reasoned that this was a sign to build a chapel for the statue at that location. Today nearly five million people annually visit the basilica to pay homage to the Virgin.

Twice a year, in May and October, masses of people make the pilgrimage from downtown Buenos Aires to the basilica, many walking the entire distance. Especially important is the *Peregrinación de la Juventud* (Youth Pilgrimage), which began as a silent protest against the military government during the "Dirty War" of the late 1970s.

Not surprisingly, one of the more popular experiences for visitors to Buenos Aires is a tour of an "authentic" *estancia* (ranch) located on the Pampas at the edge of the metropolis. Although the *gauchos* (horsemen of the Pampas) disappeared in the nineteenth century, their image, dress, and customs have become an important component of the city's mythology. Many an urbanite believes that she or he has retained some aspect of the *gaucho's* famed skills and fierce independence. Gauchos have entered national folklore as somewhat idealized symbols of freedom and autonomy. Tours from Buenos Aires to a *fiesta gaucha* generally head west or northwest to one of the *estancias* on the urban fringe. The *estancia* experience usually includes examples of regional song and dance, horse riding, *gaucho* sports, national food and wine, and country life. Urban tourists thus are exposed to a neatly packaged rural environment that symbolizes the quiet gentility of life on the pampas far from the madding crowds.

Although tourist landscapes in Buenos Aires are becoming crucial components of the city's global image, the packaging and commodification of these landscapes still are in the initial stages of development. For example, unlike London, Paris, or Tokyo, Buenos Aires does not have a tourist bus route that circulates through the city at regular intervals calling at the more important landmarks. Moreover, many of the myths, icons, and landmarks that define the urban identity of Buenos Aires are being homogenized for mass-market appeal and are losing the individuality that made them so appealing to begin with. The *gaucho* ideal, the urban angst of the tango, the controversial social justice ideology of Juan and Evita Perón, the neighborhood of the struggling immigrants, and the intimacy of the *barrio* have lost that essential character that helped to shape a unique urban identity and sense of place. Do world city and global economic processes inevitably lead to the homogenization of a city's unique characteristics? Are world cities experiencing the "Disneyfication" of their cultural and tourist landscapes? Is location the only component that distinguishes the tourist experience in Buenos Aires from the tourist experience in London or New York? For example, many international airports, hotels, restaurants, nightclubs, and packaged tours in cities around the world seem to be cast from the same mold. The internationalization of tourist landscapes in world cities certainly offers fertile ground for future research into the implications of global socioeconomic restructuring. In Buenos Aires, globalization processes are encouraging a certain level of homogenization in the cultural landscapes.

The latinamericanization of Buenos Aires

Up until the 1940s, Buenos Aires remained essentially a white European city inhabited primarily by the Spanish, Italians, Germans, European Jews, and the English. Since 1945, however, massive migration from the interior and from neighboring countries has changed the ethnic complexity of Buenos Aires. Guy Bourdé (1974) has termed this process the nationalization or latinamericanization of urban society. The influx of mestizos and indigenous peoples from the interior, as well as Koreans, Japanese, and Vietnamese from Asia, has reshaped the social and cultural dynamics of Buenos Aires and has precipitated what some have called the end of the European myth.

After the federalization of Buenos Aires in the 1880s, the urban élite began to echo the sigh of Brazilian Eduardo Prado, who contended, "Without a doubt the world is Paris" (Burns 1980, p. 20). The more Buenos Aires culturally and architecturally resembled Paris, the greater the degree of order, progress, civilization, and sophistication the city (and, by extension, the nation) could claim. Mentally, if not physically, the *porteño* aristocracy attempted to replicate the Parisian identity in Buenos Aires. To be recognized as the "Paris of Latin America" was the highest honor for Buenos Aires, and the European myth became a metaphor for the hopes, dreams, and ambitions of those who strove to shape the future destiny of the city. Throughout the twentieth century, the identity of Buenos Aires has evolved and changed in the shadow of the European myth. For many *porteños*, it is an insult to label Buenos Aires as a "Third World" city or to suggest that the city be compared to urban centers from developing countries.

As the twentieth century draws to a close, empirical evidence suggests that Buenos Aires has more in common with its regional contemporaries today than at any time in its long and eventful history. Just like other Latin American cities, Buenos Aires is attempting to cope with the growth of shantytowns, massive environmental degradation, the ongoing migration of *mestizos* and indigenous peoples from rural areas, increasing regional economic and social integration, urban deindustrialization, and with the realignment of regional political relationships. Buenos Aires is undergoing a process of latinamericanization that will have profound consequences for the city's future identity, urban relationships, and role in the global network. Buenos Aires no longer is a European city transplanted in Latin America; the European myth has ended. The city's ethnic, economic, social, and cultural composition is becoming more complex as globalization and regionalization processes change the dynamics of national, regional, and international relationships. Contemporary Buenos Aires is being reshaped by the realities of Latin America's new role in the global system.

As Horacio Vásquez Rial (1993) puts it, the crisis of a national cultural identity has hindered the development and consolidation of democracy in Argentina. A failure to acknowledge the real boundaries of national culture, boundaries which incorporate not only Buenos Aires but the interior provinces, exacerbated cultural isolationism in Buenos Aires and contributed to the structural weakness of Argentina. If both city and nation are to survive in the post-Cold War stage of finance capitalism, reinsertion into the world economy is crucial. Because economics and culture are inextricably intertwined, however, this means that the world must have access to Argentine culture and Argentine culture must be receptive to a broad array of international cultural influences. Reconstructing urban culture would be easier, for example, if *porteños* stopped comparing themselves to France, Italy, and Spain and substituted an image of their own potential for the foreign model (Martínez 1993). Adopting foreign models and ideologies without an appreciation of the implications for local culture can be extremely detrimental over time and can create a distorted sense of urban identity. What does the end of the European myth mean for future Buenos Aires? In the concluding chapter, I offer an interpretation of the likely direction of Buenos Aires' development during the coming years.

9

Future Buenos Aires

A concluding chapter on Buenos Aires seems inappropriate when one considers that the city is in dynamic flux, undergoing constant reshaping, redirection, and restructuring. Rather, this chapter serves as a statement or summary of the journey so far, with a brief analysis of the potential and possibilities for future Buenos Aires. The dynamic, ever-changing nature of world cities and the global economy make it impossible to predict with any degree of confidence the development path that Buenos Aires might follow. How citizens, politicians, institutions, and urban managers respond to the problems facing Buenos Aires depends on myriad circumstances that have yet to unfold. There is no crystal ball to foresee the likely success or failure of Buenos Aires' attempt to participate more fully in the global economy and to enhance its world city status. In the preceding pages, I have attempted to bring to the fore some of the more pressing issues for Buenos Aires as it copes with the dynamic tensions of globalization. What becomes clear in this analysis of Buenos Aires is that the urban management crisis is not new. The city has struggled to cope with megacephalous growth and rapid change since the beginning of the twentieth century. Moreover, debate over whether or not Buenos Aires is a world city in the context developed by John Friedmann (1986) seems moot. The city does exhibit fairly weak global and regional control functions by virtue of its location in the global periphery and its historical role as a primary producer and supplier of raw materials to the industrial centers of the North Atlantic economy. Yet it functions as a world city in many other important ways. Thus, the world city hypothesis has been applied not in a dichotomous way but as a method of establishing the city's position and its functions along a continuum of world city characteristics. Buenos Aires stands out in Latin America as an excellent example of how global economic change interfaces with local urban processes to shape world cities in profound and critical ways.

The realities of contemporary global economic restructuring argue for a redefinition of development strategies for Buenos Aires. As Argentina's government struggles to carve out a niche for both city and nation in the global system, it must be cognizant of the negative, neutral, and positive aspects of socioeconomic restructuring. Importantly, planning and policy making in Buenos Aires must not occur in a vacuum, as the city plays a crucial role in spatial articulation at the local, national, regional, hemispheric, and global levels. To ignore the centrifugal and centripetal implications of urban restructuring in Buenos Aires for relationships along the local–global continuum would be to invite the potential for more serious urban crises in the immediate future. Democracy in Argentina still is in a fragile condition and any major social upheavals in the nation's primary city could trigger serious challenges to the democratic process.

Perhaps the most sensitive issue to arise from Buenos Aires' socioeconomic restructuring experiences is the ongoing marginalization of distinct segments of society and of certain neighborhoods in the city. Social polarization in Buenos Aires is a reality. Increased numbers of people are living in poverty, too many children are dying from disease and starvation, crime and racism are on the increase, suicides among the elderly appear to have reached epidemic levels, and the once expansive middle-class sector of Buenos Aires has been squeezed by rising costs and declining incomes. However, the evidence from Buenos Aires does not support fully the thesis put forward by Saskia Sassen (1991) that world city processes specifically are exacerbating urban social polarization. The roots of Buenos Aires' contemporary social problems can be traced back at least to the nineteenth century. Certainly, the globalization of both the urban economy and society is having a differential impact on the city's class structure, but I contend that any type of restructuring (be it national, regional, or hemispheric) is likely to have similar effects. Many argue that capitalism, especially in its current globalized form, is the primary mechanism of social polarization. Within the free-market capitalist system, there are bound to be winners and losers if governments pursue a *laissez-faire* approach toward the provision of social services. Only by instituting strong social services that mitigate potential damage to quality of life at the lower end of the capitalist spectrum can the problems of urban social polarization be addressed seriously. Free-market globalization strategies do not have neutral spatial impacts; the outcomes often are territorially and sectorally concentrated. Although Buenos Aires has managed to avoid some of the more serious social problems that characterize contemporary México City, Lima, or Rio de Janeiro, current urban restructuring seems to be propelling the city down a development path from which there might be no easy return.

Despite the realities of ongoing social and economic polarization in Buenos Aires, there are plans and policies in place or under development to reverse (or at least to slow) the downward spiral. Buenos Aires, its managers, and citizens have the vitality, desire, and ability to effect positive change in the city. Unfortunately, the political system poses real barriers to change. Both the city and federal governments continue to be characterized by rampant corruption, unethical corporate lobbying, personal power struggles, and an almost messianic trust in the benefits of globalization, privatization, and deregulation. The economic élite and the administrative bureaucracy seem paralyzed by the apparent economic success of globalization and have been unable to articulate a clear set of policies to address Buenos Aires' social problems. Constitutional reform and new rounds of privatization may sustain the economic and political restructuring process until the end of the 1990s. Indeed, President Carlos Menem has changed Argentina's presidential term from one 6-year period with no reelection to two consecutive 4-year terms. Success in this endeavor allows Menem to pursue his globalization policies until the year 2000.

Although uncertainty exists about the long-term implications for Buenos Aires and Argentina of globalization strategies and world city restructuring, there are specific concerns that must be addressed if both city and nation are to grow and change in an environmentally and humanly sustainable manner. As a geographer, observer, and occasional resident of Buenos Aires, I would posit to the city's planners and policy makers that five broad issues exist that provide a framework upon which to build future urban management strategies. First and foremost is the need for enhanced circulation and mobility for all sectors of Buenos Aires' society. Without an integrated, multimodal transport and communication system that binds both city and nation together along the local–global continuum of socioeconomic relationships, patterns of spatial bifurcation will remain exacerbated. Buenos Aires could be further fragmented internally between enclaves of wealthy, globally connected urbanites and a turbulent sea of the poor, disenfranchised, and disconnected. Moreover, the city could become increasingly disarticulated from the interior provinces and from neighboring states as world city processes encourage the centralization of socioeconomic activities in the capital.

Second, there needs to be a major focus on social infrastructure in Buenos Aires. Housing, public utilities, access to educational facilities, and employment opportunities are the bricks and mortar of the theater within which the daily play of *porteño* life takes place. As basic social services continue to deteriorate in Buenos Aires, or at least fail to keep pace with demographic growth and change, the seeds are being sown for future social upheaval. Third, Buenos Aires desperately needs jurisdictional reform to allow for more holistic approaches to managing the Greater Buenos Aires metropolitan region. A reliance on a system of territorial management created a century ago highlights the inability of governments and institutions to adjust to the changing spatial dynamics of urban life. The functional spatial boundaries of the city must be reevaluated in the context of contemporary urban management problems. Fourth, there is a real need for a partnership of trust between local, provincial, and federal governments, the business community, and the citizens of Buenos Aires. Individuals and institutions must recognize that change has differential spatial implications and is not always neutral or positive in its impact.

Finally, governments, institutions, and individuals must realize that participation in the world city and global economic systems requires responsible long-term planning and a healthy, safe urban environment for all citizens, whatever their position in the socioeconomic hierarchy. Unfortunately, Buenos Aires has become the exclusive domain of privileged business interests, with the urban planning emphasis on corporate profits and a stable, free-market economic environment. Economic and political ideologies have focused on the critically important goal of reshaping Buenos Aires into an increasingly competitive environment for the conduct of global commerce, yet little attention has been paid to the short- and long-term social implications of restructuring. The development of a broad-based social reform program has been subordinated to the desire for economic order and progress.

Of course, these problems are not unique to Buenos Aires. Every urban environment faces the challenge of coping with the tensions of globalization. Some problems are unique to specific cities and require specific solutions, while other problems are more ubiquitous in nature and can benefit from programs and policies tried and tested in other urban milieus. Buenos Aires certainly stands as an excellent case study of the implications of rapid and profound change in social, economic, and political functions. How Buenos Aires copes with the realities of urban management crises while attempting to achieve its dreams of global status may provide a template for other cities undergoing or contemplating the restructuring process.

The changes since 1989 under the Menem government have been profound for both city and nation. Although at the end of 1995 Buenos Aires had yet to experience any major infrastructural changes in its physical landscape as a result of globalization strategies, incipient changes indicative of the future were evident. Globalization has begun to reshape Buenos Aires in profound and fundamental ways, and myriad short- and long-term plans have been proposed that if implemented certainly will reshape the city's landscapes. My hope is that this book has served not only to shed light on contemporary conditions in Buenos Aires and to bring the city's geography to the fore, but also to stand as a benchmark against which to compare the future city. Above all, I hope that the journey you have taken in this book through Buenos Aires will encourage you to visit this important world city and to follow the unfolding history of its people and culture.

References

Abbott, C. (1993) Through flight to Tokyo: Sunbelt cities and the new world economy, 1960–1990, pp. 183–212 in A. R. Hirsch and R. A. Mohl (eds) *Urban Policy in Twentieth-Century America*. New Brunswick, NJ: Rutgers University Press.

Aguirre, A. A. (1983) El traslado de la Capital Federal en el pensamiento argentino, *Participar* (Buenos Aires) Año VI (52), 22–26.

Aguirre, A. A. (1987) El desafío del traslado, *Participar* (Buenos Aires) Año IX (71), 12–13.

Ainstein, L. (1992) *Megacities in the Third World: A Research Agenda on Buenos Aires and the Question of National Urban Policy*. São Paulo: United Nations University.

Andersen, M. E. (1993) *Dossier Secreto*. Boulder: Westview Press.

Arocena, L. A. (1982) A porteño's view of his city, pp. 168–181 in S. R. Ross and T. F. McGann (eds) *Buenos Aires: 400 Years*. Austin: University of Texas Press.

Bartone, C. R., Leite, L., Triche, T. and Schertenleib, R. (1991) Private sector participation in municipal solid waste service: Experiences in Latin America, *Waste Management and Research* 9(3), 495–509.

Basco, C. A., Cerenza, T. L., Iturriza, J. E. and Valenciano, E. O. (1988) *Transporte e Integración*. Buenos Aires: Banco Interamericano de Desarrollo, Instituto para la Integración de América Latina.

Benoit, P., Benoit, J., Bellanger, F. and Marzloff, B. (1993) *Paris 1995: Le Grand Desserrement*. Paris: Romillat.

Berón, L. (1981) *La Contaminación, Factor de Desequilibrio Ecológico*. Buenos Aires: Secretaría de Medio Ambiente.

Borges, J. L. (1974) "Las calles," in Fervor de Buenos Aires [1923]. *Obras Completas*. Buenos Aires: Emece.

Bourdé, G. (1974) *Urbanisation et immigration en Amérique Latine: Buenos Aires (XIXe et XXe siécles)*. Paris: Romillat.

Bouvard, M. G. (1994) *Revolutionizing Motherhood: The Mothers of the Plaza de Mayo*. Wilmington: Scholarly Resources Inc.

Brailovsky, A. E. and Foguelman, D. (1992) *Agua y Medio Ambiente en Buenos Aires*. Buenos Aires: Editorial Fraterna.

Broek, J. O. M. (1965) *Geography: Its Scope and Spirit.* Columbus: Charles E. Merrill.

Buenos Aires Herald (1989, 1991, 1993, 1994) Various issues.

Burns, E. B. (1980) *The Poverty of Progess.* Berkeley: University of California Press.

Câmara, P. and Banister, D. (1993) Spatial inequalities in the provision of public transport in Latin American cities. *Transport Reviews* 13(4), 351–373.

Campbell, A. (1994) Despite sceptics, Argentina races ahead, *Buenos Aires Herald,* May 22, 2.

Canitrot, A. (1993) Crisis and transformation of the Argentine State (1978–1992), pp. 75–102 in W. C. Smith, C. H. Acuña and E. A. Gamarra (eds) *Democracy, Markets, and Structural Reform in Latin America: Argentina, Bolivia, Brazil, Chile, and Mexico.* New Brunswick, NJ: Transaction Publishers.

Canziana, D.F., Cordero, J.A. and Milic, E. (1989) Struggle against environmental pollution in Argentina: Updating of information, pp. 213–221, in *Man and his Ecosystems, Proceedings of the 8th Clean Air Congress 1989,* Vol. 5. Amsterdam: Elsevier Science Publishers BV.

Carlevari, I. J. F. and Carlevari, R. D. (1994) *La Argentina 1994: Estructura Humana y Economía.* Buenos Aires: Ediciones Macchi.

Carnevali, D. and Suárez, C. (1993) Electricity and the environment: Air pollutant emissions in Argentina. *Energy Policy* 27(1), 68–72.

Carty, W. P. (1981) Ring around the city. *Américas* 33(2), 3–8.

Centro de Investigaciones Ferroviarias y del Transporte (1985) *Estudio de Prefactibilidad: Ferrocarril de Circunvalación a la Ciudad de Buenos Aires.* Buenos Aires: Asociación del Personal de Dirección de Ferrocarriles Argentinos.

CONAMBA (1989) *Area Metropolitana de Buenos Aires: Proyecto 90.* Buenos Aires: Comisión Nacional del Area Metropolitana de Buenos Aires (CONAMBA).

Corradi, J. E. (1992) The Argentina of Carlos Saúl Menem. *Current History* 91(562), 80–84.

"'Corrientes' Tango," *Crítica* (October 17, 1926), p. 9.

Crawley, E. (1984) *A House Divided: Argentina 1880–1980.* London: C. Hurst.

Cuenya, B. (1988) *Inquilinatos en la Ciudad de Buenos Aires: Referentes Teóricos e Históricos y un Estudio de Caso en el Barrio de Almagro.* Buenos Aires: Cuadernos de CEUR, Numero 24.

Cuenya, B., Pastrana, E. and Yujnovsky, O. (1984) *Del la Villa Miseria al Barrio Autoconstruido: Cuatro Experiencias Organizadas de Producción del Hábitat Popular.* Buenos Aires: Ediciones CEUR.

Cuenya, B., Almada, H., Armus, D., Castells, J., di Loreto, M. and Peñalva, S. (1990) Community action to address housing and health problems: The case of San Martín in Buenos Aires, Argentina, pp. 25–55, in S. Cairncross, J. E. Hardoy, and D. Satterthwaite (eds) *The Poor Die Young: Housing and Health in Third World Cities.* London: Earthscan Publications.

D'Angelo, J. V. (1963) La conurbación de Buenos Aires, pp. 90–219, in F. de Aparicio and H. A. Difrieri (eds) *La Argentina: Suma de Geografía,* Vol 9. Buenos Aires: Ediciones Peuser.

Del Pino, D. A. (1991) *Palermo: Un Barrio Porteño.* Buenos Aires: Fundación Banco De Boston.

Earthwatch (1992) *Urban Air Pollution in Megacities of the World.* Oxford: Blackwell.

Economic Commission for Latin America and the Caribbean (1994) *Economic Panorama of Latin America, 1994.* Santiago: ECLAC.

Economist (1994) The other side of the halo, Vol. 330(7850), February 12, 38–39.

Economist (1994) Argentina Survey, November 26, A1–A17.

Etchepareborda, R. (1982) Buenos Aires: today and tomorrow, pp. 142–151, in S. R. Ross and T. F. McGann (eds) *Buenos Aires: 400 Years*. Austin: University of Texas Press.

Feagin, J.R. and Smith, M. P. (1987) Cities and the new international division of labor: An overview, pp. 5–15, in M.P. Smith and J.R. Feagin (eds) *The Capitalist City: Global Restructuring and Community Politics*. Oxford: Basil Blackwell.

Ferrer, A. (1992) Economic development in Argentina: An historical perspective. *International Social Science Journal* 44(4), 463–472.

Fisher, J. (1993) *Out of the Shadows: Women, Resistance and Politics in South America*. London: Latin American Bureau.

Flood, C. A. (1991) Agricultura suburbana en pequeña escala en el Gran Buenos Aires. *IFDA Dossier* 81, 39–50.

Friedmann, J. (1986) The world city hypothesis. *Development and Change* 17(1), 69–83.

Friedmann, J. and Wolff, G. (1982) World city formation: An agenda for research and action. *International Journal of Urban and Regional Research* 6, 309–344.

Gálvez, M. (1910) *El Diario de Gabriel Quiroga: Opiniones Sobre la Vida Argentina*. Buenos Aires: Arnoldo Möen.

Gannon, M. J. (1994) *Understanding Global Cultures: Metaphorical Journeys Through 17 Countries*. Thousand Oaks, CA: Sage Publications.

Garibotto, E. (1994) Borges-Delta revived as light rail line. *Railway Gazette International* 150(3), 180.

Gazzoli, R. (1991) Inquilinatos y hoteles en la ciudad de Buenos Aires, pp. 65–83, in Rubén Gazzoli, et al. (eds) *Alojamiento para Sectores Populares Urbanos: Buenos Aires, Montevideo, San Pablo y México*. Buenos Aires: Editorial Plus Ultra.

Giddens, A. (1984) *The Constitution of Society: Outline of the Theory of Structuration*. Cambridge: Polity Press.

Gilbert, A. (1994) *The Latin American City*. London: Latin American Bureau.

Gills, B. and Rocamora, J. (1992) Low intensity democracy. *Third World Quarterly* 13(3), 501–523.

Goldman, J. (1993) Argentine renaissance. *Architectural Record*, January, 44–46.

Goñi, U. (1994) Till Menem do us part, *Buenos Aires Herald* 22 May, 15.

Gutman, M. and Hardoy, J. (1993) *Buenos Aires: Historia Urbana del Area Metropolitana*. Madrid: Editorial MAPFRE.

Gutman, P., Gutman, G. and Dascal, G. (1987) *El Campo en la Ciudad: La Producción Agrícola en el Gran Buenos Aires*. Buenos Aires: CEUR.

Guy, D. J. (1991) *Sex and Danger in Buenos Aires: Prostitution, Family, and Nation in Argentina*. Lincoln: University of Nebraska Press.

Hall, P. G. (1966) *The World Cities*. London: Weidenfeld and Nicolson.

Hardoy, A., Hardoy, J. E. and Schusterman, R. (1991) Building community organization: The history of a squatter settlement and its own organizations in Buenos Aires. *Environment and Urbanization* 3(2), 104–120.

Hardoy, J. E. (1972) *Las Ciudades en América Latina: Seis Ensayos sobre la Urbanización Comtemporánea*. Buenos Aires: Instituto Torcuato Di Tella.

Hardoy, J. E. and Gutman, M. (1991) The role of municipal government in the protection of historic centres in Latin American cities. *Environment and Urbanization* 3(1), 96–108.

Hollander, N. C. (1990) Buenos Aires: Latin mecca of psychoanalysis, *Social Research* **57**(4), 888–919.

Ibarguren, F. (1969) *Los Orígenes del Nacionalismo Argentino*. Buenos Aires: Calcius.

Imai, K. (1992) Decentralizing government deficit finance in Argentina. *The Developing Economies* **XXX**(4), 430–449.

International Railway Journal (1993) Buenos Aires Metro Goes Private, **33**(4), 41.

Jacovella, B. C. (1953) *Fiestas Tradicionales Argentinas*. Buenos Aires: Lejouane.

Johns, M. (1992) The urbanization of peripheral capitalism: Buenos Aires, 1880–1920. *International Journal of Urban and Regional Research* **16**(3), 352–374.

Keeling D. J. (1994) Transport and regional development in Argentina: Structural deficiencies and patterns of network evolution. *Yearbook 1993: Conference of Latin Americanist Geographers* **19**, 25–34.

Keeling, D. J. (1995) Transport and the world-city paradigm, pp. 115–131, in P. L. Knox and P. J. Taylor (eds) *World Cities in a World-System*. Cambridge: Cambridge University Press.

King, A. (1990) *Global Cities: Post-imperialism and the Internationalization of London*. New York: Routledge.

King, J. (1984) Civilisation and barbarism: The impact of Europe on Argentina. *History Today*, **August**, 16–21.

La Nación (Buenos Aires) (1989, 1991, 1993, 1994) various issues.

Latin American Weekly Report (London) (1989–1995) various issues.

Le Corbusier (1947) *Proposición de un Plan Director para Buenos Aires*. Buenos Aires: Municipalidad de Buenos Aires.

Lewis, P. H. (1990) *The Crisis of Argentine Capitalism*. Chapel Hill: The University of North Carolina Press.

Lo, C. P. (1992) *Hong Kong*. London: Belhaven Press.

Ludueña, M. A. (1993) Región Metropolitana Buenos Aires: Estructuración, problemática y aspecto de cambio, pp. 284–330, in J. A. Roccatagliata (ed.) *Geografía Económica Argentina*. Buenos Aires: El Ateneo.

Lynch, J. (1981) *Argentine Dictator: Juan Manuel de Rosas, 1829–1852*. Oxford: Oxford University Press.

Lynch, K. (1960) *The Image of the City*. Cambridge, MA: M.I.T. Press.

Martin, K. (1992) Squatters take over. *The Progressive* **56**(9), 13.

Martínez, T. E. (1993) A culture of barbarism, pp. 11–23, in C. M. Lewis and N. Torrents (eds) *Argentina in the Crisis Years (1983–1990)*. London: Institute of Latin American Studies.

Meyer, J. R. and Gomez-Ibáñez, J. A. (1981) *Autos, Transit, and Cities*. Cambridge, MA: Harvard University Press.

Miller, N. (1992) *Out in the World*. New York: Random House.

Mochkowsky, J. (1991) La situación habitacional de los sectores populares, pp. 55–64, in Rubén Gazzoli, et al. (eds) *Alojamiento para Sectores Populares Urbanos: Buenos Aires, Montevideo, San Pablo y México*. Buenos Aires: Editorial Plus Ultra.

Moreno, N. B. (1939) *Buenos Aires, Puerto del Río de la Plata, Capital de la Argentina: Estudio Crítico de su Población, 1536–1936*. Buenos Aires: Talleres Gráficos Tuduri.

Mouchet, C. (1972) Buenos Aires, pp. 240–269, in W. A. Robson and D. E. Regan (eds) *Great Cities of the World: Their Government, Politics, and Planning*, Vol. 1. Beverly Hills: Sage Publications.

Official Airline Guide (1972, 1982, 1992, 1993, 1994) *OAG Worldwide Edition*. Chicago: Reuben H. Donnelly.

Pace, M. di (coordinator) (1992) Sustainable development in Argentina. *Environment and Urbanization* **4**(1), 37–52.

Padula, C. C. (1993) El proceso de integración, pp. 331–361, in J. A. Roccatagliata (ed.) *Geografía Económica Argentina*. Buenos Aires: El Ateneo.

Pastori, L. D. (1929) La construcción de subterráneos en la ciudad de Buenos Aires. *Revista de Economía Argentina* **12**(135), 197–209.

Peil, M. (1991) *Lagos*. London: Belhaven Press.

Pesci, R. and Ibáñez, E. del Acebo (1992) *Modernización y Descentralización en las Grandes Ciudades*. Buenos Aires: Concejo Nacional de Investigaciones Científicas y Técnicas (CONICET).

Pred, A. (1985) The social becomes the spatial, the spatial becomes the social: Enclosures, social change and the becoming of place in the Swedish province of Skåne, in D. Gregory and J. Urry (eds) *Social Relations and Spatial Structures*. London: Macmillan.

Prévôt-Schapira, M.-F. (1993) L'affirmation municipale dans le Grand Buenos Aires: Tensions et ambiguïtés. *Revue Canadienne D'Études du Développement* **XIV**(2), 151–172.

Púa, C. de la (1954) "Amasijo habitual" en *La Crencha Engrasada*. Buenos Aires: Editorial Porteña.

Radrizzani de Enríquez, M. (1989) La metrópoli de Buenos Aires. *Revista Geográfica* **110**, 57–104.

Rand McNally (1993) *The International Atlas*. New York: Rand McNally.

Randle, P. H. (1991a) Se cierne otra amenaza. *La Prensa* (Buenos Aires) November 25, 6.

Randle, P. H. (1991b) La desconstrucción de la ciudad contemporánea. *La Prensa* (Buenos Aires) November 8, 9.

Relph, E. (1976) *Place and Placelessness*. London: Pion.

República Argentina (1954, 1964, 1974, 1985) *Censo Nacional Económico*. Buenos Aires: Instituto Nacional de Estadística y Censos (INDEC).

República Argentina (1965) *Plan Nacional de Desarrollo, 1965– 1969*. Buenos Aires: Consejo Nacional de Desarrollo (CONADE).

República Argentina (1969) *Organización del Espacio de la Región Metropolitana de Buenos Aires: Esquema Director Año 2000*. Buenos Aires: Oficina Regional de Desarrollo Area Metropolitana.

República Argentina (1980, 1991) *Censo Nacional de Población y Vivienda*. Buenos Aires: Instituto Nacional de Estadística y Censos (INDEC).

República Argentina (1981) *Censo Socio-Económico en Villas de Emergencia*. Buenos Aires: Instituto Nacional de Estadística y Censos (INDEC).

República Argentina (1993a) *Statistical Yearbook Republic of Argentina, 1993*. Buenos Aires: Instituto Nacional de Estadística y Censos (INDEC).

República Argentina (1993b) *Argentina: A Growing Nation*. Buenos Aires: Ministerio de Economía Y Obras Y Servicios Públicos (MOSP).

República Argentina (1994) *Reflexiones y Orientaciones para la Formulación de una Política de Ordenación Territorial*. Buenos Aires: Subsecretaría de Acción de Gobierno, Proyecto Política de Ordenación Territorial, Documento de Trabajo, Tercera Edición.

Revista Mercado Inmobiliario (Buenos Aires) (1994) various issues.

Rial, Horacio Vásquez (1993) The crisis of national culture, pp. 24–34, in C. M.

Lewis and N. Torrents (eds) *Argentina in the Crisis Years (1983–1990)*. London: Institute of Latin American Studies.

Richter, F. (1993) What's next for Argentina's railroads? *Progressive Railroading* **36**(2), 74–77.

Roccatagliata, J. A. (1993) Transporte: Algunas consideraciones actuales, pp. 193–240, in J. A. Roccatagliata (ed.) *Geografía Económica Argentina*. Buenos Aires: El Ateneo.

Rock, D. (1987) *Argentina, 1516–1987*. Berkeley: University of California Press.

Rock, D. (1993) *Authoritarian Argentina: The Nationalist Movement, its History and its Impact*. Berkeley: University of California Press.

Rodríguez, M. (1956) The genesis of economic attitudes in the Río de la Plata. *Hispanic American Historical Review* **36**(2), 171–189.

Romero, J. L. (1984). *Breve historia de la Argentina*, 6th edn. Buenos Aires: Editorial Abril.

Sargent, C. S. (1974) *The Spatial Evolution of Greater Buenos Aires, Argentina, 1870–1930*. Tempe: Arizona State University Press.

Sargent, C. S. (1993) The Latin American city, pp. 172–216 in B. W. and O. M. Blouet (eds) *Latin America and the Caribbean: A Systematic and Regional Survey*. New York: John Wiley.

Sassen, S. (1991) *The Global City: New York, London, Tokyo*. Princeton: Princeton University Press.

Scalabrini Ortiz, R. (1968) Bases para la reconstrucción nacional, pp. 190–220, in A. Ciria (ed.) *La Década Infame*. Buenos Aires: Carlos Pérez.

Schneider, J. (1994) Thou shalt not kill. *Buenos Aires Herald*, May 13, 10.

Schvarzer, J. (1983) La implantación industrial, pp. 223–240, in J. L. Romero and L. A. Romero (eds) *Buenos Aires: Historia de Cuatro Siglos*, Vol II. Buenos Aires: Editorial Abril.

Schvarzer, J. (1992) The Argentine riddle in historical perspective, *Latin American Research Review* **27**(1), 169–181.

Scobie, J. R. (1971) *Argentina: A City and a Nation*, 2nd edn. New York: Oxford University Press.

Scobie, J. R. (1972) Buenos Aires as a commercial–bureaucratic city, 1880–1910: Characteristics of a city's orientation. *The American Historical Review* **77**(4), 1035–1073.

Scobie, J. R. (1974) *Buenos Aires: Plaza to Suburb, 1870– 1910*. New York: Oxford University Press.

Scovazzi, E. (1993) Carmen de Viedma. *International Journal of Urban and Regional Research* **17**(4), 516–525.

SEPLADE (1978) *Estrategias para el Desarrollo y Modernización del Eje Metropolitano*. Buenos Aires: Secretaría de Planeamiento y Desarrollo de la Provincia de Buenos Aires (SEPLADE).

Shachar, A. (1994) Randstad Holland: A "World City"? *Urban Studies* **31**(3), 381–400.

Silva, J. and Schuurman, F. J. (1989) Neighborhood associations in Buenos Aires: Contradictions within contradictions, pp. 45–61, in F. J. Schuurman and T. Van Naerssen (eds) *Urban Social Movements in the Third World*. New York: Routledge.

Sommi, L. V. (1940) *El Monopolio Inglés del transporte en Buenos Aires*. Buenos Aires: Editorial Problemas.

Stoetzel, J. R. (1993) BN,MK to move commuters. *Progressive Railroading* **36**(2), 68–70.

Thomas Cook (1974, 1994) *European and Overseas Timetables (Summer)*. Peterborough: Thomas Cook Publications.

Tobar, C. (1972) The Argentine national plan for eradicating *Villas de Emergencia*, pp. 221–228, in F. F. Rabinovitz and F. M. Trueblood (eds) *Latin American Urban Research*, Vol. 2. Beverly Hills: Sage Publications.

Torres, H. A. (1993) La aglomeración de Buenos Aires: Centralidad y sub-urbanización (1940–1990). *Estudios Geográficos* 54(211), 301–322.

Trelles, M. R. (1863) Historia del puerto de Buenos Aires. *La Revista de Buenos Aires* I, 1–28.

Tuan, Y.-F. (1974) *Topophilia: A Study of Environmental Perception, Attitudes, and Values*. Englewood Cliffs, NJ: Prentice-Hall.

Tuan, Y.-F. (1976) Humanistic geography. *Annals of the Association of American Geographers* 66(2), 266–276.

Turton, B. (1992) Urban transport patterns, pp. 67–80, in B. S. Hoyle and R. D. Knowles (eds) *Modern Transport Geography*. London: Belhaven Press.

Valdes, E. (1991) *Apuntes Para la Discusión Acerca de La Reforma de Buenos Aires*. Buenos Aires: Fundación URBE.

Wallerstein, I. (1980) *The Modern World-System II. Mercantilism and the Consolidation of the European World-Economy 1600–1750*. New York: Academic Press.

Walter, R. J. (1982) The socioeconomic growth of Buenos Aires in the twentieth century, pp. 67–126, in S. R. Ross and T. F. McGann (eds) *Buenos Aires: 400 Years*. Austin: University of Texas Press.

Walter, R. J. (1993) *Politics and Urban Growth in Buenos Aires: 1910–1942*. New York: Cambridge University Press.

Welna, D. (1988) Housing solutions for Buenos Aires' invisible poor. *Grassroots Development* 12(1), 2–7.

Wheaton, K. (ed.) (1990) *Buenos Aires*. New York: APA Publications, Insight CityGuides.

Wilkie, J. W. and Contreras, C. (1993) *Statistical Abstract of Latin America*, Vol. 30. Los Angeles: UCLA Latin American Publications Center.

World Bank (1984) *World Development Report, 1984*. New York: Oxford University Press.

Index

Page numbers given in italics refer to figures and page numbers in bold type refer to tables.

DATE DUE

MAR 1 3 2001	DEC 1 1 2002	
APR 0 8 2009		
NOV 1 8 2002		
OCT 2 3 2003		
		Printed In USA